LIQUID CAPITAL

AMERICAN BUSINESS, POLITICS, AND SOCIETY

Series Editors:
Andrew Wender Cohen, Pamela Walker Laird,
Mark H. Rose, and Elizabeth Tandy Shermer

Books in the series American Business, Politics, and Society explore
the relationships over time between governmental institutions and
the creation and performance of markets, firms, and industries large
and small. The central theme of this series is that politics, law, and
public policy—understood broadly to embrace not only lawmaking
but also the structuring presence of governmental institutions—has
been fundamental to the evolution of American business from the
colonial era to the present. The series aims to explore, in particular,
developments that have enduring consequences.

A complete list of books in the series
is available from the publisher.

LIQUID CAPITAL

Making the Chicago Waterfront

JOSHUA A. T. SALZMANN

UNIVERSITY OF PENNSYLVANIA PRESS

PHILADELPHIA

Published by
University of Pennsylvania Press
Philadelphia, Pennsylvania 19104-4112
www.upenn.edu/pennpress

Printed in the United States of America on acid-free paper
1 3 5 7 9 10 8 6 4 2

Library of Congress Cataloging-in-Publication Data
Names: Salzmann, Joshua A. T., author.
Title: Liquid capital: making the Chicago waterfront / Joshua A.T. Salzmann.
Other titles: American business, politics, and society.
Description: 1st edition. | Philadelphia : University of Pennsylvania Press,
[2018] | Series: American business, politics, and society | Includes
bibliographical references and index.
Identifiers: LCCN 2017016755 | ISBN 9780812249736 (hardcover)
Subjects: LCSH: Waterfronts—Illinois—Chicago—History—19th century. |
Waterfronts—Illinois—Chicago—History—20th century. | Land
use—Illinois—Chicago—History—19th century. | Land
use—Illinois—Chicago—History—20th century. | Human
ecology—Illinois—Chicago—History—19th century. | Human
ecology—Illinois—Chicago—History—20th century.
Classification: LCC HT168.C5 S25 2018 | DDC 304.2/097731109034—dc23
LC record available at https://lccn.loc.gov/2017016755

CONTENTS

Introduction. State Power and the Rise of Chicago   1

Chapter 1. Making a River Run Through It   9

Chapter 2. The Legal Construction of Free Marketplaces   43

Chapter 3. The Creative Destruction of the Chicago River Harbor   83

Chapter 4. Beauty and the Crisis of Commercial Civilization   117

Chapter 5. A Public Pier for Pleasure and Profit   146

Epilogue. A Waterscape for the New Millennium   175

Notes   187

Index   223

Acknowledgments   233

State Power and the Rise of Chicago

In 1818, an employee of the American Fur Company, Gurdon S. Hubbard, described a journey that traders had been making for centuries via a land route, or portage, between the Great Lakes and Mississippi River watersheds. It spanned a patch of marshland that remains a crucial crossroads today—the site of Chicago's Midway Airport.[1] The men in Hubbard's party paddled their barks from the open waters of Lake Michigan into the shallow, sand-clogged mouth of the Chicago River. From there, they ascended the main stem and south branch of the Chicago until reaching the river's source in a bog at the base of a very low ridge about half a dozen miles from Lake Michigan.

That unassuming ridge was a continental divide, formed more than thirteen thousand years ago when melting glaciers deposited heaps of debris onto the landscape. East of the ridge, water flowed into the Chicago River, Lake Michigan, and, eventually, the Atlantic Ocean. West of the ridge, water flowed into Mud Lake, a murky appendage of the Des Plaines River whose waters ran southwest toward the Mississippi and the Gulf of Mexico.[2] When Hubbard's party got to the divide, the river ran dry, and their boats had to be "placed on short rollers . . . until the [Mud] lake was reached." For three days, the men slogged through Mud Lake. Hubbard recalled the grueling trek: "Four men only remained in a boat and pushed with . . . poles, while six or eight others waded in the mud alongside . . . [and still] others busied themselves in transporting our goods on their backs to the [Des Plaines] [R]iver." All the while, the men were beset by leeches that "stuck so tight to the skin that they broke in pieces if force was used to remove them."[3]

The area surrounding that vital and miserable passageway between the Great Lakes and Mississippi River watersheds soon became the site of phenomenal urban growth. That growth was the product of collaboration between public policymakers and private businessmen. Over the course of a century, they constructed crucial water and railroad infrastructure, transforming Chicago into a massive metropolis.

Established as a town in 1833, Chicago was, at the time, a wilderness outpost of just 350 residents clumped around a small military fort on soggy land where the Chicago River trickled into Lake Michigan.[4] The site was known to local natives as *Chigagou*, or the "wild garlic place." It flooded frequently and stank. Mud abounded. Summers brought blistering heat. The bitterly cold winters were made worse by bracing winds, from which the flat, monotonous landscape offered little protection.[5]

Yet, in the course of a century, Chicagoans radically transformed the site from a desolate swamp into a vast canvas for urban experimentation, construction, and commerce. By 1933, it was a sprawling industrial metropolis of more than three million souls.[6] The city's denizens had built canals, bridges, and docks; laid railroads connecting the coasts; siphoned the nation's grain harvest into towering storage elevators; cut the tall pine forests of Michigan and Wisconsin from the earth, stacking and selling them in magnificent lumber yards; and erected cruelly efficient slaughterhouses where, as the writer Norman Mailer later observed, "they cut the animals right out of their hearts."[7] Chicagoans had built massive factories with giant blast furnaces to transform the iron ore of Minnesota's Mesabi Range into iron and steel, and they had constructed spectacular office towers filled with white collar workers who kept tabs on the rapid flow of money in and out of the city.

The point of Chicago's existence has always been to wring profit from nature. But how did the bog that Hubbard traversed in 1818 become a global metropolis? Did the natural advantages of the place call Chicago into being, or did humans build the city in spite of its sandbars, swamps, and pestilence?

Chicago's geography has always been fundamental to its story. The immense obstacles and advantages it presents have often existed in a productive tension—the natural advantages inspiring ever-greater human efforts to tame the environment and tap it for economic gain. Consequently, Chicago's chroniclers have long been ambivalent about whether nature or human agency played a greater role in the city's growth.[8]

Many of the people who witnessed firsthand Chicago's astounding rise concluded that God must have predestined it. In 1880, the former lieutenant governor of Illinois, William Bross, delivered an address to the Chicago Historical Society in which he claimed: "He who is the Author of Nature selected the site of this great city."[9] In 1923, in an address to the Geographical Society of Chicago, a University of Chicago geographer, J. Paul Goode, argued that the city's location made its rise inevitable. It was titled "Chicago: A City of Destiny."[10] Likewise, in a landmark 1991 book, the environmental historian William Cronon acknowledged the role of human decision-making in Chicago's rise, but he ultimately attributed its rapid growth to a combination of easy access to natural resources—tall timber stands, rich farm lands—and its pivotal position on the shipping lanes of the Great Lakes and the Chicago and Mississippi river systems. Cronon concluded that Chicago was, in the words of his book's title, *Nature's Metropolis*.[11]

Undoubtedly, Chicago's waterways and proximity to natural resources made the city's growth possible, but it did not make it natural, much less inevitable. In 1955, University of Chicago geographer Harold Mayer underscored this point—and pointedly took issue with Goode—in his address to the city's geographical society. It was titled "Chicago: A City of Decisions."[12] Scholars such as Harold Platt and Robert Lewis have likewise emphasized that, at every stage, Chicago's development was contingent on human actions.[13] People devised remarkable technologies, crafted new laws, and created innovative political and economic institutions to harvest the timber, cattle, hogs, coal, iron ore, and grain produced in the city's hinterland. At the same time, Chicago's development demanded that humans transform the urban landscape, or the metropolis's nature. Above all, they had to radically alter the waterfront and waterways—especially Lake Michigan, the Chicago River, and the Calumet River—to make the wretched landscape habitable and to make the continent's resources exploitable by the city's enterprising businessmen.

The power to command water often resides with the elite.[14] In this regard, Chicago was not exceptional. The people and institutions that changed the flow of Chicago's watercourses and constructed its waterfront included the arch-conservative Supreme Court Justices Melville Fuller and Stephen Field, the idealistic urban planner Daniel Burnham and his colleagues in the Chicago Commercial Club, the pioneering landscape architect Frederick Law Olmsted, the expansive Illinois Central Railroad, the resourceful Army Corps of Engineers, the enterprising Chicago Board of Trade, Chicago's crafty Common Council, and the creative, cash-strapped state of Illinois.

Their achievements were monumental. They fused the Great Lakes and Mississippi watersheds with a canal; piped in drinking water from the depths of Lake Michigan; constructed sewers, docks, piers, and bridges; blasted through sandbars at the mouths of the two rivers; dredged, straightened, and widened the rivers; reversed the flow of the Chicago River; built railroad

tracks, depots, and grain elevators along the city's watercourses; and decorated the lakefront with verdant parks and splendid civic spaces.

Even more remarkably, Chicagoans used the same resources for seemingly incompatible purposes, thereby serving stakeholders with divergent
agendas. The city's inhabitants drank from the very watershed fouled by
their sewers and by the animal blood and guts from their meatpackers. Even
as the city and industry clogged the river channel with waste, large boats
dragged their hulls through the slop, shuttling cargoes to and from businesses. Chicagoans, moreover, demanded that the river banks and lakeshore
serve as sites for factories, grain elevators, and railroad depots—as well as
civic monuments and "natural" beauty. Thus, the city's waterways and waterfront simultaneously facilitated mass production, commodity circulation,
public health, tourism, and social harmony. Chicagoans engineered a waterscape to reconcile the environmental contradictions of the urban economy.
They created a new ecology for a new urban industrial capitalism. The waterscape, in turn, became a resource for moneymaking, a form of liquid
capital.[15]

The story of Chicago's growth, then, is largely about the contentious politics of creating and managing the urban environment. And, it presents something of a paradox. Chicago's waterfront, the hub of economic activity in a
city renowned as an archetype of crass industrial capitalism, was also the site
of several of the nation's precedent-making decisions about public land use,
economic regulation, and environmental protection. A dispute over storage
rates at the grain elevators along the banks of the Chicago River, for instance,
led to the Supreme Court's 1877 ruling in *Munn v. Illinois*, which dramatically
expanded state legislatures' ability to regulate any businesses deemed "affected with a public interest."[16] Another dispute over the ownership of the
lakeshore resulted in a Supreme Court ruling in *Illinois Central v. Illinois*
(1892), which mandated that states hold vital natural resources "in trust" for
the public. Contemporary environmentalists have, in turn, used this ruling
to argue for protection of air, water, and forests.[17] Meantime, Chicago's
waterfront—developed in accord with the recommendations of Burnham's
monumental 1909 *Plan of Chicago*—has become a model civic landscape for
urban planners throughout the world.[18]

Chicago's waterfront, in sum, was both a critical moneymaking enterprise and the site of several precedents for economic regulation and environmental stewardship. That fact is difficult to square with master narratives
about American history and economic policy, which draw sharp—and ulti-

mately misleading—distinctions between the public realm of government and the private sphere of the market.

Historians often tell the story of the growth of the state as a reaction to private market excess. During the nineteenth century, the narrative goes, America had a "weak" state, and public officials seldom intervened in the private marketplace. Unbridled industrial capitalism, in turn, produced class conflict, pollution, workplace accidents, and consumer exploitation. In the early twentieth century, though, well-educated middle-class political reformers came to the rescue, leveraging the power of state and federal governments to enact regulations that mitigated the effects of the industrial revolution. Progressive reforms were a public, state-centered response to the vagaries of the private marketplace.[19]

This narrative is inscribed in the very terms historians use to describe the late nineteenth and early twentieth centuries. In the 1920s, liberal, "progressive" historians disparaged the late nineteenth century as "the Gilded Age," after the title of Mark Twain and Charles Dudley Warner's 1873 satire of the era's greed and corruption. Meanwhile, they celebrated the early twentieth century as "the Progressive Era." These terms continue to shape how many Americans think about the rise of the state: as a reaction to industrial capitalism, with the state-centered reforms of the early twentieth century correcting the excesses of the late-nineteenth-century free market.[20] It would indeed be ironic, within the framework of this narrative, that Chicago's waterfront was simultaneously a site of economic dynamism and muscular assertions of state power.

The irony, though, is not in what transpired on the shores of Lake Michigan and along the Chicago and Calumet Rivers. It lies in the space between what that master narrative of history and economic policy reveals—and hides. The "Gilded Age and Progressive Era" framing is powerful because it is partly true. The state did grow larger after the industrial revolution, and state-imposed economic regulations have often served as checks on market excesses. Historians of progressivism have thus rightly described the growth of the regulatory state as the critical development of the era. Yet these facts too often obscure another key part of the story of American political economy. Namely, the state played a crucial role in promoting economic development long before the Progressive Era, and industrial capitalism thrived because of—not in spite of—public policy, which was as crucial to its emergence as the initiatives of private business leaders.

Over the last three decades, scholars have become increasingly focused on the state's role in promoting industrialization. For much of the twentieth century, though, state power figured little in the works of business historians who trained their attention on individual capitalists, big firms, and corporate middle managers.[21] Beginning in the 1980s, historians and political scientists began to, in the words of Theda Skocpol, "bring the state back in" to studies of economic development.[22] Since then, scholars of American political development and historians of capitalism have shown that the market economy was not just a wild creature to be tamed by the state; rather, it was largely a product of monetary policies, infrastructure, and laws crafted by the state well before the Progressive Era.[23]

The recognition of a large, powerful state prior to the early twentieth century suggests that progressivism was not so sharp a break with the past, as some scholars have suggested, and that social and economic engineering were hardly new. Chicago's waterfront is an example of what might be termed earthy pragmatism—that is, experimentation with the landscape as an instrument of social and economic change. The city's existence depended on it.

For Chicago to function as a site of production and exchange, several threats to economic development had to be eliminated: sandbars and swamps that blocked travel to and from Chicago; railroad and grain elevator monopolies over crucial waterfront spaces; and the virulent class conflict that threatened the socioeconomic order. From the start of the city's history in the 1830s, Chicago's brand of buccaneering industrial capitalism depended on Chicagoans' success at making the city's waterways and its waterfront into ports, points of railroad connection, sewers, sources of drinking water, and grounds for pleasure and public life. Yet, the elemental relationship between Chicago and its waterways is often overshadowed by the city's storied past of soaring skyscrapers, mass production, and deadly confrontations between workers and capitalists at sites such as Haymarket Square and Pullman.

How did the desolate swamplands that Hubbard slogged through in 1818 become, long before his death in 1886, an intensely managed waterscape supporting the life and economy of a massive metropolis? The history of Chicago and its relationship to water suggests that—contrary to claims made by some of Chicago's chroniclers and the historians' master narrative of the era—markets and cities do not sprout up in the absence of strong government. Instead, Chicago and the markets that constituted it were creatures of the state, in large part because they required significant environmental engineering and regulation to flourish.

The history of Chicago's waterfront suggests that the conventional dualisms—private versus public and free enterprise versus state regulation—do little to explain the rise of nineteenth-century industrial cities. Chicago was created by a state that blended public and private institutions, personnel, and agendas.[24]

In Chicago, governmental power was often an extension of the interests, agendas, and efforts of a small number of business leaders. The sandbars, monopolies, and class violence that might have thwarted Chicago's economic growth were largely contained through creative collaborations between government officials and business leaders. Together, they fashioned public infrastructure to make Chicago accessible, established economic regulations to facilitate trade, and created public spaces on the waterfront to spur tourism and ease class tensions. In so doing, they transformed a muddy, desolate bog into a waterscape conducive to exchange, accumulation, leisure tourism, and class harmony—a means for profit making, a form of liquid capital.

Liquid Capital: Making the Chicago Waterfront travels through time across one of North America's most pivotal economic spaces: from the canal construction boom of the 1830s; to the great legal and economic battles over monopoly in the late nineteenth century; to the grittiest, smoke-filled days of the Industrial Revolution; and to the dawning of a prettier, leisure-centered capitalism at the start of the twentieth century. It tells the story of a waterscape continually transformed, of poet Carl Sandburg's Chicago: "Building, breaking, rebuilding."[25]

CHAPTER 1

Making a River Run Through It

Until deep into the nineteenth century, it was uncertain that Chicago would become the continent's preeminent inland metropolis, but even so, the promise and pitfalls of its geography were immediately obvious to the first Europeans who surveyed the center of North America. In 1673, the French explorer Louis Joliet and Jesuit missionary Jacques Marquette made the portage at *Chigagou* after having explored the upper Mississippi River Valley.[1] Marveling at the route's imperial possibilities, Joliet reported to the governor of French Canada, "we can quite easily go to Florida in boats . . . There would be only one canal to make by cutting only half a league of prairie, to pass from the lake of Illinois, [Lake Michigan] into the St. Louis River, [the Des Plaines and Illinois Rivers]." Such a canal would link Quebec to the fertile lands of the continental interior where, Joliet advised the governor, there would be "great advantages . . . to founding new colonies."[2]

The French, however, soon realized that constructing just a canal might not suffice to give them access to the center of North America. The explorer René-Robert Cavelier Sieur de La Salle, who camped at the site in the winter of 1682–1683, was similarly enthusiastic about the location, predicting that it would become a "gate of empire" and "the seat of commerce."[3] Yet, he saw obstacles to using the canal proposed by Joliet. In a letter to New France's governor general, La Salle quipped that Joliet's "proposed ditch" would do nothing to remove the "sand bar at the mouth of the channel [of the Chicago River] which leads to the lake of the Illinois [Lake Michigan]."[4] If the river's mouth remained clogged with sand, most boats would never reach the canal imagined by Joliet.

Together, La Salle and Joliet had identified the main challenges to capitalizing on the site's transportation advantages: it would be necessary to dig a canal across the portage and to dredge the sand-clogged mouth of the

Chicago River. Those were matters of statecraft no less than feats of engineering, and the French lacked the incentive and the capacity to build in so re-
mote a place. It was not until 1718 that the French-Mississippi Company
founded New Orleans, completing the imperial arc from Montreal to the
mouth of the Mississippi River. The expanse of territory between those two
cities was, moreover, only a sparsely populated fur trading region over which
the French state had limited administrative control.[5]

Marshalling the money and manpower to construct the canal envisioned
by Joliet—and remove the sandbar observed by La Salle—is, of course, a story
of American, not French, politics. French-claimed and Indian-controlled,
Chigagou became the Anglo-American fur trading post of Chicago in the
eighteenth and early nineteenth century. From the 1830s to the 1850s, American policymakers worked in tandem with private investors to transform that
little outpost into a great port city by making a river run through it, one connecting Chicago to the Atlantic and to the Gulf of Mexico.

By the middle of the nineteenth century, the state, city, and federal governments, as well as numerous private individuals, seemed to have resolved
the environmental paradox of Chicago—that the city's location both beck-
oned and repelled waterborne travelers. Through their combined efforts, the
Army Corps of Engineers, Chicago alderman, and various individual property owners had transformed the Chicago River from a sluggish stream into a
navigable waterway—albeit one that required constant, costly upkeep—
complete with bridges and wharves. Even more critically, the state's canal
commissioners and investors had replaced the portage that was at once so
convenient and so unpleasant to use with a canal grander, by far, than the one
imagined by Joliet in 1673.

These feats of engineering transformed the waterfront into an asset with
great commercial value. At the same time, though, they caused unintended
changes in the shape of the shoreline and in the city's commercial geography
that threatened to undermine the value of the waterfront.

The Changing Imperial Landscape

In the second half of the eighteenth century, the site of the portage remained
a backwater as great imperial powers fought to establish dominion over the
center of North America.[6] In 1763, at the conclusion of the Seven Years War,
the French lost their tenuous grip on most of their lands east of the

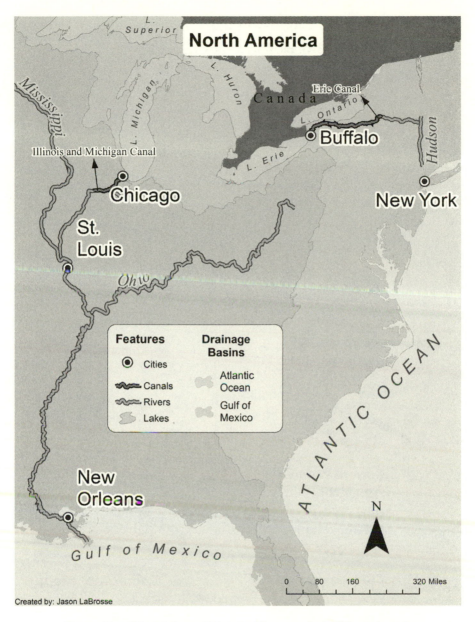

Figure 1. Map of Great Lakes and Mississippi River watersheds. Chicago sits on the cusp of the subcontinental divide between the Great Lakes and Mississippi River watersheds. After the construction of the Erie Canal in 1825, it was possible to travel by water from Chicago to New York City. The completion of the Illinois and Michigan Canal between the Chicago River and the Illinois River in 1848 made it possible to travel from Chicago to New Orleans via water. Chicago thus became a key hub for waterborne commerce in North America. Map created by Jason LaBrosse.

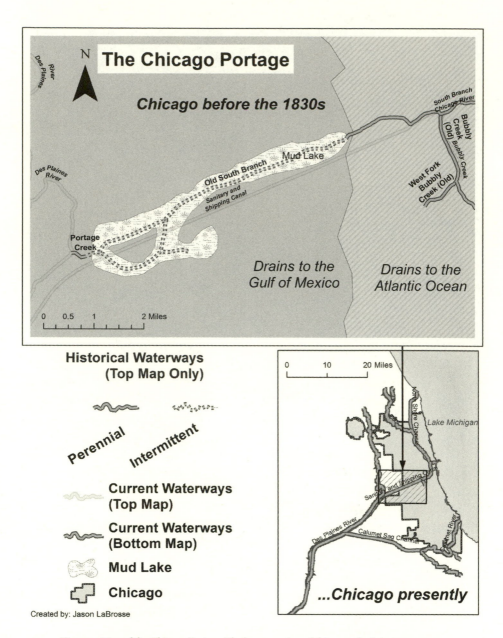

Figure 2. Map of the Chicago Portage. The lower portion of this map depicts contemporary
waterways and boundaries of the city of Chicago. The upper portion of the map is a
detailed representation of the land route, or portage, that travelers used to drag their
boats through to pass between the South Branch of the Chicago River in the Great Lakes
watershed and the Des Plaines River in the Mississippi River watershed. The Illinois and
Michigan Canal (1848) replaced the portage route. Map created by Jason LaBrosse.

Mississippi River to the British—who, in turn, lost their holdings south of the Great Lakes and east of the Mississippi to the Americans after the Revolutionary War. Throughout these imperial transfers, the Chicago Portage remained a lonely wilderness crossroads for Francophone and Native American traders. In fact, it did not have a permanent settler until 1779, when a black man thought to have been born in St. Domingue, Jean Baptiste Pointe Du Sable, established a farm and trading post on the north bank of the river. Du Sable took the daughter of a Potawatomi chief as his wife, and he prospered.[7]

Du Sable's French and Native American *Chigagou* became the Anglo-American settlement of Chicago during the eighteenth and early nineteenth century wars for the Great Lakes region. When the American Revolution ended in 1783, the British retained numerous forts in the area that would come to be Indiana and Illinois, trading with Native Americans and encouraging many of them take up arms against the United States in an effort to contain American settlement. To resist American control of the Great Lakes region, Native American tribes banned together, forming the "Western Confederacy." After a decade of conflict known as the Northwest Indian War, the United States military won a resounding victory against the Western Confederacy and their British allies at the Battle of Fallen Timbers in 1794 in present-day Maumee, Ohio. In the subsequent Treaty of Greenville (1795), the Native Americans ceded much of Ohio, the site of Detroit, and the small area that would become downtown Chicago.[8]

To counter the British presence in the western Great Lakes region, the United States Army built Fort Dearborn in 1803 at the spot where the sluggish Chicago River dribbled across a sandbar and into Lake Michigan. Fort Dearborn became a site of battle when the United States declared war on the British in 1812. Six hundred British-allied Native Americans ambushed ninety-four white Americans and their Miami guides, burning the fort and killing fifty-two people. The carnage of what Anglo-Americans dubbed the "Fort Dearborn Massacre" fed many whites' hostility toward Native Americans.[9]

The U.S. Army rebuilt Fort Dearborn in 1816–1817 as a defense against the region's Native Americans, a move that foreshadowed a broader shift from coexistence with, to removal of, Native Americans.[10] The policy of removal in this region followed the transformation of the region's political economy from fur trading to farming.[11] Fort Dearborn thus became an instrument of removal, opening lands to Anglo-American farmers.

In 1832, the U.S. military used the fort as a staging ground for a war against the Sauk chief Black Hawk, who was resisting American settlement in northwestern Illinois. Fort Dearborn's proximity to Lake Michigan made it a natural choice for shipping soldiers and supplies to the region. Yet, the sandbar that La Salle had lamented in the 1680s prevented ships from entering the mouth of the Chicago River. Ships anchored a mile off the coast, and men shuttled their cargos to shore on smaller boats. These complications notwithstanding, American forces—Abraham Lincoln and Jefferson Davis among them—defeated Black Hawk. The federal government and Native Americans negotiated the 1833 Treaty of Chicago. Native Americans exchanged five million acres of land in northeastern Illinois and southeast Wisconsin to the United States government for five million acres west of the Mississippi. With that, Native American tribes were driven from the region that would soon be dominated by the city of Chicago.[12]

At the time, Saint Louis's geographical strengths—its proximity to the Ohio and Missouri Rivers and its easy connection to the bustling port of New Orleans—suggested that it would dwarf Chicago as an economic force. In light of the nation's growing sectional crisis, however, Yankee merchants became increasingly reluctant to invest capital in the slave state of Missouri, instead favoring Illinois.[13] Meanwhile, Illinoisans engineered a new economic geography for Chicago—one conducive to transportation of people, goods, and information—by building a canal and establishing a harbor in the Chicago River.

Remarkably, these monumental projects were completed in a polity where city, state, and federal governments shared authority, and at a time when questions about the balance of power pushed the nation ever closer to cataclysm. It is not surprising that political leaders failed to reach definitive agreements over which governing body should bear the costs of engineering a new geography for Chicago's waterways. Instead, the city, state, and federal governments created a patchwork of power over the landscape, sharing authority and costs even as they continually renegotiated their responsibilities for building infrastructure. Oftentimes, lawmakers resolved funding questions by selling land and bonds to private investors to raise money for infrastructure. The Illinois and Michigan Canal offers a case in point.

The Illinois and Michigan Canal

The same year that Hubbard first waded through the muddy Chicago Portage, 1818, Illinois congressional delegate Nathaniel Pope redrew the state's boundaries in anticipation of a canal. In so doing, he radically altered the political and economic geography of Illinois.

Like most early Illinois settlers, Pope hailed from a slave state and gravitated to the more prosperous and populated southern portion of the territory. Born into a prominent Kentucky family, he traded on his family influence to gain a post as Illinois's territorial secretary in 1809, a post he held until his 1816 election as territorial delegate to Congress. In that role, Pope negotiated key terms of Illinois's 1818 bid for statehood, including an eight-thousand-square-mile extension of the state's northern border. According to the Northwest Ordinance, that border was to extend due west from Lake Michigan's southern tip, thereby depriving Illinois of the Lake Michigan shoreline and the Chicago Portage.[14]

Pope could envision the canal imagined by French explorers soon becoming a reality. President James Madison had spoken of the possibility in his 1814 inaugural, and in an 1816 treaty the federal government had forced the Potawatomi Indians to relinquish a twenty-mile-wide strip of land for a canal between Ottawa and the Chicago River.[15] Pope, determined to pluck that canal from the as-yet-to-be organized territory of Wisconsin, requested a forty-mile extension of the state's northern border, telling Congress that the lake frontage would "afford additional security to the perpetuity of the Union, inasmuch as the State would thereby be connected with the States of Indiana, Ohio, Pennsylvania, and New York, through the Lakes."[16]

Congress obliged, and Pope's prediction that water transportation would help seal Illinois to the Union proved true. From the 1850s on, migrants and capital from New England and New York poured into northern Illinois.[17] By the eve of the Civil War, Illinois had begun to shed its southern character and forge bonds of culture, commerce, and politics with the North. Thus, Illinoisans like Lincoln who were born in southern states would side with the cause of union.[18]

The movement of the state line notwithstanding, the canal's course was still not set. That remained contingent on the decisions of Illinois officials, surveyors, and eastern financiers. In 1827, the state received a land grant from Congress of 284,000 acres, the sale of which would be used to finance construction.[19] Two years later, the governor of Illinois appointed canal commissioners to oversee the project. The commissioners began laying out towns, including Chicago, along the proposed route. The Canal Commission hired surveyor James Thompson to make a plat of the town of Chicago. The Thompson Plat of 1830 established a grid of sixty-six-foot-wide streets, interspersed with lots dissected by sixteen-foot alleyways. The three branches of the Chicago River wound through the map, interrupting its otherwise perfect symmetry. By creating a series of relatively uniform segments, Thompson and the canal commissioners transformed Chicago's land into a salable commodity for which there would soon be plenty of credit.[20]

The prospect of the canal, combined with the increasing availability of credit, drove investment in Chicago real estate. In 1832, President Andrew Jackson broke the power of the Second Bank of the United States, freeing western banks to offer credit for land purchases on liberal terms. Speculators with pockets full of easy credit bought and sold Chicago lots at a fever pitch, with buyers from as far away as Europe, New England, and New York snapping up property they had never even seen at continually rising prices. A Lake Street lot, for instance, cost three hundred dollars in 1832 and sold for sixty thousand dollars in 1836.[21] These grand sums were mainly pocketed by land speculators who flipped lots, not the Canal Commission, which had sold most of its holdings before prices soared. Consequently, land sales did not generate enough capital to build the costly canal, and the state legislature began to consider if there was a cheaper, alternate route for the waterway.[22]

In the 1830s, members of the Illinois state legislature debated whether to fix the location of the canal on the basis of construction cost, politics, or topography. Viewed from ground level, the most obvious canal route seemed to follow the portage from the Chicago River to the Des Plaines. The surface of the upper Des Plaines was on a level with that of Lake Michigan, and the land in-between the two waterways rose to a maximum elevation of fourteen feet. Thus, the original plan was to make a thirty-mile "deep cut" in the earth from the Chicago River directly to the Des Plaines, letting gravity pull the water southwest. This plan, if enacted, would have reversed the flow of the Chicago River—a feat that engineers achieved in 1871. But during the 1830s, the deep-cut plan literally foundered on the rocks.

Viewed from beneath the earth's surface, the proposed route had critical drawbacks. The soil consisted of dense clay called "hard pan," and worse still, limestone bedrock lurked just below the earth's surface at key points. The cost of blasting through the bedrock would be enormous: An 1833 estimate put the canal project cost at four million dollars, up significantly from estimates of seven hundred thousand dollars in 1823–1824. With cost projections soaring, some legislators suggested building a railroad or finding a less-rocky alternative canal route. The state, however, simply jettisoned the entire project until its 1835–1836 legislative session, when Hubbard—now a

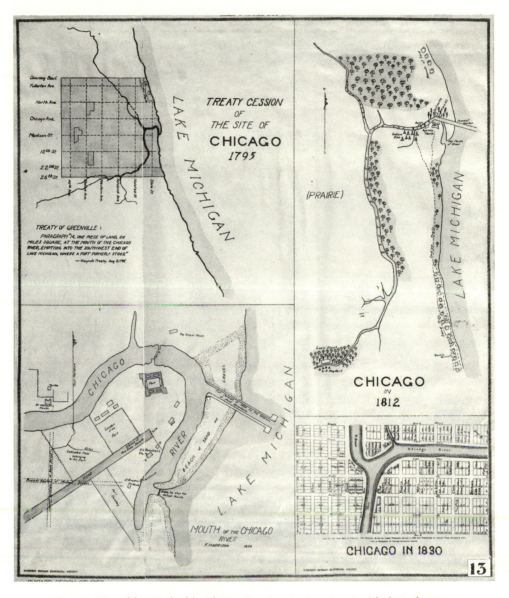

Figure 3. Maps of the mouth of the Chicago River in 1795, 1812, 1830, 1834 (clockwise from top left). These maps depict the Chicago River at four crucial points in the city's early history. The map at the top left shows the six square-mile area of land ceded by American Indians to the United States government in the 1795 Treaty of Greenville. The next map depicts Fort Dearborn and the settlements clumped along the Chicago River in 1812. The third map illustrates how surveyor James Thompson laid out the streets and lots of Chicago in 1830. The final map illustrates where the U.S. Army dredged a channel through the sandbar at the mouth of the Chicago River in 1834. Charles A. Kent compiled these maps in 1915 for use in the Chicago Public Schools. This compilation of maps is housed in and was reproduced by the Chicago History Museum.

state representative—successfully argued that even if the original canal route was rocky and costly, both political and long-term economic logic argued for making Chicago the terminus of the canal.[23]

Since his first slog through Mud Lake in 1818, Hubbard had prospered trading furs and selling livestock to the soldiers garrisoned at Fort Dearborn. Having moved to Chicago permanently in 1834, Hubbard won election to represent the town in the state legislature. In the renewed debate over the canal, a faction of cost-conscious representatives argued for rerouting it through the Calumet River, which was located about a dozen miles south of the Chicago River, along the Illinois-Indiana border, and ran from Lake Calumet into Lake Michigan. The plan's advocates explained that engineers could cut a channel from the Calumet River through the adjacent Saganashkee Slough, or "Sag," to the Des Plaines.[24] Advocates of the Calumet-Sag route promised that the route would circumvent much of the bedrock, thereby reducing construction costs. Hubbard countered this geological argument with a lesson in political geography. Taking out a map, Hubbard showed his colleagues in the chamber that the mouth of the Calumet River sat only a few hundred yards from the border of Indiana. Hubbard, according to one account, then noted that "it was expected that wherever the canal terminated, a great city would grow up" and asked "whether it was desirable that the coming city should be as much of it in the state of Indiana as in Illinois, when the entire expense of construction would devolve upon our state[?]" Hubbard's argument prevailed, and on July 4, 1836, the state of Illinois began making the "deep cut" between the Des Plaines and the Chicago River.[25]

While political considerations dictated that the Illinois and Michigan Canal flow through Chicago, the imperatives of finance forced engineers to abandon the deep cut. Hubbard and his legislative colleagues' insistence that the canal run through Chicago meant that engineers and laborers had to proceed with the arduous and frequently deadly work of cutting through the hard pan and bedrock along the route, which was carried out largely by Irish laborers. To finance the undertaking, the state of Illinois borrowed great sums. In 1835, the legislature granted Governor Joseph Duncan power to negotiate a five hundred thousand dollars loan for money to build the canal. In 1837, the legislature passed the Internal Improvement Act, authorizing the state to borrow four million dollars for canal construction and millions more to build an intricate railroad network across the state, known as the Illinois Central Railroad (a private corporation would later bear that name).[26] Just when the state began to accrue enormous debts, the Panic of 1837 struck, stalling the economy and driving the cost of borrowing higher.[27] By 1840, the cash-strapped state of Illinois halted work on the canal and railroads. By 1842, the state was in financial ruin with $10.6 million in public debt, annual interest payments of eight hundred thousand dollars, and a yearly income of just ninety-eight thousand dollars.[28]

Illinois was not alone. Inspired by New York's Erie Canal, Ohio and Indiana had also launched ambitious internal improvement projects. In 1832, Ohio completed a canal between Lake Erie and the Ohio River, and its tremendous success galvanized political support for new public works projects. In 1837, the state legislature passed a Loan Law that virtually required the state to match private investment in internal improvements. Hoosiers, meanwhile, started building a "Mammoth System" of railroads, canals, and turnpikes. The Panic of 1837 was a devastating blow to all these Midwestern projects, and to state economies across the nation.

For years, western banks had been making unsound loans to land speculators in Chicago and throughout the nation. In 1836, President Jackson put an end to easy credit with his "specie circular," an executive order that required western banks to redeem paper money in gold or silver. Deflation ensued. The cost of borrowing soared as many states became mired in expensive internal improvement projects. By 1841, Indiana had spent over eight million dollars on just 281 miles of its proposed 1,289 mile transportation system; it would need twelve million dollars more to complete the work. Already burdened with a total public debt of fifteen million dollars and annual interest payments of at least $615,000, the state of Indiana defaulted. Ohio fared a little better. In the decade after 1836, it spent thirteen million dollars on canals and aid to transportation companies. Meanwhile, the Loan Law alone forced the state to take on three million dollars of debt by 1842. The law, moreover, created numerous opportunities for corruption and misuse of public money. In 1842, the legislature repealed what had come to be called the "Plunder Law." A combination of New York investors and the economy's rebound in 1843 saved Ohio from bankruptcy.[29]

As public debt wrought havoc on the finances of states throughout the Midwest, businessmen supplied private capital to resurrect the Illinois and Michigan Canal project. In June 1842, a New York City land speculator named Arthur Bronson journeyed to Chicago to assess the status of the Illinois and Michigan Canal. In 1833, Bronson had begun buying up Chicago real estate, betting on the successful completion of the canal. As he toured Chicago, Bronson met with business leaders, including William B. Ogden, a real-estate speculator and Democratic politician who served as the city's first mayor (1837–1838). The men discussed how to secure money to finish the canal. Bronson and Ogden determined that they would appeal to investors in Boston, New York, and London for an additional $1.6 million in loans. In exchange for the capital, the investors required, among other things, that the state abandon the deep-cut plan for a cheaper, shallow-cut channel eight feet above the level of Lake Michigan. In other words, the investors demanded that water run uphill. A canal engineer named Ira Miltimore figured out how to comply. Using giant steam pumps, the engineer would force water from the south branch of the Chicago River into the canal.[30]

That engineers would make water run uphill at the behest of financiers symbolized the growing role of private businessmen in building public infrastructure. Lawmakers in Ohio, Indiana, and Illinois were deeply shaken by the financial crises of the 1830s and 1840s, and they moved to severely limit their states' capacity to build new infrastructure. In 1851, Ohio lawmakers established a new state constitution that prohibited the state from borrowing money. Hoosiers likewise rewrote their constitution in 1850–1851 to forbid the state of Indiana from taking on public debt.

Increasingly, new infrastructure would be built by private corporations.[31] For instance, when Democratic Senator Stephen Douglas renewed the push for an Illinois railroad in the late 1840s, he assumed that a private corporation, not taxpayers, should raise the capital. In 1851, the state granted a corporate charter to the Illinois Central Railroad, a private version of its defunct publicly funded predecessor.[32] The new Illinois Central would, like the Illinois and Michigan Canal, link New Orleans to the mouth of the Chicago River Harbor. Before that could happen, however, Chicago required a navigable harbor.

Public Property, Private Capital, and Wharves

As laborers dug the Illinois and Michigan Canal out of hard rock and clay, the city of Chicago worked on a related project: transforming the sluggish, sand-clogged Chicago River that would link the canal to Lake Michigan into a viable harbor. The river needed to be widened and dredged to allow for the passage of boats. The banks of the Chicago River required wharves for handling cargo and bridges to facilitate overland travel. These feats of construction required effective regulation of public space. They also posed a financing dilemma: how to split the costs of infrastructure between all of Chicago's tax-payers and the specific individuals who would make money from the harbor.

At first, legal ambiguity over waterfront access delayed its development.[33] In the 1830s, the trustees of the town of Chicago promised to commit public funds to river dredging in order to encourage business owners to construct docks and wharves. The trustees thus tried to channel both public and private money into harbor construction. In 1835, the town trustees, with the consent of the state legislature, leased public riverfront lots to the highest bidder for a period of 999 years. Under the terms of the lease, the lessees had four years to pay for access to the lot and two years to build five-foot-wide docks three feet above the water line. The trustees, on the other hand, agreed to dredge the river channel ten feet in front of the docks within four years of the leasing agreement.

The economic panic that struck in 1837 made it nearly impossible for the city, incorporated in March of that very year, to incur the enormous expenditures required to dredge the river. Nor could the lessees pay for their lots. Since both sides reneged on the terms, the contracts were ignored until 1844, when the Chicago Common Council launched an inquiry into the status of the wharfing leases. It discovered that the city's wharves were mired in legal chaos. Some lessees had built on and occupied their lots, while others had sold them to third parties. Still others had abandoned them to squatters.[34]

The Common Council consisted largely of merchants, bankers, lumber dealers, and real estate brokers who had come to Chicago from the northeast in hopes of making fortunes, and many of the aldermen had a stake in port development. Their success depended on the city's growth, which required a working harbor.[35] Seeking an end to the confusion over wharfing rights, in 1845 the Common Council ordered that all wharfing privileges be surrendered to the city, since most of the original lessees had failed to pay.[36] It was forced to back off this plan to seize the wharves, since it too had violated the 1835 leases. In 1846, the council issued a new order levying a fifty dollar quarterly penalty against "any person . . . in possession of any portion of the public landings or wharfing privileges" until "some further settlement be made."[37] With this act, the Common Council acknowledged that the claims to wharf privileges required careful, individualized adjudication. In February of 1847, the state legislature passed "An Act to adjust and settle the title to all wharfing privileges in Chicago," which returned riverfront lots to the city and established a procedure whereby claimants could negotiate a settlement.[38] By 1850, the city had settled the claims and issued a series of new wharf leases with the expectation that business owners would construct the docks necessary for the port.[39]

After establishing property rights on the riverfront, the city was able to condemn certain lots in order to deepen and widen the channel of the Chicago River. This was essential for the city's growing harbor. The confusion over wharf leases notwithstanding, the commerce in Chicago's harbor had increased in value from three hundred thousand dollars in 1836 to five million dollars in 1847.[40] With the imminent completion of the Illinois and Michigan Canal, the city of Chicago and the canal trustees anticipated even greater increases in Chicago River commerce. In October of 1847, the Common Council began to redraw the map of the riverfront to accommodate the new channel. The city evacuated several streets—all of North Water Street west of Wolcott, Carroll Street east of the river's north branch, and east of Water Street from North Water to Kinzie—to permit the canal trustees to widen and deepen the Chicago River and build a turning basin on the north branch of the river at Carroll Street. By resolving the uncertainty over property rights, then, the city destroyed an older landscape and created a new one more suitable for the demands of a growing commerce.[41]

Through river dredging and the offer of long-term leases, Chicago's Common Council enticed private parties to build wharves on public lands. The Chicago River Harbor, constructed as a joint public and private enterprise, became a dynamic marketplace.

The Chicago Common Council pinned the costs of wharf construction on those who wished to use them—as opposed to all the city's taxpayers. This was a matter of fairness, an acknowledgement by the city's alderman that creating new infrastructure benefitted some people more than others. Even so, the construction of new infrastructure was sometimes a matter of intense dispute. If it was not a matter of cost, it was often a matter of space. Commerce followed infrastructure, as goods flowed into harbors, over roads, and across bridges. Consequently, the power to build or destroy infrastructure on public land was often tantamount to the power to establish or destroy a marketplace. Recognizing this fact, Chicagoans fought bitterly over where to locate the city's bridges.

Breaking and Building Bridges for Commerce

Before daybreak one morning in July 1839, a "large crowd" gathered on the banks of the Chicago River to destroy the bridge at Dearborn Street. The precise identity and number of the people who came to the riverbank brandishing axes and sledge hammers that morning is unknown, but the crowd likely consisted mostly of Southsiders embroiled in in the great "Bridge War" with Northsiders.[42]

Ostensibly the Southsiders were acting in the interest of public safety. Built in 1834 on the order of the town trustees, the structure at Dearborn Street was the only bridge that spanned the main stem of the river. It was a rickety, three-hundred-foot-long "gallows" draw with two frames that loomed "like instruments of death" and a sixty-foot passageway for ships that could be opened by a team of six men pulling chains. For years its supports had been pummeled by the "blows of passing vessels," and its planks worn underfoot of pedestrians and animals, causing the bridge to begin to disintegrate.[43] The city had made repairs in 1835 and 1837, but structural problems persisted. In 1838, Alderman Henry Rucker reported on the city's options: repair the bridge again for a cost of between $135 and $300, insert a float between its piers for $650, or replace it with a floating bridge at Clark Street for $1,090.[44] In July of the following year, the Chicago Common Council ordered that the hazardous bridge be torn down and replaced with a ferry. The next morning an enthusiastic crowd "chopped the bridge to pieces."[45]

The crowd's eagerness to tear down the bridge owed less to concerns over safety than to its desire to control the corridors of commerce in Chicago and, with them, the city's burgeoning grain market. Before railroads and canal boats stitched Chicago to the Midwestern interior, farmers brought their produce to the city on wagons known as "prairie schooners." According to the *Chicago Times*, "Every night there came up out of the south a great fleet of prairie schooners that . . . often numbered five hundred, and came laden with wheat and corn." The farmers came in from the south and, since the city's principal grain warehouses lay north of the main stem of the river, they had to cross a bridge or sell their crops to a middleman on the Southside. Southsiders eager to insert themselves into that lucrative intermediary role were delighted when bridge defects led the Common Council to authorize the destruction of the draw at Dearborn Street. Those Southsiders, however, were not content to merely destroy one bridge. They also wanted to prevent the construction of any new bridges.[46]

During the late 1830s and early 1840s the Chicago Common Council debated not how to fund bridge construction but whether to even have bridges binding the sections of the city. As the Dearborn Street Bridge continually deteriorated, Northside businessmen led by Ogden spearheaded plans for an alternative bridge at Wells Street, for which they promised to pay.[47] The Common Council included two aldermen from each of the city's six wards. Its members, evenly split between Northsiders and Southsiders, rejected the proposal.

The council agreed that the Dearborn Street Bridge had to go, but it argued bitterly over whether to replace the span, and, if so, where the new bridge should be located. Southside Alderman Augustus Garrett led the charge against a new bridge; he even went so far as to claim that a span across the river would help British troops enter the city if they attacked from Canada.[48] Northside real estate moguls Ogden and Walter Newberry, in turn, tried to win Southside aldermen's support for the bridge. According to the *Chicago Times*, Ogden and Newberry gifted two blocks of Southside land to the Catholic Church for the purpose of building a cathedral with the understanding the aldermen would acquiesce to a bridge.[49]

By April of 1840, workmen were driving piles for a new span at Clark Street. Even so, the debate over the bridge continued. In 1841, the Common Council considered moving a new bridge from Clark to Dearborn, but took no such action.[50] When a flood damaged the Clark Street Bridge in 1844, Garrett argued that it should be removed. Northsiders silenced him, however, by repairing it. With financing from private property owners like Newberry, the city constructed several new bridges across the river before the end of the decade, although not without the typical wrangling over location.[51] With each new bridge, it became easier to shuttle people, goods, and information across the Chicago River.

The Shifting Sands of the Chicago River Harbor

As Chicago's city leaders successfully harnessed public and private funds to build key infrastructure—bridges, wharves, and a deeper, wider river channel—in the 1830s and 1840s, and the Chicago River became a thriving harbor, one vexing barrier to commerce remained. The sandbar, described by La Salle over a century earlier, still stubbornly clogged the mouth of the Chicago River. Because it abutted the army's Fort Dearborn and Lake Michigan, an interstate body of water, the sandbar was a federal responsibility, but the federal government failed to consistently allocate money to keep the channel open, which continually refilled with sand. Some influential political leaders from the south did not want to spend money developing a northern city, and Chicago's leaders grew frustrated.

The river was the lifeblood of their city's economy, and it had the potential to be a key harbor on expansive Lake Michigan, which runs 307 miles in length and up to 118 miles in width, with a maximum depth of 923 feet.[52] On an 1821 visit to the Chicago River, geographer and ethnologist Henry Schoolcraft observed that "after passing the Manitou Islands [off the cost of northern Michigan] there is no harbor or shelter for vessels in the southern part of Lake Michigan, and that every vessel which passes into that lake after the month of September, runs an imminent hazard of shipwreck." But, Schoolcraft noted, the "sand which is driven up into the mouth of the Chicago Creek" blocked deep draft vessels from entering that potential harbor.[53]

The mouth of the Chicago River had to be cleared of sand to permit ships to pass from the waters of Lake Michigan to the proposed canal. In 1830, surveyor William Howard told Congress that "The formation of a good harbor at this place [the mouth of the Chicago] is . . . indispensable to the efficiency of the proposed canal from Lake Michigan to the Illinois river."[54] To establish such a harbor, however, engineers would have to contend with an incessant barrage of water and sand. The force of Lake Michigan's current drove sand across the mouth of the Chicago River, closing off the stream from all but the smallest of vessels. When he made his survey of the Chicago River in 1830, Howard was surprised to discover that the sandbar did not owe to the sediments carried by the river into the lake. "A remarkable circumstance connected with the formation of this bar is," Howard observed, "that these deposits of sand seem to be brought almost entirely from the North [by lake currents]."[55]

The Chicago River was generally too sluggish to carry much sand to its mouth. The south branch originated five or six miles southwest of the lake on a low prairie bog and the north branch ran south along a low muddy plain parallel to Lake Michigan for about thirty miles. The two branches met a mile or so from Lake Michigan and flowed east past a settlement of about a dozen houses and Fort Dearborn. After Fort Dearborn, the river then turned south and dribbled over the sandbar and into Lake Michigan.[56]

As Howard had noted, Lake Michigan's currents had created the sandbar through a process of littoral drift. According to the historical geographer Libby Hill, Lake Michigan's current often flowed for two hundred nautical miles from Michigan's Leelanau Peninsula before it pummeled the Chicago lake shore from the northeast. As the lake waters flowed toward Chicago's shoreline, sometimes aided by storms or great winds, they gained momentum and swept sand and other debris along with them. As a wave washed ashore, however, it lost its energy, dropping much of the debris. Some debris collected on the shoreline and some rolled back into the lake with the receding waves. As the receding waves bounced off the shoreline, they rolled back into the lake, not toward their origin in the northeast, but easterly and slightly to the south, continually moving the sands southeast along the shoreline. That littoral drift clogged the Chicago River's mouth with sand and bent the channel southward.[57]

In the 1830s, the Army Corps of Engineers cut a channel through the sandbar at the mouth of the Chicago River, forever altering the shoreline in unforeseen ways. To open the harbor, Howard suggested to Congress that the Army Corps of Engineers cut a channel across the sandbar, so that the Chicago River flowed due east into the lake. Howard proposed building two long piers on either side of the river mouth that extended out into Lake Michigan, thereby, Howard hoped, protecting the river's opening from sand.[58] In 1833, Congress appropriated money. Army engineers, first commanded by Major George Bender and after 1834 by Lieutenant James Allen, cut a two-hundred-foot-wide channel through the sandbar so that the river flowed almost due east into Lake Michigan about one thousand feet north of its former outlet. By 1835, the south pier ran 700 feet into the lake and the north, or weather, pier extended 1,260 feet. Lieutenant Allen could already see that just north of the weather pier, a new sand bar was forming that threatened to encroach on the river channel as it grew. As the lake currents rolled in from the northeast, the north pier trapped sand, growing the north shoreline of the city by 320 feet between 1833 to 1837 and another 400 feet between 1837 and 1839, creating an area known as the "sands" and later Streeterville. South of the piers, however, the effect was just the opposite. The piers prevented the currents from depositing new sands and created an eddy that eroded the existing southern lakeshore, an area occupied by the U.S. Army Fort Dearborn and the city's only public parks.[59]

The city of Chicago acquired the valuable but eroding Fort Dearborn lands from the federal government in 1839. By 1833, American forces had crushed the band of Sauk and Fox Indians led by Chief Black Hawk and forced Native Americans to relinquish their lands east of the Mississippi River.[60] Fort Dearborn, therefore, became largely obsolete except that it housed the army engineers who worked to clear the mouth of the Chicago River. In 1838, Chicagoans petitioned the federal government to relinquish the fort because it was "useless for a military post."[61] In 1839, the Secretary of War granted 90 percent of the Fort Dearborn land to the city, reserving only a small parcel south of the mouth of the Chicago River for military buildings. The Fort Dearborn Addition to Chicago consisted of valuable waterfront lots and public lands. The addition consisted of seventy-six acres extending northeast from the intersection of State and Madison Streets to Lake Michigan and the Chicago River, most of which the city subdivided into lots and sold to private parties.[62]

President Martin Van Buren, however, ensured that some of the Fort Dearborn Addition lands were reserved for the public. Campaigning for re-election, the New York Democrat worried that he would lose western votes if eastern speculators bought up too much choice waterfront land in Chicago. Van Buren therefore ordered the General Land Office to designate the block west of Michigan Avenue between Randolph and Madison Streets a "public square," which became known as Dearborn Park. The land office marked the parcel east of Michigan Avenue "public ground." This ground became known as North Lake Park since it adjoined a strip of lakeshore land to the south, between Madison and Twelfth Streets. The land had been set aside just three years earlier when the state's canal commissioners elected not to sell it, instead deeming the space "Public Ground—A Common to Remain Forever Open, Clear and Free of any Buildings or other Obstruction Whatever." In 1844, the canal commissioners transferred control of that public space to the city of Chicago. By 1847, the land had become known as Lake Park, a popular promenading ground.[63] The Fort Dearborn Addition therefore extended the city's park space and endowed it with additional lakeshore and riverfront lots. But these assets were imperiled because the Army Corps of Engineers' efforts to open the Chicago River Harbor had precipitated the erosion of the shoreline.

The city of Chicago had contradictory political and environmental imperatives. The city required a harbor. Yet, the acts of dredging the river and extending piers into Lake Michigan caused the erosion of valuable lake shore lands south of the mouth of the river. The city's position highlights a common environmental and economic tension: the transformation of a landscape often simultaneously increases its value and sows the seeds of its destruction. Even if those goals were contradictory, though, the city had little choice. It had to simultaneously maintain the harbor and protect valuable private and public lands on the lakeshore, and it attempted to achieve these goals—without imposing heavy taxes on its population—by appealing to the federal government for lakeshore protection.

Within months of acquiring the Fort Dearborn Addition, the city of Chicago asked the federal government for the remaining federal lands as compensation for damage done to the shoreline. The mayor and Common Council complained to Congress that the "extension of piers forming the harbor . . . have caused such a change in the action and effect of the water on this shore of Lake Michigan that . . . land . . . on the south side [of the piers] . . . is rapidly disappearing." To save "a large portion of the best part of our city" from the lake waters, the petition requested that Congress grant the city additional federal lands to compensate the city for the cost of "erecting a permanent barrier against this invasion." The petition fell on deaf ears.[64]

If Lake Michigan's currents posed a threat to the Chicago River Harbor, so too did the shifting sands of congressional politics. From 1839 to 1841, Congress, mired in sectional conflict over the distribution of internal improvement funds, allocated not a cent for harbor improvement. Meanwhile, in Chicago, sand crept around the north pier into the river's mouth, clogging the channel and putting commerce in peril. In 1842, Chicago's Democratic mayor, Francis Sherman, and the Common Council petitioned Congress for harbor improvement money. Anticipating a debate over the national significance of the harbor, the mayor and aldermen highlighted Chicago's emerging position as a gateway between east and west. "The agricultural prospects of all of Illinois, Indiana, Iowa, and Missouri," noted the petition, "are . . . greatly dependent upon facilities for business . . . on the southwest part of Lake Michigan: which lake is part of the great channel by which the staples of these States will best reach the eastern market."[65]

Indeed, the city of only about six thousand residents already boasted annual imports in excess of $1.5 million and exports of $348,362. The petition warned, however, that "serious and immediate evils threaten the . . . harbor for the purposes of commerce." Critically, "the action of the wind . . . has formed a sand-bar across the pier."[66] Congress granted a modest ten thousand dollars in 1843 for Chicago harbor repairs.[67] Even so, it mattered little in the grand scheme of things. For the harbor to remain open Congress would have to continually pour money into dredging and pier renovations designed to preserve the harbor from an incessant barrage of wind, water, and sand (Table 1).

Growing increasingly frustrated with Congress's lack of sustained funding for harbor improvements, the Chicago Common Council challenged the federal government's control of what remained of Fort Dearborn. In April of 1845, on motion of the lawyer and Whig alderman J. Young Scammon, the Chicago Common Council ordered that "the street commissioner be directed forthwith to open the street (Michigan Avenue) and remove the obstructions therefrom."[68] So ordered, Street Commissioner Phillip Dean would have to extend the city's street grid through the Fort Dearborn reservation. In order to carry out this order, Dean needed to destroy up to eight Fort Dearborn buildings—a feat that had not been repeated since Pottawatomie warriors burned the fort in 1812. Perhaps not coincidentally, one of the buildings Dean would have to wreck to execute the Common Council's order was the Office of Public Works, which housed the army engineers.

Table 1. Federal Spending on Chicago River Improvement, 1833–1843

Year	Federal Appropriation
1833	$25,000
1834	$30,000
1835	$30,000
1836	$25,000
1837	$30,000
1838	$40,000
1839	$0
1840	$0
1841	$0
1842	$30,000
1843	$10,000

Sources: The data from 1833 to 1842 are from Jesse B. Thomas, *Statistical Report*, in *Chicago River-and-Harbor Convention*, ed. Robert Fergus (Chicago: Fergus Printing Co., 1882), 192; the data from 1843 is from Mendelsohn, "The Federal Hand in Urban Development," 259.

Before city workers began wielding their axes and sledge hammers, however, U.S. government agent Charles Schlatter secured an injunction from the district court judge to halt the destruction of federal property. Four years later, the Supreme Court ruled, in *United States v. Chicago*, that the city's right to build streets did not endow it with the power to seize federal lands.[69] In the meantime, Schlatter voluntarily removed several federal buildings in 1845 and 1846 so the city could extend River Street along the main stem of the Chicago River.[70]

Schlatter's actions eased tensions between the federal government and the Chicago Common Council over waterfront policies, but the détente was short lived. In 1846, President James Polk, a Democrat from Tennessee, vetoed a bill that would have allocated $1,378,450 to over forty different river improvement projects throughout the American north and west, including dredging the sandbar that choked the mouth of the Chicago River Harbor.[71] The veto placed Chicago at the center of a virulent partisan debate over federal power, slavery, and the physical dimensions of the American economy. It centered on the question of who should pay for government services: all taxpayers, or just those who directly benefitted?

The National Politics of Internal Improvement

Polk's veto was just the latest episode in a larger debate over internal improvements that centered, in part, on distinctive conceptions of political and economic space. Inspired by Thomas Jefferson's ideals of limited federal power and local self-governance, Polk believed that congressional authority to improve rivers and harbors depended on a geographic assessment of the shape of the market. If a river or harbor carried interstate or foreign commerce, it possessed a "national" character, and Congress could allocate money for improvements. If, on the other hand, a river or harbor carried primarily intrastate commerce, improvements were merely a "local" matter, and Congress could not fund them without breeching the constitutional limits of its power. Thus, Polk's 1846 veto hinged on his determination that "Some of the objects of appropriation contained in this bill are local in their character, and lie within the limits of a single State."[72]

Polk's language parroted that of Andrew Jackson's famous veto of the Maysville Road Bill. In 1830, Jackson had denied federal funding to build a road between Maysville and Lexington, Kentucky, the home of political rival

Henry Clay, on the basis that the project was of a "purely local character." Jackson's veto rejected the integrated approach to internal improvements championed by Whigs such as Clay. Rooted in a Hamiltonian vision of centralized government and economic institutions, Clay's "American System" advocated funding internal improvements that, even if confined within one state, would function as parts of an integrated, national transportation network.[73]

Polk and Jackson's positions on internal improvements proved geographically problematic, but politically astute. It was difficult to distinguish between improvements of a local versus national character as rivers, harbors, or roads in one state might nonetheless handle national commerce.[74] Polk, moreover, linked his critique of federal support for local improvements to yet another muddy geographic distinction. He suggested that the federal government could improve "natural," but not "artificial" waterways.[75]

A key problem with the 1846 Rivers and Harbors Bill, Polk noted, was that it made harbors out of some waterways "at the expense of the local natural advantages of another in its vicinity."[76] Polk's position begged the question: How was a statesman to draw the distinction between a natural harbor and an artificial one if both needed improvement? These geographic distinctions, local versus national and natural versus artificial, made little environmental or economic sense, but their malleability made them politically potent. Democrats could claim to stand for limited government and justify spending federal dollars on improvements projects by pointing to, either cynically or earnestly, the national or natural characteristics of the waterway.

Even under Democratic presidents in the 1830s and 1840s, the federal government had poured money into improvement projects. Jackson, for instance, authorized more than sixteen million dollars of federal expenditures between 1830 and 1837 on roads, canals, rivers, and harbors.[77] Democrats' previous willingness to fund internal improvements raised doubts as to whether several of Polk's stated objections to the 1846 bill—the local character of the improvements, the artificiality of some of the waterways, and a desire to limit federal power—could be taken entirely at face value.

Polk's critics were also deeply skeptical of the president's claim that he sought to discourage sectional rivalry with his veto. Polk maintained that limiting appropriations for improvements would discourage "combinations of local and sectional interests" from forming in Congress to compete in a "disreputable scramble for public money."[78] Without federal spoils to fight over, there could not be sectional rivalries. But, the president's critics could not accept that logic at the same time he was leading a war against Mexico to acquire the proslavery Republic of Texas. The Whig *Chicago Daily Journal*, for instance, chaffed at Polk's exhortations of fiscal restraint, asking: "Are not the treasury doors unbarred whenever the '*open sesame*' is whispered by the slave-driver?" The president's "real hostility to the Bill," charged the paper, owed to the fact that "the objects of improvement lie north of Mason and Dixon's line." Polk, the paper concluded, had denied Chicago an effective harbor for commerce not out of political principle, but "because he wants the money for the Mexican War!"[79] The veto had enflamed the very sectional tensions Polk wished to avoid.

Polk's veto also drove a wedge between the northern and southern wings of the Democratic Party. Jackson's views on Indian removal, public lands, and the virtue of the common man had helped the party consistently carry Illinois in presidential elections from 1824 to the 1844 run of Polk.[80] Polk's 1846 veto created tensions between the party's southern leaders and Illinois Democrats like congressmen John Wentworth and Stephen Douglas.

Illinoisans required infrastructure for economic development. Wentworth and Douglas had therefore thrown their considerable political weight behind the effort to pass the 1846 Rivers and Harbors Bill. When Polk vetoed the bill, Douglas and Wentworth found themselves in a difficult position. The congressmen neither wanted to accede to the veto nor reject outright the principles of their party's leader. Congressman Douglas accepted Polk's argument that the constitution forbade federal appropriations for local improvements, but he maintained that many improvements called for in the bill were significant to the nation. Wentworth, on the other hand, denied that the veto rested on constitutional grounds. Rather, he charged Polk with sectional prejudice, noting that "this harbor question is one between north and south."[81]

Frustration over Polk's veto stirred political action. Shortly after Polk's veto, an agent of the Lake Steamboat Association, William Hall, called on politicians to assemble in protest at a national rivers and harbors convention. Through their attendance, speeches, and resolutions, the delegates would make their message clear: The federal government should pay for internal improvements in the north and west.[82]

The 1847 Chicago River and Harbor Convention

Many Chicago boosters eager to showcase their growing city clamored to host the event. Political and personal rivals like Democratic Congressman Wentworth and Whig attorney Scammon worked together to organize what came to be known as the 1847 Chicago River and Harbor Convention.[83] The two men maintained that their city, with a canal and an accessible harbor, would become the hub of a commercial corridor stretching from New York to New Orleans along the Great Lakes and Mississippi River watersheds. "These great waters, for whose safe navigation this Convention is called," noted Wentworth and Scammon in a promotional statement, "are soon to be united by . . . the Illinois & Michigan Canal." That union of waters, they argued, would bind the nation together in a common political economy: "The commerce of Boston, of Philadelphia, of Baltimore, of New York, of New Orleans . . . indeed of the whole country, thence becomes in a great measure connected. It has common interest."[84]

It was far from clear to all Chicagoans, though, that paying for the convention was in their best interests. As city leaders planned for the convention, some citizens and aldermen hesitated over shouldering the costs of the event. Their concerns echoed the national debate over internal improvements. They wished to pin the costs of the convention on those who stood to benefit. To do so, Chicagoans needed to determine whether the convention served the entire city's interests or those of a few citizens.

In May, a convention organizing committee of 110 citizens asked the Chicago Common Council to help pay for the River and Harbor Convention. The Council's Whig Finance Committee chairman, Levi Boone, made a five hundred dollar appropriation, noting that the convention was of an "entirely public & national character." But, when the organizing committee requested an additional thousand dollars, Boone resisted. He noted that the use of additional public money for the convention was opposed by "some of our fellow citizens, who pay taxes." Boone's deference to these citizens was consistent with a principle of antebellum Chicago governance: The bill for city services should be sent to the beneficiaries.[85]

Boone's opponents did not dispute this principle. Rather, they claimed that the convention was indeed in the city's interest. On June 18, 1847, a convention organizer and Democratic Illinois state senator, Norman Judd, led a public rally calling on the Common Council to allocate thousands more

dollars for the convention. Judd maintained the convention was "of para-
mount importance to the best interests . . . of the city."[86] He and fellow members of the organizing committee regarded the convention as an opportunity
to promote Chicago among the nation's political and economic elite. Convention organizers therefore distributed pamphlets trumpeting the city's
growth from 4,853 in 1840 to more than 16,000 in 1847 and boasting of Chicago's three libraries, three hundred dry goods stores, five bowling saloons,
six foundries, fifty-six attorneys, twenty-four lumber dealers, fourteen news-
papers, nineteen schools, and three shipbuilders.[87]

Many aldermen agreed that hosting the River and Harbor Convention
would benefit Chicago. One-third of the city's aldermen joined the 110-
member citizens committee that organized the convention. It successfully
pressed Boone to allocate more money for the convention, but it did not get
as much as it wanted. The convention was funded, like so much of Chicago's
infrastructure, with a mixture of private and public money. Private donors
gave an untold sum, and the city relinquished thirteen hundred dollars from
its coffers.[88]

As the city's aldermen squabbled over who should pay for the convention,
Whig Party leaders used the occasion of their trip to Chicago to highlight the
commercial potential of the north and west. The Albany journalist and party
boss Thurlow Weed, for instance, described Chicago's economic utility for
residents of New York State in his dispatches to readers of the *Albany Evening
Journal*. With the completion of the Erie Canal between Albany and Buffalo
in 1825, Weed noted, New Yorkers had a direct water route from the Atlantic
Ocean to the Great Lakes. They could harvest the natural resources of the
nation's interior and ship their products to western cities, thereby building a
commercial empire.[89]

Weed traveled to Chicago from Buffalo in 1847 aboard a "magnificent"
steamship aptly named *Empire*, steaming west across Lake Erie, turning
north to ascend the Detroit River, Lake St. Clair, and the dangerously shallow
St. Clair River, before bursting out onto the deep blue waters of Lake Huron.[90]
It was at that point, "passing out of the St. Clair River into broad and deep
Huron," Weed reported, that "you *begin* to comprehend something of the
vastness of the West." To Weed, the landscape seemed a divine gift. "That
America is to be the 'seat of empire,'" Weed suggested, "'is a fixed fact.' A
wisdom above that of man has prepared for the inhabitants of worn-out, im-
poverished, and over burthened Europe, a fresh, fertile, primeval land, whose
virgin soil and graceful forests will wave over millions of people." As the

Empire chugged around Michigan and turned southwest toward Chicago, Weed marveled at the seemingly limitless timber stands, highlighting how they might be used to drive commercial progress with his observation that the *Empire*'s crew pitched six hundred cords of wood—the equivalent of ten acres of heavily forested land—into the boat's furnace during the trip to Chicago.[91] Indeed, much of the timber described by Weed would, in the coming decades, be chopped down and shipped to the lumber yards along the banks of the Chicago River.[92]

Weed's suggestion that a divine logic ordained the commercial growth of the Midwest and its soon-to-be leading metropolis of Chicago belied the gritty political, financial, and environmental realities of building cities and marketplaces. That, of course, was the point. Weed's account was a political text designed to persuade voters and politicians of the wisdom, even the inevitability, of spending money on rivers and harbors to help chart a particular economic geography. The existence of the city to which Weed traveled in the summer of 1847 was anything but foreordained. Rather, the Chicago of 1847 was the contingent outcome of a series of political and financial decisions, made over the course of several decades, about how to reshape the landscape and waterways for commerce. That project continued in 1847, which is why the attendees of the River and Harbor Convention wanted the federal government to pay for improvements.[93]

Weed's colleague at the *New York Tribune*, Horace Greeley, exaggerated the level of support for the convention in his dispatches from Chicago, giving the impression that Chicagoans had a singular purpose in hosting the event, which began with a Fourth of July parade. Greeley praised the "magnificent" procession of musicians, military ships on wheels, and fire engines that snaked through city streets along a route that had been shortened "in deference" to the blistering heat. He did not mention that Chicagoans had quarreled over who should pay for it; perhaps he did not know.[94] In any case, Greeley painted a picture of a city dedicated to staging a grand event. He claimed the western city of sixteen thousand residents had been overrun with between ten thousand and twenty thousand visitors, even though other estimates put the figure at just over two thousand.[95] There was, Greeley noted, "scarcely a spare inch of room in any public house," and many of Chicago's "citizens had . . . thrown open their dwellings" to accommodate the guests.[96]

Greeley's account reinforced the twin purposes of the convention: western boosterism and protesting the policies of President Polk. The delegates first met to discuss these issues formally on July 5. The heat had broken, giving way to a pleasant lake breeze, which cooled the delegates crammed into a tent in Chicago's Dearborn Park.[97] They contemplated the power of government to build new, public infrastructure and, in so doing, to create new markets.

To Regulate and Create a Marketplace

On July 6, David Dudley Field transformed the convention from an act of political theater to a substantive policy debate by challenging a position widely held by the delegates: that the federal government had the constitutional authority and responsibility to build waterways and harbors.[98] The day began with the reading of letters of support for the aims of the convention sent by absent politicians such as Missouri Democratic Senator Thomas Hart Benton, Kentucky Whig Senator Henry Clay, and former Democratic President Martin Van Buren.[99] Then Pennsylvania Whig Congressman Andrew Stewart made a "vigorous" speech calling on the federal government to spend money on infrastructure, a theme that met with the majority of the crowds' approval, but that also incited a rare show of opposition.[100]

Field voiced a fear common among Jacksonian Democrats that government policies might privilege favored citizens. Field, a prominent New York City attorney, was the son of a Congregationalist minister who had been raised in Stockbridge, Massachusetts. Growing up, Field had been schooled in law and Jacksonian politics by several members of the prominent Sedgwick family. As a student at Williams College, he had studied under Henry and Robert Sedgwick, impressing his mentors so much that they later entered into a legal practice with him in New York City. While in New York, Field cultivated a relationship with perhaps the most influential member of the Sedgwick family, Theodore, who was an attorney, *New York Evening Post* columnist, and author of influential legal and economic treatises. Sedgwick's writings hit key Jacksonian themes, especially an aversion to government redistribution of wealth through "*legal privileges given to some, and denied to others.*"[101] Field, too, shared this concern; the fear that government policies would privilege some citizens over others formed the core of his objection to federal funding for internal improvements.

He argued that the federal government had the power "to *regulate* not to *create*" new commercial arteries—an act that redistributed wealth.[102] Field warned the delegates, not unwisely, that political power tends "ever toward accumulation."[103] He thus believed it critical to mark the limits of federal power. The Constitution, Field reminded his audience, accorded the federal government the power to "regulate commerce with foreign nations, and among the several states."[104] That interpretation had been affirmed in Chief Justice John Marshall's famous ruling in *Gibbons v. Ogden* (1824), which denied the state of New York the power to grant a monopoly on ferry service between New York City and New Jersey on the basis that only Congress, not the state, had the "power to regulate, that is, to prescribe the rule by which commerce is to be governed."[105] Incident to the power to regulate commerce, Field continued, Congress must also protect it, "because protection is indispensable to the effect of the regulations."[106] Thus, Field concluded that the federal government had the power to erect lighthouses and piers, and to dredge the "natural channels" on which commerce flowed.[107]

Field then turned to what he considered the limits of federal power, provoking his audience. He asked rhetorically: "Can the government open new avenues for commerce? Can it enter upon the soil of the states, and dig canals, build railways, and scoop harbors out of the unindented coast for new marts of trade?" The majority of the delegates no doubt answered in the affirmative, but Field declared: "I deny that it has any such power."[108] Field's audience bristled at this.[109] The lawyer nonetheless tried to pull them over to his side by speculating on the potentially radical economic implications of permitting the federal government to create new markets, or "marts." If given the power, he commented, nothing could stop the federal government from buying up vast quantities of grain to manipulate its market price.[110] Field believed that whether the federal government manipulated grain prices or transformed the landscape to create new "marts of trade," the effect was the same. The federal government would take wealth from some and shower it on others, exactly what Theodore Sedgwick and other Jacksonian Democrats feared.[111]

The Whigs in attendance at the convention immediately challenged Field's distinctions between legitimate government regulation and illegitimate government creation of commercial arteries, demonstrating that they broke down on a practical, spatial level. The New York Whig and former member of President John Tyler's cabinet, John Spencer, for one, noted that most Democrats, including Field, accepted the federal government's power to establish lighthouses for purposes of safety. If the federal government could build a lighthouse to protect commerce, Spencer reasoned, it could certainly "provide harbors of shelter on these lakes."[112] The act of establishing a safe harbor for stormy weather would, of course, also create a new artery for commerce.

Greeley expanded on the link between safety regulation and creating new harbors, arguing that environmental conditions dictated that the federal government establish ports in places like Chicago. The journalist inverted the Democratic Party position that the federal government should improve only "natural" harbors. The absence of natural harbors on the Lake Michigan coastline was not, Greeley maintained, reason to deny federal funding for improvements. Rather, it meant that federal harbor funding was all the more critical for safety. Since natural harbors did not exist, harbors of refuge would have to be "made entirely—scooped out of the shifting sands and fortified by expensive piers." The "greater the natural deficiency," Greeley reasoned, "the more palpable the necessity and thus the Constitutionality of National interposition."[113] If the federal government had the duty to protect a ship's safety, then it had to make harbors in places where nature had not. Regulation then would be equivalent to creating a new marketplace, a point lost on Field.

Field's distinction between market regulation and creation indicates that he believed commercial arteries existed on their own, independent of government. The Chicago of 1847, however, belied that view. That city and its principal arteries of commerce were products of intense environmental engineering carried out by public and private actors alike. The harbor Field entered in July 1847 was dredged by the Army Corps of Engineers and the city of Chicago. The dock he disembarked upon was leased from the city and built by a private individual. The bridges Field used to cross the Chicago River were constructed by the city, on public land, with private capital. Commercial centers like Chicago were not created primarily by market forces.[114] Rather, government leaders and private businessmen collaborated to build the infrastructure that made the city a marketplace.

The Opening of the Illinois at Michigan Canal

In 1848, Joliet's vision from two centuries earlier finally came to fruition. The state of Illinois and private investors completed the commercial artery that linked the Chicago River to the Mississippi River system. They replaced the portage that was at once so convenient, and so unpleasant to use, with a canal. So great was that achievement that, at three o'clock on April 10, 1848,

Chicagoans crowded the river bank to witness its completion and wonder about its meaning.

As one reporter wrote, it was as if the "whole city had been emptied down at 'Lock No. 1." A crowd had gathered on the banks of the south branch of the Chicago River to greet the arrival of the very first boat to pass over the summit of the Illinois and Michigan Canal and enter the Chicago River. As the crowd waited, the onlookers inspected two "splendid" 160-horsepower pumps. Those pumps, the brainchild of engineer Miltimore, reconciled the canal financiers' demand for a cheaper, shallow-cut channel with the laws of gravity; each minute they pushed seven thousand cubic feet of water out of the river channel upward into the canal.[115] At about half past four o'clock, the crowd turned its gaze from the pumps to the horizon where it glimpsed a boat on the "ribbon like sheet of water which was stretching to the southwest." A little after five o'clock, the propeller *A. Rossiter* pulled the *General Fry* and its cargo of leading citizens from Lockport, Illinois, into the south branch of the Chicago River. They were greeted by cheering Chicagoans and Mayor James Woodworth, a Democrat from upstate New York who had worked as a dry goods merchant as well as a contractor on the Erie and Illinois and Michigan Canals. The opening of the Illinois and Michigan Canal linked Chicago's economy and ecology more closely than ever before to the large swath of continent between New York and New Orleans.[116]

The canal was the region's foremost commercial artery until it was eclipsed by the use of railroads, which moved goods faster and seldom shut down due to winter ice or shallow waters in dry summers. On April 24, 1848, the first cargo boat to arrive in Chicago by canal, *General Thornton*, hauled sugar from New Orleans through the city on the way to Buffalo, New York. While the canal handled southern goods like sugar from New Orleans, the majority of shipments consisted of products from the upper Midwest, including five and a half million bushels of wheat, twenty-six million bushels of corn, twenty-seven million pounds of pork, 563 million feet of lumber, and fifty thousand tons of coal during the first ten years of operation.[117] The Illinois and Michigan Canal was Chicago's largest feeder of wheat until 1851 (when it was surpassed by the Galena and Chicago Union Railroad) and of corn until 1868 (when the Illinois Central and the Chicago, Burlington, and Quincy Railroads eclipsed it). The canal also hauled the most timber from Chicago's lumber market to the treeless prairie until the winter of 1863–1864.[118]

The Illinois and Michigan Canal's role in making Chicago a key commercial center highlights the tensions in the Democratic position on internal improvements. Democrats like Field and Polk supported limited government and opposed wealth redistribution. Consequently, they tried to contain the costs of internal improvements within the boundaries of neighborhoods, cities, and states. Yet, internal improvements like the Illinois and Michigan Canal facilitated movement of people, goods, and information across political boundaries. The growing interconnectedness of the nation made it increasingly difficult to determine who exactly benefitted from the improvement of a given river, harbor, or canal. Many political leaders nonetheless persisted in trying to bill the beneficiaries of government services. This goal was foremost in the mind of Chicago Mayor Woodworth after the destruction of the city's bridges in the flood of 1849—and of Democratic Senator Douglas when he pushed for the construction of a railroad in Illinois during the 1840s and 1850s.[119] Woodworth and Douglas alike would find ways to shift more of the costs of constructing new bridges and railroads onto private investors. At the same time, the mayor and the senator tried to ensure that the private parties who financed new infrastructure were held accountable to public officials.

Billing the Beneficiaries of Internal Improvements

On March 12, 1849, around nine o'clock in the morning, residents of the Southside of Chicago heard "loud reports as of distant artillery" out on the prairie. Soon thereafter, the sound of "crashing timbers" rang loudly through the city.[120] An ice pack on the Chicago River had burst, unleashing a flood.

It all began a few days earlier, when the winter snowpack melted after a soaking rain. The Des Plaines River and Mud Lake swelled with water, spilling onto the prairie and then filling the Illinois and Michigan Canal and the Chicago River. On March 10, a logjam of ice, wood, and other debris formed on the south branch of the Chicago River beside a packinghouse two miles from the city limits. Water welled up behind the dam for two days before bursting with a sound like cannon fire.

The torrent swept through the river channel with "great violence," smashing canal and lake boats to pieces and pulverizing the bridges at Randolph, Wells, Clark, and Madison. As the rushing waters toppled the bridges at Clark, Madison, and Randolph, four boys and one man perched on those structures drowned. When the current drove a schooner into the side of the *Oneida*, the canal boat's captain was crushed to death. The force of water and snapping timbers hurled a spar from the river channel which struck a man dead as he stood on Clark Street. Five steamships, nineteen sail boats, and thirty canal boats were destroyed, along with the bridges of the south and main branches of the river. At the river's mouth, a "mass of floating material was hurled together at a point near the piers, in a confused jam" of what used to be the contents of the city's harbor.[121] The death toll was unknown.

The sudden destruction of the bridges drove city leaders to adopt more efficient, less democratic methods of decision making. In the 1830s and early 1840s, decisions about where to build infrastructure were made chiefly in the Common Council, and the debates often degenerated into intercity, sectional disputes like the one surrounding the Dearborn Street Bridge. After the 1849 flood, Mayor Woodworth and private property holders took charge of such decisions. The mayor asked owners of riverside property to pay one-third of the cost of new bridges. If they paid, the city would build the span, and the property owners would reap the transportation benefits. If they declined, Woodworth would propose building the bridge elsewhere, near property owners who were willing to pay. In the four years after the flood, the city erected eight new bridges.[122]

Woodworth and the city of Chicago thus effectively blended the Whig and Democrats' approaches to internal improvements. By paying two-thirds of the cost, the city acknowledged the Whig view that infrastructure was a public good, benefitting the whole city. At the same time, the city conceded the point championed by Polk and Field—namely, some property owners gained more from new infrastructure than others, and should pay more—by making the primary beneficiaries of new infrastructure pay a third of the cost of a bridge.

At the state level, too, antebellum political leaders devised strategies to build infrastructure that would benefit the public without taxing those who did not stand to directly benefit. The corporation became one of their favored legal mechanisms. More than merely a private, profit-seeking institution, the corporation was an institution that received special privileges from the state, like rights of way, in exchange for providing a crucial service to the public. It therefore sought, simultaneously, to serve the public while enriching its shareholders.[123]

When Senator Douglas renewed the push for an Illinois railroad in the late 1840s, he determined that a private corporation, not taxpayers, should raise the capital. To realize that vision, he orchestrated the transfer of public lands to the railroad. In 1850, Douglas and Congressman Wentworth mus-cled through Congress a bill that transferred a two-hundred-foot-wide strip of land running from Cairo, Illinois, to LaSalle, Illinois, the terminus of the Illinois and Michigan Canal, as well as 2,595,000 acres of land to the state of Illinois for the purposes of laying track and selling land to raise money for constructing a railroad. The state of Illinois, in turn, issued a corporate charter to the Illinois Central Railroad on February 10, 1851.[124] The state granted the railroad corporation the acreage it had received from Congress, with the stipulation that it construct lines 380 miles from Cairo to Galena and 271 miles from Centralia to Chicago, where it would establish a terminal on the rapidly eroding Chicago lakefront.[125]

The Illinois Central Railroad's entrance into Chicago during the 1850s highlighted just how fast the city's economic geography was changing. During the 1830s and 1840s, Chicago's leaders fretted over how to build infrastructure to make the city accessible. By the 1850s, the city's waterfront had become one of the preeminent hubs for people, goods, and information traveling across North America by water and rail alike.

The waterfront's centrality presented city, state, and business leaders with a new challenge: ensuring that private property owners did not monopolize this crucial site of exchange. Some policymakers and businessmen urged the state to pass laws making key waterfront spaces and infrastructure public—and therefore accessible to all who wished to use them for making money. Others countered that such laws would violate the private property rights protected by the U.S. Constitution. The disputes over private property rights and access to the Chicago waterfront culminated in two landmark Supreme Court cases, *Munn v. Illinois* (1877) and *Illinois Central v. Illinois* (1892). In both rulings, the court crafted an expansive definition of public space and dramatically expanded the state's power to regulate commerce. The court reasoned that broader public powers were essential for protecting Chicago's position as a site of exchange.[126]

CHAPTER 2

The Legal Construction of Free Marketplaces

Situated at the nexus of critical water and rail arteries, Chicago grew with astonishing speed, from a frontier crossroads of 350 in 1833 to a metropolis of 300,000 by 1870. When fire scorched and leveled much of the city in October of 1871, Chicagoans rebuilt, bigger and faster, and the population soared past one million by 1890.[1] The city's waterways and railroads stretched into the countryside like tentacles, greedily sucking nature's bounties—the fruits of fertile farmlands and tall pine forests—into the city, where they were either consumed by the city's exploding population or shipped out along the same waterways and railroads, supplying the nation's expanding economy and population with raw materials and finished products.

Chicago's vitality would not have been possible without its vast network of commercial arteries, but the rise of Chicago as the preeminent commercial hub of the North American interior involved more than digging canals and fashioning structures of timber, brick, iron, and steel. Chicago's rise was a product, too, of political cataclysm. The Civil War deprived Chicago's chief rivals, Saint Louis and Cincinnati, of their lucrative trade with the South. As its challengers withered, Chicago profited from the bloodshed. In 1862 alone, the Union Army spent more than $4.7 in the city on supplies of clothing, meat, lumber, and, most critically, grain.[2] By war's end, Chicago had become the nation's preeminent east-west commercial hub, and the city's harbor was the busiest in the nation by far. More boats arrived in Chicago during 1871, for instance, than in the ports of New York, San Francisco, Philadelphia, Baltimore, Charleston, and Mobile combined.[3]

The ships that called at those great seaports tended to be larger than the canal and lake boats that frequented Chicago, but the fact remained: the waterfront of the nation's great inland metropolis had become a fulcrum on which significant parts of the American economy turned. The Chicago

River's banks had, for example, become the site of leading world markets for lumber and grain. On the South Branch of the Chicago River, lake ships deposited cargoes of timber from the great stands of Wisconsin and Michigan in massive lumber yards clustered around river slips south of Twenty-Second and west of Halsted Street. By 1879, the stock in Chicago's lumber yards exceeded four hundred million board feet, or over one-fifth of all the milled timber in the region stretching from Cleveland to Minneapolis. Much of this lumber from Chicago would, in turn, be shipped to farmers and merchants on the treeless prairie.[4]

The main branch of the Chicago River, meanwhile, formed the geographic center of the city's rapidly growing trade in grain. In 1850, Chicago handled half as much wheat and flour as passed through St. Louis, but within just four years, Chicago handled three million bushels of wheat to its rival's 2.1 million.[5] Midwestern farmers sent even more wheat to Chicago during the years leading up to and during the Civil War. Using mechanical reapers forged in Cyrus McCormick's factory beside the Chicago River, farmers harvested enough wheat to feed the Union Army. "Without McCormick's invention," noted Secretary of War Edwin Stanton, "the North could not win and . . . the Union would be dismembered."[6] In the first two years of the conflict, grain exports from Chicago soared from thirty-one million to sixty-five million bushels.[7] These levels of production continued after the war, with global economic ramifications. In 1873, for instance, the city handled over sixty-eight million bushels of grain, and Chicago wheat flooded markets as far away as Central Europe and Russia.[8]

These great commodity flows were made possible through feats of engineering—the dredging of the river and the construction of the Illinois and Michigan Canal, for example—as well as the development of new technologies, like steam-powered grain storage elevators and railroads, which linked the nation's watercourses to a rapidly growing transportation network centered largely on Chicago.[9]

No less important than these, though, were feats of legal and political engineering undertaken by Illinois lawmakers, some business leaders, and state and federal judges. Methodically and very intentionally, they created well-regulated, *public* waterfront spaces through which the Midwest's bounty could freely flow.[10] Their efforts culminated in two landmark Supreme Court cases, *Munn v. Illinois* (1877) and *Illinois Central v. Illinois* (1892), which declared public, state control over Chicago's riverside grain elevators and its lakeshore harbor.[11] These rulings helped spur Chicago's economic development by making the city's waterfront accessible to those who wished to use it for profit. *Illinois Central* and *Munn* also shaped how jurists made the often-subjective distinctions between public and private sectors. Those distinctions defined late nineteenth- and early twentieth-century American law.

Monopolizing Space and Information
at the Gateway of Commerce

In 1848, the Chicago waterfront became what Supreme Court Justice Morrison Waite would later call the "very gateway of commerce," when the Illinois and Michigan Canal breached the continental divide, making it possible to ship grain and other goods from points on the Mississippi River watershed to Chicago.[12]

Just as the canal brought goods from the city's hinterland to its busy waterfront, so too did railroads; Chicago's waterfront thus became a critical junction between North America's waterways and its growing web of railroads. In November 1848, Ogden's new Galena and Chicago Union Railroad sent the first locomotive steaming out of the city, connecting its waterfront to a new agricultural hinterland. Starting at the railroad's terminal near the Chicago River, the *Pioneer* pulled a single baggage car carrying a cadre of prominent Chicagoans to a point eight miles west of the city. On the outskirts of town, the train encountered a farmer bringing a wagon load of wheat and hides into Chicago. Two of the *Pioneer*'s passengers purchased the goods and transported them to the city aboard the train. By 1848, then, a new economic geography had been established. Grain traveled from the farms of the Midwest by rail and by canal to the banks of the Chicago River where it awaited transshipment to consumers.[13]

Businessmen such as Ira Munn and George Scott erected large warehouses—with rails flanking one side and the Chicago River on the other—to store the grain in route from the Midwest to consumers in the eastern United States and Europe. As grain sat in those elevators awaiting rail or water shipment, Munn and Scott not only charged farmers storage fees, they harbored immensely valuable information about the supply of a crucial global commodity. Their control of this market information owed to economic geographies, technologies, and business practices developed in the 1840s and 1850s—all of which had made the Chicago waterfront a critical bottleneck in the global grain trade.

Chicago's grain elevator operators made their private riverfront property—
and information—the subject of broad, public concern by using it to manipulate markets. The men came to epitomize the nineteenth-century "robber
baron." Though often associated with pitchfork-wielding populists, the term
was actually coined by scions of two elite Boston families, Charles Francis
Adams Jr. and Josiah Quincy Jr., who dubbed the businessmen who monop-
olized transportation corridors "robber barons," recalling the medieval Ger-
manic warlords who had allegedly strung iron chains across the Rhine River
and taken toll from all who passed.[14]

The grain elevators built by men like Munn and Scott provided railroads
with a critical, labor-saving technology that, for legal reasons, they could not
directly harness themselves. When the *Pioneer* brought the first load of wheat
to Chicago, it was most likely stored in sacks by the farmer who grew it.
Sacked wheat required an enormous amount of labor to transport. Each sack
had to be loaded onto a railcar or boat, transported to Chicago, offloaded for
inspection and purchase, reloaded for shipment to the consumer, and, at its
destination, unloaded again. These steps required human muscle, but this
changed in the 1850s when Chicagoans adopted the steam-powered grain elevator introduced in 1842 by Buffalo warehouseman Joseph Dart. A conveyor
belt with affixed buckets carried grain to the top of the multistory structure
where an operator weighed it before dumping it into one of several great,
vertical storage bins. When it came time to transport the grain again, the elevator operators simply opened a chute at the bottom of the bin and poured its
contents into a waiting ship or railroad car below.[15]

Even though the railroads that handled grain required elevators, their
corporate charters seldom permitted them to enter the storage business.[16]
Consequently, railroads often rented waterfront lands to elevator operators.
In the early 1860s, for example, the massive Chicago and Northwestern Railroad, which had since subsumed the Galena and Chicago Union, leased a
parcel of land on Chicago's Water Street near the Kinzie Street Bridge to
Munn and Scott. In 1862 Munn and Scott erected the Northwestern Railroad
Elevator with fifty bins capable of holding up to six hundred thousand bush-
els of grain.[17]

The adoption by Munn, Scott, and other warehousemen of steam-
powered elevators depended on organizational innovations that transformed
the fruit of the prairie into a form of currency. As elevators became larger, it
proved impractical to store just one individual's grain in a single, voluminous
bin. Warehouse owners therefore sought to mix the grains of various owners.

This presented a problem. If different grains were mixed, how could property be returned to its rightful owner? This question was taken up by the Chicago Board of Trade. The board was founded in 1848 by eighty-two businessmen, from a wide-range of occupations, 38 percent of whom had served as members of the organizing committee for the 1847 River and Harbor Convention.[18] In keeping with the members' interest in transportation, the board became increasingly focused on the city's growing grain trade during the 1850s and 1860s. Grain elevator operators, in turn, assumed positions of power in the Board of Trade; Munn, for instance, served as its president from 1860 to 1861. To help elevator operators maximize their storage space, in 1856 the board established categories and grades, or quality measures, for wheat. Thus, when a farmer deposited his crop into an elevator, it would not be segregated. Rather, the elevator operator would mix it with wheat of a like grade and category, "no. 2 winter wheat," for example. This practice helped maximize storage space as well as facilitated transactions. The person who deposited grain into the warehouse received a receipt not for the very same grain but for a like amount of the same category and grade.[19] The elevator receipt became a form of currency. Farmers sold them to grain merchants. Grain traders bought and sold receipts in the trading "pits" at the Board of Trade, and banks accepted them as collateral and for deposit.[20] In effect, a warehouseman who issued a grain receipt printed money.

Chicago elevator owners colluded to cheat farmers and grain traders alike. In 1862, the owners of the city's north and west side elevators established a secret pool; they divided ownership of seven elevators into four hundred shares, bought interlocking portions, and distributed dividends. Munn and Scott, majority owners of four elevators, managed the warehouses on the city's west side, keeping books and distributing dividends.[21] Through the pool, Chicago's warehousemen helped eliminate price competition and negotiated favorable shipping agreements with railroads. Farmers had virtually no control over which elevator received their grain or the cost of storage. This made them susceptible to even greater abuses. Elevator operators shortchanged farmers by rigging scales, arbitrarily downgrading wheat, and lying about crop spoilage.[22] With their cunning and their control over a commercial gateway, grain elevator owners became extremely wealthy. In the 1860s, a typical elevator charge for receiving, twenty days storage, and shipping grain amounted to two cents per bushel, or approximately 5 percent of the total cost of transportation from a Midwestern farm to New York City. In 1864 *The Prairie Farmer* estimated that Chicago's warehousemen reaped one million

dollars in annual income or an average of eighty thousand dollars per elevator.[23] By the late 1860s, Munn's dividends from the pooling agreement averaged one hundred thousand dollars per year, an income he sought to augment
through market manipulation.[24]

A Chicago grain elevator bestowed upon its owner the ability to control
market information—a power warehousemen frequently abused. As the
grain of the American Midwest passed through Chicago, elevator owners issued storage receipts. Those texts not only functioned as a claim check, they
told a story about the quality and supply of a commodity. And, as that story
changed, so too did prices. In the hands of a duplicitous elevator operator
then, the storage receipt took on a literary form best described as market fiction. Sometimes an elevator owner issued bogus receipts. Other times, an
owner simply neglected to retire a receipt after a client claimed a lot of grain.[25]
In either case, the effect was the same. The elevator owner circulated receipts
not backed by actual grain, thereby profiting from a lie.

That lie also created the impression of larger grain supplies, driving prices
lower. An elevator owner could profit from buying low on his own reports of
large supplies, leaking the truth about the actual amount of grain in store,
and selling to hapless traders as the prices rose. If an elevator owner wanted
to put upward pressure on prices, he could fabricate a story of scarcity. An
elevator owner might falsely report that grain supplies in his care had
spoiled—and sell high on the news.[26] Whatever the market fiction, an elevator operator's word was made both plausible and unverifiable by the space he
controlled. His elevator contained the truth about grain supplies, but by invoking his private property rights, he could deny others the opportunity to
confirm his word.

Public Space and Access to Market Information

After the Civil War, Midwestern farmers belonging to cooperative organizations known as Granges successfully pressed Midwestern state legislatures
to enact railroad and grain elevator rate restrictions, leading to a series of six
cases testing the legitimacy of statutory economic regulation. The court's
ruling in *Munn* was the first in the "*Granger Cases*," which upheld the state
rate regulations.[27] Illinois farmers did advocate grain elevator rate restrictions, though the more powerful impetus for elevator regulation came from
Chicago grain traders who wished to peer inside the bins. The story of this

strange alliance of farm and finance shows that critical economic spaces like the Chicago waterfront were the site of fierce contests over more than just goods. In *Munn*, the court used the language of space—the "gateway of commerce"—to pronounce upon a conflict over information.[28]

That fight began in the Board of Trade during the 1850s, and it spilled out into state politics. The board's members comprised, in part, grain traders who wanted a public accounting of supplies and elevator operators who sought to hide their stores from prying eyes. In 1857, the grain traders took the upper hand, compelling the board to appoint inspectors to enter the warehouses and report on the quality and condition of stores. At the same time, the Board of Trade also began to act as a clearinghouse for market information by recording incoming and outgoing grain shipments to prevent the issue of false receipts.[29] Two years later, the Illinois state legislature enhanced the Board of Trade's powers by granting the organization a special charter as "a body politic and corporate." The board thus assumed a quasi-governmental status with legal authority to compel its membership, which included the elevator owners, to comply with its inspection rules and standards for weights and grades.[30]

Elevator owners nonetheless sidestepped board regulations. Since the elevators were private property, board inspectors depended on the permission of their owners to enter. Consequently, elevator operators could arrange for inspections at times when they were in compliance with regulations or their abuses could be masked.[31] In light of these evasions, a growing faction of board members began to call for state regulation of the warehouses. That faction drove the grain elevator operators out of power during the 1870 Board of Trade officers' election. Thus, the board that Munn had headed ten years earlier was now committed to using the state government to, in the words of its president, break "a monopoly highly detrimental to every interest of the city."[32]

The Chicago Board of Trade immediately pressed the state of Illinois for regulation. At the same time as the pro-regulation faction had gained power in the Board of Trade, Illinois lawmakers were in the midst of drafting a new state constitution. Constitutional convention delegates were being bombarded by petitions from merchants and farmers calling for passage of an article regulating grain elevators.[33] The convention did not take action, however, until the Board of Trade threw its weight behind the effort. At its urging, Delegate William Cary introduced an article calling for warehouse regulation, the text of which, some alleged, had actually been drafted by members of the board. The Board of Trade's support for the measure made some delegates uneasy. Claiming to represent famers, delegate Thomas Turner, for one, decried the article as a means to help grain traders who he described as "leeches upon commerce and the community, that suck the life blood out of the farmers and dealers in grain."[34]

Even if the article was drafted for the benefit of grain traders, other delegates noted that farmers too would profit from accurate market information. Delegate William Coolbaugh, for instance, asked, "Can it wrong the farmer in Fulton county who ships a thousand bushels of grain to Chicago and holds it there, subject to the market, to require the warehousemen there to inform him and the public how many bushels of grain are in store, so that he may exercise his judgment about the best time to sell it?"[35] Coolbaugh's rhetorical question not only described farmers' need for market information, it underscored the challenges they faced operating over time and distance. The farmer had to pay to transport his crop to Chicago before he knew what price it would fetch on the grain market. The rapid price fluctuations brought about by the market manipulations of grain elevator operators could make this all the worse. Farmers, like commodities traders, had an interest in securing accurate information about grain supplies.

The delegates to the Illinois State Constitutional Convention designated grain elevators as "public" spaces in order to ensure access to market information. They passed an article stating, "All elevators or storehouses where grain or other property is stored for a compensation . . . are declared to be public warehouses." If warehouses were public, the delegates reasoned, elevator operators could not invoke their private property rights to prevent inspection. The constitution not only designated the warehouses public, it mandated that their operators take responsibility for disseminating market information by making daily reports of the quantity and quality of grain stores. It also required elevator operators to permit the holders of grain receipts to inspect stores as well as the elevator's account books. To give "full effect" to this article, the constitution called on the state legislature to "pass all necessary laws to prevent the issue of false and fraudulent warehouse receipts."[36] Members of the state legislature, in turn, invited the Chicago Board of Trade to draft laws regulating warehouses and railroads. With the board's proposals as a framework, the Illinois General Assembly passed the 1871 Warehouse Act designed to curtail railroad rate discrimination, set maximum storage fees, and prevent the issue of false elevator receipts. The legislature also required warehouse owners to obtain a state operating license and submit to the regulatory power of a new Board of Railroad and Warehouse Commissioners.[37]

Grain elevator operators resisted state regulation, but Chicago's Board of Trade and its banks ultimately forced them to comply with the law. Munn and Scott, for instance, refused to obtain an operating license or to let state inspectors enter their elevators. The state sued and won. In July of 1872, the court ordered Munn and Scott to pay a fine of one hundred dollars. The warehousemen appealed the ruling to the Illinois State Supreme Court, beginning the case that would culminate in the U.S. Supreme Court's 1877 decision in *Munn v. Illinois*.[38] Even before the high court ruling, however, bankers and the Board of Trade forced elevator owners to comply with the regulations intended to prevent the issue of bogus receipts. Chicago banks refused to accept receipts from elevator operators that did not register them with state inspectors, and the Board of Trade barred unregistered receipts from the trading pits.[39] Thus, state law did not, in and of itself, solve the problem of bogus receipts; rather, it gave financial institutions a means to stop accepting unverified receipts as currency. By the summer of 1872 it was all but impossible for grain elevator operators to issue false receipts. They did, however, commit fraud by failing to retire old receipts from circulation after grain had been claimed.

Munn and Scott recycled receipts in order to raise money to speculate with a financial instrument designed to eliminate spatial and temporal risk from grain trading, the futures contract. Buyers and sellers of commodities like grain had long been plagued by the fact that the price could change wildly during the time it took to conduct a transaction over great distances. With the use of a telegraph, however, buyers and sellers could sidestep this problem by contracting to deliver a set amount of grain at an agreed-upon price on a future date. While the futures contract eliminated the risk of price fluctuation, it created new opportunities for speculation. Historian William Cronon offers this hypothetical example: "Imagine, for instance, that Jones sold Smith a futures contract for 10,000 bushels of No. 2 spring wheat at 70 cents a bushel, to be delivered at the end of June. If that grade was in fact selling for 68 cents a bushel on June 30, Jones could either purchase 10,000 bushels at the lower price and deliver the receipts to Smith or—more conveniently still—accept a cash payment of $200 from Smith to make up the difference between the contract price and the market price." These speculations also created the possibility of a market "corner." A corner occurred when a group of speculators surreptitiously bought up nearly all the real grain supplies as well as the contracts for delivery at a future date. When the futures contracts came due, those who were obligated to deliver grain discovered that they could purchase it only from the very speculators they owed. In other words, cornerers forced their marks to buy grain from them in order to deliver it to them. When that happened, the victorious speculators would bleed their victims dry by charging exorbitant prices.[40]

During 1872, Munn and Scott joined a group of speculators in an attempt to corner wheat that they financed by selling old grain receipts. The group included warehouse owner Hugh Maher, Munn and Scott's former broker F. J. Diamond, grain merchant Thomas H. Chisholm, and commission merchant John B. Lyon. In the spring, Lyon began buying contracts for future delivery at the end of August. By July, the trading pits were buzzing with news of Lyon's maneuvers, and the price of wheat shot up from $1.16 a bushel to $1.35 by the end of the month. As the price rose, more farmers sent their crops to Chicago, making it more difficult for the group to buy up the physical stores of wheat before the August futures contracts came due.[41] In order to raise the capital to support their corner, Maher, Munn, and Scott recycled elevator receipts rather than retiring them from circulation after the owner claimed the grain. This practice came to light when fire destroyed Maher's "Iowa Elevator" located near the confluence of the north and main branches of the Chicago River. The postfire property loss investigations estimated that Maher had circulated receipts for three hundred thousand more bushels of grain than the Iowa Elevator had in store.[42]

Maher's duplicity led many Board of Trade members to suspect Munn, Scott, and other elevator operators of the same. The board demanded inspectors be allowed into all the city's elevators to confirm that receipts matched stores. Munn and Scott acquiesced, or so it seemed. The warehousemen requested some time before the inspection to consolidate their holdings into a few bins. Their request was granted, and Munn and Scott set to work. But, rather than consolidate their grain, the warehousemen installed false bottoms in the bins of their great Northwestern Elevator. By raising the floors of the bins much higher, Munn and Scott made it seem as if their elevator was brimming with all the grain for which they had issued receipts. Their deception went undetected until November. In the meantime, Munn and Scott persisted in their wheat corner attempt, which brought financial ruin upon them.[43]

Some of the very Midwestern farmers who accused elevator operators of exploitation likely contributed to Munn and Scott's downfall. As Lyon continued buying up all the wheat supplies, prices soared to $1.50 a bushel on August 10 and to $1.61½ by August 15. At these prices, farmers hastily unloaded their stores; receipts in Chicago rose from 75,000 bushels a day in the second week of August to as many as 179,000 bushels per day in the third week of the month. Acting on behalf of the cornering syndicate, Lyon kept buying, but he was running out of cash. Lyon turned to Chicago's banks, seeking a large, short-term capital infusion to support the corner until the futures contracts came due at the end of the month. All through business hours on August 19, Lyon bought wheat, spending the very last of his money. Then at five o'clock, he got devastating news. Chicago's bankers denied him credit, citing provisions in their corporate charters that prohibited lending more than 10 percent of their capital to one borrower. With no more money to buy up wheat supplies, the corner collapsed.[44] The men were ruined. Diamond skipped town with his account books. Chisholm drowned himself in Lake Michigan.[45] Munn and Scott sold their holdings to grain magnate George Armour in a transaction that netted Munn only ten dollars. The low price reflected the fact that Armour had to honor the receipts issued by Munn and Scott for hundreds of thousands of bushels of grain not contained in the elevators. On October 29, 1872, a court forced Munn and Scott into bankruptcy, and in December they were expelled from the Board of Trade.[46] Disgraced, the men faded from public view. Munn last surfaced in Denver, Colorado, where he signed an affidavit just six months before the United States Supreme Court issued its landmark ruling in the case that bears his name, but in which he had no stake.[47]

Public Space and the Making of a Free Market

In *Munn v. Illinois*, the Supreme Court confronted the reality of an increasingly complex, interconnected economy. The private property of the few—particularly if located at a transportation bottleneck like the Chicago waterfront—could threaten that of the many. Those few—Chicago's warehouse owners—brought the case before the courts.

In 1872, Munn and Scott appealed their conviction for violating the Warehouse Act by refusing to acquire an operating license. In 1874, the Illinois Supreme Court rejected their appeal, upholding the constitutionality of the Warehouse Act. By that time, Munn and Scott had gone bankrupt, but Chicago's remaining warehousemen appealed the state's ruling to the United States Supreme Court. The elevator operators were particularly interested in overturning the provision of the act limiting maximum charges for grain storage.[48] The rate limits, they protested, reduced the value of their private property. Yet those very limits aimed to protect the private property of the traders, farmers, and merchants who, by necessity of economic geography, had to store their grain in Chicago's elevators.

There was no escaping the fact that the private property rights of the elevator owners and of grain traders, merchants, and farmers were mutually exclusive. The conservative *Chicago Tribune* cringed at the prospect of state intervention in the economy, but saw no alternative. When the Illinois Supreme Court upheld the Warehouse Act in 1874, the paper lamented: "we have to contemplate a novel and in some respects dangerous decision [upholding statutory economic regulation] on the one hand or we have to face an omnipresent and hitherto invulnerable monopoly on the other."[49]

The *Tribune*'s lament over having to choose between dependence on a monopoly or state meddling in the economy reflected a broader crisis of liberalism. The liberal economic dogmas of the first half of the nineteenth century no longer seemed to apply. In antebellum America, monopolies were widely considered to be products not of private property, but of state grants of special privileges. Antimonopolists during the ages of Jefferson and Jackson therefore embraced laissez faire as a radical, democratic doctrine that protected common people from elites otherwise capable of using their political capital to secure economic favor. Following the logic of classical liberal political economists like Adam Smith, American political leaders such as Jefferson and Jackson believed that private property would serve as a means of self-sufficiency and political independence. By the 1860s, however, it was becoming clear that, as the *Tribune* noted of Chicago's grain elevator operators, laissez faire, and even some forms of private property ownership, could be means not of independence, but of dependence.[50] The conflict over private property on the Chicago waterfront that led to *Munn* therefore invited the Supreme Court to weigh the merits of laissez faire against a new liberalism, rooted in a pragmatic understanding of economic space, where the state wielded its power to prevent some private property owners from using their geographic advantages to exploit others.

The warehousemen of Chicago advanced a classical liberal, laissez faire defense of private property rights in *Munn*, claiming that strict constitutional protections for private property would foster investment in business. To argue their case, the elevator owners hired the esteemed attorney John N. Jewett.[51] A native New Englander with a serious demeanor, Jewett became a pillar of the Chicago legal community, cofounding the Chicago Bar Association in 1873, serving as the organization's president in 1877, and holding the position of dean of the John Marshall Law School from 1899 until his death in 1904.[52] In *Munn*, the attorney insisted that by setting maximum storage rates the state was depriving warehousemen of income, or taking their property without due process. If the Supreme Court upheld that precedent, Jewett worried, it would set "the government . . . on . . . the highway to the plundering of individual wealth, and the destruction of private enterprise." Jewett wondered what incentive anyone would have to invest in business.[53]

If Jewett's more philosophical argument about the sanctity of property rights swayed the justices, his second, jurisdictional claim only underscored the practical reality his clients wished to deny. Namely, the public had an interest in Chicago's waterfront grain elevators. Jewett argued that Chicago's elevators were so critical to the flow of grain across the continent that their use constituted a form of interstate commerce, even though all the warehouses were located in the state. Thus, Jewett suggested the elevators could not be regulated by the Illinois legislature, only Congress.[54] Jewett seemed to have gambled on the fact that he could not realistically deny the economic centrality of the waterfront elevators. His strategy backfired. The court rejected Jewett's jurisdictional argument and readily accepted his point about the geographic centrality of Chicago's grain warehouses, which played into the hand of Illinois Attorney General James Edsall. Edsall claimed that location was the very thing that made the grain elevators a form of public, not private, property. Chicago's warehousemen, Edsall noted, "can impose such rates upon shippers and producers of grain as they see fit," because they are "in the possession of the very 'gateway to commerce.'" Without regulation, elevator operators could extort the whole nation. Edsall insisted that setting grain storage rates, like those of draymen, hackmen, or ferry operators, would facilitate the flow of an essential commodity through Chicago's waterfront, thereby safeguarding the grain market.[55]

The Supreme Court concurred with Edsall's view that economic geography had transformed Chicago's elevators from a private business to one "affected with a public interest." With that phrase the author of the seven to two majority opinion, Chief Justice Morrison Waite, established a precedent for state legislatures to respond to the new economic realities of the Industrial Age with statutory regulations. His ruling in *Munn* was among the most significant events of his career. Waite grew up in Connecticut where his father practiced law and earned a seat on the state's Supreme Court. Morrison Waite attended Yale before settling in Toledo, Ohio, practicing law, and serving one term in the Ohio Senate from 1849 to 1850. The Whig-turned-Republican lawyer was little known on the national political stage until President Ulysses S. Grant nominated him to the nation's highest court in 1874. Grant had already attempted to appoint four other men to the post; two had declined and two had faltered in their attempts at congressional confirmation. By nominating Waite, Grant satisfied many Ohio Republicans, including his distant relative and Secretary of the Interior Columbus Delano. Waite served on the bench from 1874 to 1888, distinguishing himself with good humor and able management.[56] He showed his pragmatism in his ruling in *Munn*.

Waite's decision highlighted the specific economic and geographic factors that had made the public dependent on Chicago grain elevators. The justice observed, "the great producing region of the West and North-west sends its grain by water and rail to Chicago, where the greater part of it is shipped by vessel for transportation to the seaboard by the Great Lakes . . . some of it is forwarded by railway to the Eastern ports . . . [and some vessels are] sailed through the St. Lawrence directly to Europe . . . The quantity [of grain] received in Chicago has made it the greatest grain market in the world." The elevator firms "located with the river harbor on one side and the railway tracks on the other" thus controlled a world market through their small parcels of riverfront land. From these facts, Waite and the majority of the court concluded that warehousemen "stand . . . in the very 'gateway of commerce,' and take toll from all who pass." For the grain market to function, Waite reasoned, elevators needed to be regulated by the state.[57]

Waite's ruling was novel in that it endowed state legislatures with greater regulatory power, but the principle that private businesses served a public function was not. It had roots in the recent and distant past. In the 1840s, after the widespread failure of state-funded internal improvement projects, state governments chartered many private corporations like the Illinois Central Railroad to build critical infrastructure. It was therefore no stretch for Waite and other members of the court to conclude that private businesses also served public functions.[58] Waite's ruling, moreover, cited older English practices of granting public access to waterfront lands, which were described in Lord Chief Justice Matthew Hale's circa 1670 legal treatise *De Portibus Maris*.[59] Hale observed that even in cases where private subjects controlled waterfront lands, English law dictated that they provide reasonably priced access to a port, especially when no alternative points of access existed.[60] In *Munn*, Waite quoted Hale directly: "If the king or subject have a public wharf, unto which all persons . . . must come . . . because there is no other wharf in that port . . . there cannot be taken arbitrary and excessive duties for . . . wharfage . . . . but the duties must be reasonable and moderate." By regulating Chicago grain elevator rates, the state of Illinois, Waite concluded, was simply enforcing this centuries old principle that the public had a right to gain access to navigable waterways.[61]

Waite, moreover, noted that the United States itself had a longstanding tradition of public regulation of the use of private property. He pointed out, for instance, that in 1820 Congress had granted the city of Washington, D.C., the power to regulate the weight and quality of bread as well as to set rates for chimney sweeps and, critically, wharves. Waite observed that none of these regulations was ever judged a violation of the Fifth Amendment's "takings clause," which prevented government confiscation of private property without compensation. The chief justice did not see the new Fourteenth Amendment's due process clause in different terms. Waite observed "it is apparent that, down to the time of the adoption of the Fourteenth Amendment, it was not supposed that statutes regulating the use, or even the price of the use, of private property necessarily deprived an owner of his property without due process of law."[62] Waite reasoned that the Fourteenth Amendment simply reaffirmed the property protections contained in the Fifth Amendment, rather than redefining regulation as a taking without due process. Rate regulation did not, in Waite's view, deprive warehousemen of their property; it protected people from the actions of businessmen who made their affairs a matter of concern to the public. "If they did not wish to submit themselves to such interference [rate regulation]," Waite suggested "they should not have clothed the public with an interest in their concerns" by leveraging their private property to control the stream of grain flowing through the Chicago waterfront.[63]

Waite's cantankerous colleague, Stephen Field, disagreed sharply. Field's dissent in *Munn* was part of a larger body of jurisprudence dedicated to limiting state power to confiscate or redistribute wealth, which he developed over a long career.[64] Field's tenure on the Supreme Court stretched from before the Civil War to the dawn of the Progressive Era. When he was a young man, Field set out for Gold Rush-era San Francisco armed with a degree from Massachusetts's Williams College. From his upbringing in Stockbridge, Massachusetts, where his father preached Puritan religious doctrine from a pulpit once occupied by Jonathan Edwards, Field developed an uncompromising style of thinking; he saw moral right and wrong fixed along clear lines and he maintained a Puritan notion of a moral aristocracy that translated into a procapitalist ideology that justified the ascendancy of a business elite.[65]

Field began his political career as *alcalde*—a post similar to a mayor—in Marysville, California, during the 1850s and soon secured a position on the state Supreme Court. With the support of railroad tycoon Leland Stanford and the California congressional delegation, Field became the nominee for a post on the United States Supreme Court during the Civil War. Field's elevation to the bench also owed to the relationship between his elder brother David Dudley Field and Abraham Lincoln, who had met at the 1847 Chicago River and Harbor Convention.[66] According to Stephen Field's biographer Paul Kens, "Family lore has it that, in a personal interview with the president, a prominent New Yorker named John Gray recommended [Stephen] Field's appointment. 'Does David want his brother to have it?' Lincoln was said to have asked. 'Yes,' said Mr. Gray. 'Then he shall have it,'" replied the president.[67] By nominating Field, a pro-union Democrat, Lincoln drew the fortunes of California Democrats closer to the administration and the cause of union. Congress approved Field, and the justice began his thirty-five-year career on the bench in May of 1863.[68]

Field earned a reputation as a principal architect of laissez faire jurisprudence for his interpretation of the new Fourteenth Amendment to the Constitution. Written by radical Republicans seeking to extend the rights of citizens to freed slaves, the amendment prevented government from taking a citizen's life, liberty, or property without due process of law. Field, however, considered the amendment applicable beyond the freedmen. He crafted an interpretation that protected citizens from economic regulations that interfered with contractual freedom or took private property. In an 1873 dissent in the *Slaughterhouse Cases*, Field argued that the Fourteenth Amendment rights of butchers had been violated by an 1869 Louisiana law granting one company a meatpacking monopoly in exchange for compliance with public health practices. The state-granted monopoly, Field contended, interfered with butchers' liberty to sell their labor.[69] By articulating an interpretation of the Constitution that privileged individual, contractual freedom over state power, Field created a roadmap for lawyers and judges wishing to shield businesses from state regulation in future decades.[70] Historian Robert McCloskey therefore identified Field's dissent in the *Slaughterhouse Cases* as "the point in our intellectual history at which the democratic strain in the American tradition begins its subservience to political conservatism."[71]

Field extended his idea of substantive due process in his 1877 *Munn* dissent. He argued that rate restrictions on grain elevators constituted government seizure of private property without due process.[72] At the root of Field's quarrel with Waite and the majority was his contractual understanding of economic regulation—as an exchange of state-granted rights for meeting certain public responsibilities. "When Sir Matthew Hale, and the sages of the law in his day, spoke of property as affected by a public interest," Field argued, "they referred to property . . . granted by the government, or in connection with which special privileges were conferred."[73] Yet, the state had granted nothing to Munn and Scott; and, they had promised nothing to the state. Field therefore saw rate regulation as expropriation, an act "subversive of the rights of private property," which should be protected by the Fourteenth Amendment.[74] Field expressed deep concern over Waite's claim that a legislature or even the Supreme Court could distinguish between a wholly private business and one "affected with a public interest" simply by evaluating economic and geographic conditions. The defiant judge thus declared, "The defendants were no more public warehousemen . . . than the merchant who sells his merchandise to the public is a public merchant, or the blacksmith who shoes horses for the public is a public blacksmith; and it was a strange notion that by calling them so they would be brought under legislative control." Field quipped "One might as well attempt to change the nature of colors, by giving them a new designation."[75]

Field was right. His colleagues were trying to give state lawmakers the power to simply designate a business "affected with a public interest" and enact economic regulations accordingly. Almost a decade after Waite's ruling, Justice Samuel Miller revealed that his colleagues had made a calculated decision to issue the court's ruling in *Munn* before releasing opinions on the other *Granger Cases*. They wanted to challenge Field's contractual view of economic regulation through corporate charters. Munn and Scott presented an opportunity to do so because they were not incorporated, unlike the railroads involved in the other *Granger Cases*. While the railroad corporations involved in the other *Granger Cases* challenged rate restrictions on the basis that they had not agreed to such provisions in their charters, Attorney Jewett could make no such claims on behalf of Munn and Scott. Thus, Miller recalled that *Munn* clearly presented the question of regulating a "private citizen, or unincorporated partnership . . . free from any act of incorporation of any State whatever."[76] When Waite and the majority ruled that the state of Illinois could regulate an unincorporated business, it legitimized statutory economic regulation. With that act the court acknowledged that economic power stemmed as much from private property as from state-granted privileges. The court, moreover, gave state legislatures the power to respond to new economic geographies—especially ones that endowed unscrupulous men like Munn and Scott with the power to take a toll from all those whose grain passed through the Chicago waterfront.

In *Munn*, the Supreme Court confronted an irony of classical laissez faire; economic actors could not exchange goods freely when crucial economic spaces remained privately held and unregulated. The State and Illinois and the Supreme Court thus attempted to create a free market by establishing economic spaces that were public. By designating Chicago grain elevators public, lawmakers justified regulations that ensured cheap, routine access to market information and crucial transportation infrastructure. In other words, they made grain elevators public spaces so that everyone could use them to make a profit.

At the very same time that Chicago's warehousemen were consolidating their control over the grain trade, the Illinois Central Railroad was bribing state legislators to grant it a monopoly over the city's outer, or lakeshore, harbor. In 1869, the state of Illinois granted the railroad the submerged lands beneath between Twelfth and Randolph Streets, a significant portion of the harbor of a city at the center of an international network of railroads and waterways. In 1873, the state legislature, under pressure from antirailroad Grangers, revoked this grant, setting off a decades-long legal battle over the outer harbor that culminated in the 1892 Supreme Court ruling in *Illinois Central v. Illinois*.[77] The court held that the submerged lands beneath Chicago's lakeshore harbor must forever remain public. As in *Munn*, the court wished to create a free market by making the harbor public and, therefore, accessible to everyone who wished to use it to make a profit.

The Illinois Central on the Lakefront

The Illinois Central gained a foothold on the lakeshore in the 1850s, when political leaders throughout the country traded access to public lands to corporations willing to build expensive infrastructure. In Chicago, the Common Council offered a waterfront right of way to the railroad. In exchange, the Illinois Central would build an expensive breakwater to solve one of the city's gravest environmental problems: the rapid erosion of valuable shoreline south of the mouth of the Chicago River. Alas, this great benefit for the city came at significant costs, a fact not lost on Chicago Mayor Walter Gurnee, a Democrat who had worked his way into the city's elite by establishing a profitable tannery, helping found the city's Board of Trade, and living on the city's stylish Michigan Avenue.

During the 1851 Christmas season, Mayor Gurnee contemplated signing an ordinance that would anger his wealthy neighbors. It would permit the Illinois Central to build and run its trains across a trestle in the waters of Lake Michigan, parallel to the shoreline between Twelfth and Randolph Streets. In return, the Illinois Central would construct a costly breakwater to stop the erosion of the shoreline inadvertently caused by the Army Corps of Engineers' dredging of a ship channel through the sandbar at the river's mouth.[78]

The promise of lakeshore protection might have pleased Gurnee's neighbors in the elegant, cream-colored townhouses along Michigan Avenue; after all, a breakwater would stop the erosion that threatened the Fort Dearborn Addition—the area stretching northeast from State and Madison Streets to the Chicago River and Lake Michigan—and the two nearest parks, Dearborn Park and Lake Park. Those parks remained undeveloped, barren, and littered, but the open spaces—gifts of President Van Buren and the Illinois and Michigan Canal Commissioners—nonetheless held promise of a day when green spaces would dot the city's front yard. If the railroad built the breakwater, moreover, Michigan Avenue property owners would escape having to pay for lakeshore protection themselves, a fate they had resisted for nearly a decade.

Yet many of Gurnee's well-heeled neighbors objected to the ordinance. What mattered most to them was the aesthetics of the lakefront and preserving their spectacular waterfront views, uninterrupted by unsightly scenes of industry. Gurnee vetoed the ordinance.[79]

The latest episode in a decade-long fight over who would pay to protect the lakeshore, the 1851 veto aggravated sectional and interest group tensions across the city. Congressman Wentworth, for instance, lashed out at the mayor, accusing him of putting the interests of a few wealthy property owners above those of the city at large. It is tempting to see Wentworth's reproach of Mayor Gurnee as hypocrisy because as the owner of one fortieth of the Illinois Central Railroad's stock, he stood to gain from passage of an ordinance enabling the railroad to conduct commerce on the busy Chicago waterfront. Even so, the congressman raised a good point. Michigan Avenue property owners wanted all the city's taxpayers to spend money protecting the shoreline. Chicagoans who did not live along Michigan Avenue, however, did not enjoy lake views from the comfort of their homes, for the most part, or relish paying taxes to protect those who did.[80]

Over the previous decade, the Chicago Common Council had vacillated on the question of who should pay to protect the shoreline from Lake Michigan's unrelenting current. In 1840, the Common Council treated lakeshore protection as a public responsibility to be paid for from general tax funds. At this time, many of the city's 4,470 residents were "boosters" who had invested heavily in real estate, hoping that urban growth would enrich them. The recent Panic of 1837 had driven land prices down sharply. Many Chicago property owners thus supported public works spending in hopes of spurring a real estate recovery. In September of 1840, owners of lots in the Fort Dearborn Addition offered the city a $1,048 loan for breakwater construction. The Common Council accepted the money, and, with it, public responsibility for lakeshore protection.[81]

In 1845, however, the Common Council took the opposite position, determining that lakeshore protection was the responsibility of private property owners. Two things had changed. First, Lake Michigan had destroyed the breakwater, and its currents had begun to thrash the open land east of Michigan Avenue, which would later become Lake Park. Second, the city's population had topped twelve thousand. Consequently, Chicagoans' economic interests had become far more differentiated, making it harder to determine whether it would benefit the entire city to spend money protecting one particular area of the lakefront. Michigan Avenue property owners who did not want to shoulder the burden of lakeshore protection alone said it would. Without a new breakwater, they argued, Chicago would be "deprived of one of the most extensive Public Parks that can be found in any American city." This appeal to the public interest fell on deaf ears, however. Chicago alderman had come to regard lakeshore protection as the responsibility of the property owners who enjoyed views of Lake Michigan. The Common Council ordered Michigan Avenue property owners to pay special tax assessments and subscriptions to raise the seven thousand dollars needed for a new breakwater. Michigan Avenue property owners protested the assessments, but the city proceeded, constructing the new breakwater by November of 1845. Lake Michigan's currents pummeled the new breakwater in short order. By August of 1846, a large chunk of the structure had washed away.[82]

In 1850, the Chicago Common Council crafted a new, hybrid public-private financing scheme to construct yet another breakwater. North Side Alderman John Dodge led a special committee charged with determining who should pay for it. Dodge concluded that both private property owners and the broader public had an interest in lakeshore protection. "Lots upon

Michigan Avenue," Dodge observed, "would be much more benefitted by such improvement than owners of Lands in other portions of the City." The alderman also believed that a breakwater would benefit "all the citizens," because it would save Lake Park, which had already lost twenty of its original thirty-five acres to the pounding currents of Lake Michigan. Dodge's committee therefore proposed that the city and the lakeshore property owners share the cost of building a new, ten-thousand-dollar breakwater. The Common Council agreed with Dodge, and the city began construction. Lake Michigan Avenue property owners, however, protested the plan, arguing that Dodge's special committee did not have the legal authority to tax and spend. Frustrated by Michigan Avenue property owners' continuing reluctance to pay for lakeshore protection, the Chicago Common Council welcomed a proposal from a business corporation.[83] The Illinois Central Railroad had received a charter from the state in 1851, which granted it lands and rights of way in unincorporated areas. To gain a right of way in an incorporated city like Chicago, the railroad had to negotiate with its aldermen. Railroad officials proposed to trade a right of way along the city's waterfront for breakwater construction.[84]

Illinois Central attorney Mason Brayman worked to convince the Chicago Common Council that the railroad would serve the public interest. He walked a fine line, though, in attempting to define the Illinois Central as an agent of the public interest, while protecting its bottom line. The railroad's admitted desire to build a terminal on the waterfront made it susceptible to extortion by the Common Council. Chicago's shrewd aldermen thus proposed that in addition to the breakwater the railroad construct retaining walls and heap land fill into the water to extend the city's park lands east from Michigan Avenue. Brayman firmly rejected the proposal, calling it "wholly inadmissible" that a corporation chartered to operate a railroad would spend money building a public park. "May not the Company," he quipped, "be required to level the Hills of Galena, pave the streets of Bloomington, and fill up the low grounds of Cairo, as well as make a 'public promenade' at Chicago?" Brayman maintained, "Railroads are not constructed for the purpose of building cities, nor of adorning cities, nor of repairing . . . damages which . . . [cities] have suffered from fire or water." But, the attorney added, "all these results may follow the construction of lines of Railroads to favored points." Thus, while city building and repair were not objectives of the railroad's operations, they could be incidents of them in cases where the interests of the Illinois Central and the city of Chicago aligned.[85]

Brayman insisted the railroad and the city had two common interests: protecting the lakeshore and augmenting the city's "natural" transportation corridors with railroads. The attorney pledged the Illinois Central would erect "a permanent sea-wall which will afford the City adequate security against the further advances of the Lake." At a cost of "several hundred thousand dollars," the railroad's seawall promised to be far sturdier than those previously built by penny-pinching aldermen and lakeshore property owners. The city would therefore gain lakeshore protection at no cost. Brayman did not mention it, but the breakwater would presumably also protect the railroad's trestle. The meeting of rail and water in Chicago would, Brayman thought, be of the greatest benefit to the Illinois Central and the city of Chicago. Brayman regarded the growth of cities and railroads as mutually reinforcing, organic processes, occurring at waters' edge. "Railroads like streams," Brayman lectured the Common Council, "seek navigable waters." For, "There transshipments take place; there is created a demand for labor, capital, enterprise;" there, at waters' edge, with the clustering of labor and capital, Brayman concluded, "Cities are made." The railroad, in the attorney's formulation, merely followed and enhanced this otherwise natural process. "While a railroad for its own convenience and advantage seeks a termination at a point where natural advantages have already created a City, it confers double benefits upon the favored point." In his formulation, the railroad was simply the logical culmination of a process of city building that resulted from geographic conditions preordained by the creator.[86]

While Brayman's logic of city building rightly emphasized the centrality of water and importance of clustering, it denied the essential roles of individuals, governments, and, ironically, corporations like the Illinois Central. City making was not an inevitable, natural process. In fact, some of the very waterways—the Chicago River Harbor and the Illinois and Michigan Canal—that Brayman described as "natural" were actually marvels of modern statecraft, finance, and human engineering. Urban growth, moreover, largely followed rather than preceded the creation of a new aquatic geography. Perhaps out of ignorance or, more likely, out of cunning, Brayman naturalized city building. By describing railroad construction as the culmination of a natural process of urban development, Brayman attempted to make the Illinois Central's entry seem like the inevitable next step.[87]

The clever lawyer naturalized the entrance of the railroad into the city at a time when some powerful Chicagoans worried the railroad might ruin the natural beauty of the lakeshore. Mayor Gurnee and his neighbors in the elegant townhouses along Michigan Avenue, in particular, worried the railroad would be an eyesore. That concern had, in large part, caused the mayor to veto the 1851 ordinance granting the Illinois Central a right of way. Gurnee's objections were brushed aside, however, by a large majority of alderman under pressure from cost-conscious residents of the north and west sides whose views of the lake were not in jeopardy. The Common Council granted the Illinois Central a right of way in 1852.[88] Aldermen nonetheless responded to his aesthetic concerns, crafting an ordinance that attempted to reconcile industry and beauty. The ordinance specified, for instance, that the railroad not place "any obstructions to the view of the lake from the shore" or "occupy, use or intrude upon the open ground known as Lake Park." And in the areas south of Twelfth Street, where the railroad tracks would run on dry land, the Illinois Central would have to erect "fences . . . [to] prevent damage to persons and property." The ordinance also stated that nothing in the agreement constituted an abdication of the city's power to "use and control . . . the Harbor of the City." Ironically, these provisions did not forestall conflicts; rather, they anticipated the subjects of conflict. Over the next century, Chicagoans would fight over park construction, erecting buildings, rail traffic, train smoke, noise on the lakeshore, and, above all, whether the city and the state could abdicate control of the harbor to the Illinois Central Railroad. The latter issue would, of course, be settled by the Supreme Court in 1892.[89]

In the meantime, the Illinois Central Railroad became the defining manmade feature of the city's lakefront south of the mouth of the Chicago River. In 1861, *London Times* reporter William H. Russell described his entry to the city on the Illinois Central. The train sped toward Chicago from the south, traversing lands the railroad had purchased from Illinois Senator Douglas and real estate developer Paul Cornell. "As we approached Chicago," Russell observed, "the prairie subsided into swampy land, and thick belts of trees fringed the horizon; on our right glimpses of sea [Lake Michigan] could be caught." The train crossed into the city at Twenty-Second Street and the lakeshore, hugging the shoreline until Twelfth Street where, Russell noted, "the train leaving the land altogether, dashes out on a pier and causeway built along the borders of the lake." From the trestle, Russell could see "lines of noble houses, [and] a fine boulevard," where Gurnee and other opponents to the railroad's entry into the city resided. Russell also spotted a "forest of masts" poking up from the lake and the waters of the Chicago River as well as some of the "famed grain elevators by which so many have been hoisted to fortune." As the train approached Randolph Street, it ran back up onto dry

GREAT CENTRAL DEPOT GROUNDS.
With Entrance to Harbor.

Figure 4. Lithograph of the Great Central Depot grounds on the Chicago lakefront,
1866. The image shows the Chicago lakefront from Lake Park looking northeast toward
the train station on Randolph Street. The Illinois Central Railroad tracks are set on a
trestle in the waters of Lake Michigan. To the right of the station are two grain elevators.
Behind the station and the grain elevators are the masts of the sailboats clogging the
mouth of the Chicago River. The Illinois Central Railroad claimed titled to the lands
beneath the railroad trestle in its legal dispute with the city and state that culminated
in the 1892 ruling in *Illinois v. Illinois Central*. This lithograph was created by Jevne and
Almini in 1866. It is housed in and was reproduced by the Chicago History Museum.

land and onto the railroad's extensive waterfront complex. The site consisted
of seventy-three acres of old Fort Dearborn lands between Randolph Street
and the Chicago River that the railroad had purchased in 1852. It contained
two towering grain elevators, a maze of railroad tracks, a lake slip, and the
four-story "station of the Central Illinois Company."[90]

At the same time that the Illinois Central developed its facilities on the
Chicago lakefront, American judges began to craft new interpretations of riparian, or shoreline, law that called the railroad's right of way into question.

Jurists in the United States were attempting to adapt British law to North American geography. The key issue was whether riparian owners' property rights would extend only to the shoreline or all the way to the lands beneath the water. Depending on how courts answered this question, the city of Chicago may not have had the legal authority to grant the Illinois Central a right of way to build a trestle across the lands underneath Chicago's harbor.

American jurists had long followed English riparian law, but there was ambiguity about how it translated to the North American environment. In English law, riparian owners held titles that extended to the edge of all tidal waters and to the lands beneath all nontidal waters. With its long coastline and short rivers, nearly all of England's commercial waterways rose and fell with the tides. Thus, when English jurists spoke of "tidal" waters, they assumed them to be navigable; whereas they assumed that nontidal waters were not. In the late seventeenth century, the English judge Hale authored a legal treatise, *De Juro Maris*, explaining British riparian law. Hale noted that the lands submerged beneath navigable, tidal waters were owned by the king. By contrast, the submerged lands under nontidal lakes and rivers, which Hale assumed not to be commercially navigable, were held by the owners of the shoreline, with their property rights extending to the center line of the body of water.[91] These rules informed American law as well. Joseph Angell's 1824 *A Treatise on the Common Law in Relation to Water-Courses* observed that American courts adhered to the practices described by Hale and followed in the English courts.[92] In two cases, *Martin v. Waddell* (1842) and *Pollard v. Hagan* (1845), the United States Supreme Court adapted the English law to the American political context, ruling that in the absence of a king state governments would hold title to lands beneath tidal waters. What the high court and Angell did not say, however, was how English law would apply to bodies of water like Lake Michigan that were not tidal, but were nonetheless critical for navigation. Did the state hold title to the lakebed or did the owners of the shoreline?[93]

In the middle of the nineteenth century, American courts began to deviate from English riparian law. The existence of so many commercially navigable, nontidal bodies of water as well as the construction of many canals led some judges to begin crafting a distinct, American interpretation of the law.[94] In *Propeller Genesee Chief v. Fitzhugh* (1851), the United States Supreme Court held that admiralty jurisdiction extended to all navigable waters, not just those affected by the tides. While the case did not comment upon ownership of submerged lands, it demonstrated that the court recognized navigability was not limited, as in England, principally to tidal waters.[95] Angell, moreover, noted in his fourth edition of the *Law of Watercourses* published in 1850 that courts in New York and New Hampshire had begun to draw property lines at the edge of circular lakes and ponds because the English "law of boundary [extending property titles to the center line of the waterway], as applied to rivers, is without doubt inapplicable to the *lakes* and other large natural collections of fresh [nontidal] water in this country." In some instances, American courts vested title of lands beneath nontidal waters in state governments. In others cases, however, American courts still followed the English precedent of assigning title to lands beneath nontidal waters to riparian owners.[96]

The Illinois Supreme Court followed the English precedent until 1860 when it acknowledged the difficulty of drawing property boundaries beneath large, circular bodies of water like Lake Michigan. Along relatively straight rivers and streams, it was a simple matter to extend the shore owners' property line outward to the middle of the waterway. In *Middleton v. Pritchard* (1842), the Illinois Supreme Court, for instance, ruled that the owner of land on the Mississippi River shoreline could claim ownership of all the land on the riverbed and all of the timber on an island.[97] Yet, in 1860, the court took a markedly different stance. Noting the difficulty of tracing property lines out into the center of very large, circular bodies of water like Lake Michigan, the Illinois Supreme Court held in *Seaman v. Smith* that riparian property rights extended only to the lake's shoreline.[98]

The court's opinion in *Seaman* cast doubt on whether the Illinois Central had legal authority to build infrastructure on the lakeshore. The city of Chicago had granted the railroad the right of way to lay tracks across the bed of the lake. But, if one followed the court's logic in *Seaman v. Smith*, lakeside property owners' claims ended at water's edge and the state held title to lands underneath lakes. Thus, it was possible that the city of Chicago had granted the Illinois Central a right of way across lands that it did not own. If, on the other hand, the courts followed the English view that the riparian owner held title to the lakebed, the city's right of way grant would be legitimate as long as the city of Chicago owned the land beside the lake, Lake Park.[99] But, as it turned out, it was not even clear who really owned Lake Park.

In 1867, the *Chicago Tribune* suggested that the city did not hold title to Lake Park, as had been previously assumed. The *Tribune* noted that "it has been supposed that the city of Chicago had an unquestionable title to this important piece of property; but an examination of the subject will show that there are some interesting, if not doubtful, points in the case." The paper noted that the area Chicagoans commonly referred to as Lake Park—the vacant land between Michigan Avenue and the lake stretching for about a mile between Madison to Twelfth Streets—was granted to the state of Illinois by Congress for the purposes of raising funds for canal construction. Congress had ordered that the lands be used only "for the purpose of aiding the said State in opening a canal to unite the waters of the Illinois River with those of Lake Michigan . . . and no other."[100] In 1836, the state appointed canal commissioners to sell the federally granted lands to raise money for building the Illinois and Michigan Canal. The state told the Canal Commission "'to sell the lots in the town of Chicago . . . as also fractional section fifteen [where Lake Park was located] . . . it being first laid off and subdivided into town lots, streets and alleys.'"[101] Despite this order, the canal commissioners declined to sell part of the ground in North Lake Park, setting it aside as "vacant ground to remain forever free and clear of buildings."[102] The *Tribune* wrote in 1867 that "it is perfectly apparent that a public park is neither a "town lot," "street" or "alley," and it is an interesting question whether, in setting this land off as vacant, they exceeded the discretion allowed them by law."[103] The paper suggested that since the state had not fulfilled the conditions of the grant, the title to Lake Park might actually revert back to the federal government or still belong to the trustees of the canal.

If the state's title to Lake Park was clouded, so too was the city's. Chicago's title derived from the state legislature's inclusion in the city charter of an ambiguous clause that, the *Tribune* noted, might have conveyed Lake Park to the city. Therefore, it was unclear who owned Lake Park—the city, the state, or the federal government. It was, moreover, unclear whether the riparian owners' rights stopped at water's edge or extended to the lands beneath the outer harbor. As a result, nobody knew if the city of Chicago had had the authority to trade a right of way to the Illinois Central in exchange for a breakwater.[104] Legal ambiguity abounded. Politically connected individuals, the Illinois Central Railroad, and the Chicago Common Council looked to state legislators in Springfield to secure their rights to the valuable lakeshore.

Legislative Capture and State-Granted Monopoly

During the 1867 legislative session, a well-connected Chicago lawyer, Melville Fuller, attempted to gain a monopoly on the city's outer harbor. His law partner, Illinois legislator Henry Shepard, introduced a bill that would permit Fuller to develop massive port facilities on the lakefront between the mouth of the Chicago River and Sixteenth Street. It would have been, the *Chicago Tribune* noted, "a grant by the state of Illinois to Melville W. Fuller . . . [which] gives him the authority to practically close the present river, and thereby . . . authorizes him to collect duty . . . for the privilege of entering his estate."[105] The bill failed, but Fuller's attempt to claim the harbor worried members of the Chicago Common Council and managers of the Illinois Central.[106]

The city and the railroad alike sent representatives to Springfield during the next legislative session to secure their claims to the lakeshore, but only the Illinois Central prevailed. At the outset of the 1869 state legislative session, state legislator and Chicago alderman Joshua Knickerbocker introduced a bill granting the city title to the submerged lands along Chicago's waterfront and Lake Park. The purpose of the bill was to establish Chicago's title and thereby "enable the city to enlarge its harbor."[107] The city's proposal died, however, at the hands of the Illinois Central's formidable lobbyist, Dr. Alonzo Mack. In lieu of the Knickerbocker bill, Mack persuaded state legislators to support another law, granting the lands beneath the outer harbor to the Illinois Central Railroad.[108] Mack's bill also ordered "the city of Chicago to alienate and convey" the northern part of Lake Park to the railroad for the sum of eight hundred thousand dollars so that the railroad could build a depot. In return, the Illinois Central would pay a state tax of 7 percent of its gross income from its use of Lake Park and the submerged lands.[109] If the prospect of tax revenue was not enough to sway state legislators to support the bill, Mack allegedly swapped cash for their votes.[110] Whatever his tactics, the lobbyist grew smug with the prospect of success, boasting "the gates of hell and Governor Palmer cannot prevail against . . . [the bill]."[111]

With Mack on the brink of success, Knickerbocker staged a protest, drawing Michigan Avenue property owners who wished to keep the shoreline free of unsightly scenes of industry. At eight o'clock on a winter night, Knickerbocker and an estimated five hundred Chicagoans, including former Republican Lieutenant Governor Bross and former mayor and Congressman John Wentworth, rallied at Chicago's Farwell Hall to sound their objections.[112] Knickerbocker, Bross, and Wentworth all condemned the bill for granting the Illinois Central an outer harbor monopoly.[113] Yet, the crowd of lakeshore property owners seemed even more concerned about the effect that selling North Lake Park to the railroad for depot construction would have on their views and access to the park. When Knickerbocker declared that "this space [North Lake Park] was left open for the purpose of opening a lake view to the lots which fronted upon Michigan Avenue," applause rumbled through the hall.[114] Bross, who counted among those Michigan Avenue property owners, argued that parks offered broad public health and social benefits. His claims reflected the thinking of contemporary landscape architects like Olmsted who had, during a chance meeting in the Sierra Nevada mountains, inspired Bross to become an advocate of building parks in Chicago.[115] Bross thus commented on the public value of Lake Park, observing that "our clerks, our laboring men, our serving girls . . . are found in crowds . . . enjoying the beauty and freshness and health of that lake."[116] In the 1890s, similar arguments would inspire city officials and business leaders to cooperate in building massive parks along the city's lakefront. In the 1860s, however, industry prevailed over aesthetic and social concerns. The state legislature passed the bill granting North Lake Park and the outer harbor to the Illinois Central Railroad.[117]

Illinois Governor John Palmer vetoed the bill known as the 1869 Lake Front Act. Born to a poor family in Kentucky in 1817, Palmer's family migrated to Alton, Illinois, in 1831. Palmer earned a college degree and worked as a cooper, salesman, school teacher, and a lawyer. He was a Democrat before switching to the Republican Party in 1856. During the Civil War, Palmer enlisted in the Union Army, earning the rank of general. Two years after the conflict, he won election as Illinois governor. Palmer's opposition to the Lake Front Act hinged on his view that the legislature had bestowed an "imperial gift" upon the Illinois Central without getting enough in return. The governor claimed that while the railroad was only compelled to pay eight hundred thousand dollars for North Lake Park, it "had a market value of two millions, six hundred thousand dollars." The scope of the outer harbor grant, moreover, disturbed Palmer, who observed that it extended "along the lake shore from the Chicago River for a distance of nearly two miles, and for a distance of one mile from the shore . . . cover[ing] the great business center of the city." Palmer marveled at the fact that the legislature would grant the railroad such choice waterfront space without requiring the corporation to build a public harbor. He suggested to the legislature "that no grant be made . . . which does not couple with the grant the condition that the work of improvement shall be commenced within a reasonable time . . . so as to meet the fair demands of business."[118] The state legislature nonetheless overrode Palmer's veto, leaving Chicago's outer harbor in the hands of the Illinois Central Railroad.[119]

Federal officials shared Palmer's concern that Chicago's outer harbor needed development. In November of 1869, Major J. B. Wheeler, the head of the Chicago district of the Army Corps of Engineers, predicted that the city would have to add harbor facilities to accommodate new traffic. The "greater depth of water over the St. Clair flats," the "enlargement of the Welland Canal" between Lakes Erie and Ontario, and the potential construction of "a steamboat canal," between Chicago and the Mississippi Rivers would soon make it possible for ships with deeper drafts to journey to Chicago, creating more "direct trade with Europe."[120] Any increase in waterborne commerce would crowd the Chicago River, which Wheeler noted, "is taxed to its utmost to accommodate the present condition of affairs and that it is utterly inadequate to meet the want of commerce rapidly growing."[121] Given the situation reported by Wheeler, Congress made appropriations for the construction of breakwaters surrounding the mouth of the Chicago and just off the lakeshore in front of downtown Chicago. This created a safe anchorage basin surrounding the submerged lands newly acquired by the Illinois Central.[122]

As the Army Corps of Engineers constructed the anchorage basin, the federal government successfully challenged some provisions of the Lake Front Act, preventing the Illinois Central from developing Lake Park. An officer of the U. S. Attorney General, G. O. Glover filed a suit on behalf of the United States challenging the legality of the transfer of North Lake Park to the railroad. District court Judge Thomas Drummond issued an injunction prohibiting the transfer because North Lake Park had, in the 1830s, been dedicated by the canal commissioners as public land to remain free and clear of buildings.[123] That injunction prevented the Illinois Central from building a large railroad depot at that location. Meanwhile, Glover also challenged the Illinois Central's ownership of the submerged lands on the basis that their property rights might interfere with the Army Corps' efforts to build a protected basin on the lakefront. This case was settled in January of 1872 with the railroad and the federal government drawing a line between the area within the breakwater open to navigation and the area that the Illinois Central could claim for the construction of docks and railroads.[124] The Illinois Central began constructing piers and additional breakwaters along the lakefront, but before the railroad developed a large outer harbor, the state legislature challenged its title.[125]

In 1873, amid the Granger backlash against railroad power across the Midwest, state legislators considered repealing the Lake Front Act.[126] Proponents of repeal saw it as a means of reversing a corrupt bargain. As state representative Bradwell put it, "every member should know the act was the biggest steal that was ever brought through the Legislature."[127] For its part, the Illinois Central did not bother to deny the claims that it had secured the lakefront through bribery. Rather, it dispatched lawyer Jewett to Springfield to try to convince legislators to bury the repeal bill in the judiciary committee.[128] Jewett warned state representatives that it was unconstitutional for one legislature to revoke a contract made by a previous legislature. Jewett's argument was echoed by Representative Rountree who advised his colleagues that "It was of no importance whether the bill was carried by fraud and corruption. . . . the State had renounced all its right to the land . . . [and] Men who were mindful of their constitutional obligations could not vote against referring it to the Judiciary [Committee]." Representative Herrington shot back with accusations of collusion: "The gentlemen [Rountree] was co-operating with the paid attorneys and friends of the Illinois Central, and was particeps criminus with that Company in attempting to defend its robbery of the City of Chicago."[129] This antirailroad animus defined the session, and the legislature soon repealed the Lake Front Act.[130]

The repeal of the Lake Front Act only added new uncertainties to existing ambiguities over title to the submerged lands. As Jewett had argued, it might have been unconstitutional for the legislature to repeal the grant; it might have been a taking of the railroad's private property without the due process of law afforded by the Fourteenth Amendment. Even if the repeal was legal, it was still not clear who owned Lake Park—the city, state, or federal government. It was also not clear whether the riparian owner's title extended to the lands submerged beneath the waters of Lake Michigan, or if they ended at the shoreline. Thus, nobody knew who the riparian owner was or if that owner had the right to grant the Illinois Central a right of way.

The Public Trust Doctrine and the Free Marketplace

Ambiguity over property rights on the lakefront arrested harbor development. Port traffic, meanwhile, increased steadily on the Chicago River during the 1870s and 1880s. Amid growing calls for lakeshore port development, the Illinois attorney general brought suit against the railroad in 1883, in hopes of determining who had title to the submerged lands. With a clear title, the city or state might build an outer harbor along Chicago's downtown lakeshore, thereby relieving congestion on the river. From its inception, then, the "Chicago Lake Front Case" was an attempt by government officials to designate the lakeshore as a public space and build a harbor accessible to all those who wished to use it for profit making.

During the 1870s and 1880s, Chicagoans, the federal government, and the Illinois Central all launched building projects on the lakeshore near, but not on, the contested submerged lands between Randolph and Twelfth Streets. A key development in Lake Park occurred after the long, hot summer of 1871. On October 8, the bone dry city of wooden structures was engulfed by a blaze that began on Saturday evening in a barn near the intersection of Jefferson and Taylor. The fire traveled north on the wind, burning a four-square-mile area in the heart of Chicago before it was dampened by a cool Tuesday morning rain.[131] Chicagoans cleared some of the debris by heaping it into the basin of stagnant water between Michigan Avenue and the Illinois Central's railroad trestle, thereby expanding Lake Park.[132]

After the Great Chicago Fire, the city's economy boomed, and so too did waterborne commerce. Tonnage in the port of Chicago soared, from 6,077,542 in 1872 to 9,754,949 tons in 1882.[133] The Illinois Central, in turn, built three large piers between the river's mouth and Randolph Street and one more south of Twelfth Street.[134] The Army Corps of Engineers, meanwhile, constructed a large breakwater, sheltering the outer harbor from the currents of Lake Michigan (see map). Even so, most of the traffic in the city's port went to the Chicago River, because there were comparatively few docks on the Chicago lakefront. Nobody would build an outer harbor on the submerged lands between Randolph and Twelfth Streets. Ambiguity over property rights had simply arrested development.[135]

The state of Illinois brought suit against the Illinois Central in order to respond to the increasing demand for harbor development. The city's leading Republican newspaper had agitated for such action. Joseph Medill's *Chicago Tribune* suggested the state and the railroad go to the courts to determine the owner of the submerged lands so that "the work of [harbor] construction, in accordance with some plan . . . , may be commenced at once."[136] In March of 1883, the Illinois attorney general filed a suit against the railroad, which also named the city of Chicago and the federal government as defendants because of their interests in Lake Park. After years of litigation in 1888, Justice John Harlan, writing for the U.S. Circuit Court, handed down a ruling declaring Lake Park the property of the city and the submerged lands that of the state of Illinois.[137] The Illinois Central took two years to prepare before it began the long appeal process, which culminated in the 1892 Supreme Court case *Illinois Central v. Illinois* argued by Attorney Jewett.[138]

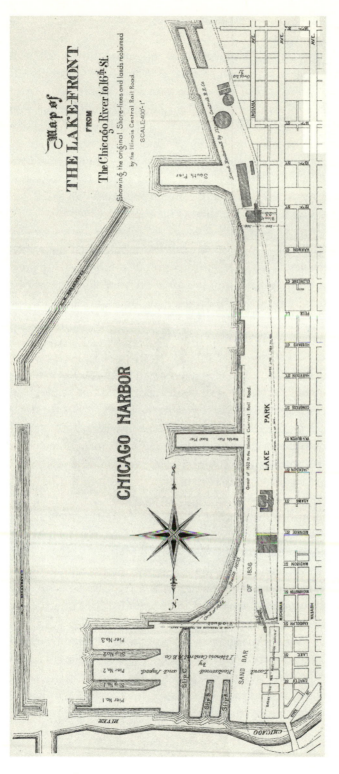

Figure 5. Map of the Chicago lakefront south of the mouth of the Chicago River, 1894. This map shows the shoreline south of the mouth of the Chicago River, which was occupied and filled-in by the Illinois Central Railroad. The map is turned so that east is at the top, north is to the left, south to the right, and west at the bottom. The Supreme Court determined that the state of Illinois owned the lands under Lake Michigan's waters between Twelfth and Randolph Streets in its 1892 ruling in *Illinois Central v. Illinois*. The map dates to 1894. Its creator is unknown. The map is in the collection of and was reproduced by the Chicago History Museum.

Jewett might have thought that the tide of opinion on the Supreme Court had turned his way since his loss in *Munn v. Illinois*. The court, under Chief Justice Morrison Waite, would not concede that the Fourteenth Amendment's due process clause prohibited statutory regulation of business. Waite, however, had died in 1888, ushering in one of the court's most conservative, antiregulatory eras under the leadership of Chief Justice Melville Fuller. A Chicagoan, Fuller had been integrally involved in the wrangling over Chicago's lakeshore. During the 1867 legislative session, he had tried to gain that prize for himself, and in 1887 the city of Chicago employed him to defend its claim against the Illinois Central in the Circuit Court. Given his prior involvement, Fuller would have to recuse himself from the Lake Front Case deliberations. The Fuller Court was nonetheless a bastion of conservative thinking.[139] Consequently, Stephen Field's vision of substantive due process was in the ascent.[140] By 1905, it would become accepted doctrine when the Fuller Court struck down a New York regulation limiting bakers' hours in *Lochner v. New York*.[141]

Jewett framed the Illinois Central's appeal as a test of the principle of substantive due process that was so central to Field's jurisprudence. The railroad's attorney claimed the city's 1869 submerged land grant constituted a valid contract. A valid contract, Jewett contended, could not be overturned by the Illinois state legislature without violating the Fourteenth Amendment's due process clause or the Constitution's contract clause, which prevented states from retroactively altering a contract. Thus, Jewett maintained the 1873 repeal of the Lake Front Act was invalid. For its part, the state of Illinois argued the repeal had been a valid exercise of its police powers. Justice Field, in contrast, did not see the case in either of those terms.[142]

A feeble, aged Justice Field delivered the court's four-to-three majority ruling on December 5, 1892. Justices Joseph Lamar, John Harlan, and Field's nephew Justice David Brewer concurred with the decision. Horace Gray, Henry Billings Brown, and George Shiras dissented. Samuel Blatchford, an Illinois Central shareholder, abstained from ruling in the case. So too did the conservative Fuller who had once tried to secure a lakefront harbor grant from the state legislature for himself and then represented the city of Chicago in earlier litigation over the lakeshore.[143] Field unraveled a scroll from which he read his decision in a voice so withered that it failed to carry his pronouncements to the ears of the reporters hovering on the fringes of the chambers.[144] Although his body was frail and his voice wavered, his logic was keen and forceful and betrayed a characteristic independence of thought.

Field resisted Jewett's attempts to frame the case in a way that would force him to either uphold the 1869 grant or contradict his strong defense of private property in his dissents in *Munn* and the *Slaughterhouse Cases*.[145]

Field held that neither the contract clause nor the Fourteenth Amendment's due process clause applied to the case.[146] The Illinois Central had not been stripped of its property because, Field argued, the state legislature had made an invalid grant in 1869. To substantiate this point, Field relied on a legal doctrine that had its roots in ancient Roman law. The "public trust doctrine" barred sovereign powers from alienating particular lands, such as those under navigable waters, from the people. Field concluded, "So with trusts connected with public property, or property of a special character, like lands under navigable waters; they cannot be placed entirely beyond the direction and control of the state."[147] In sum, the state did not possess the authority to give away submerged lands that belonged to the people. Field's position was consistent with Jacksonian Democrats' fear that government officials would dispense special privileges. The justice struck down the grant for the same reason Jackson disbanded the National Bank. He saw legislative power as the source of a monopoly that benefited special interests.[148] While Field's jurisprudence was consistent with Jacksonian principles, his antipathy to state-granted monopoly does not entirely explain the ruling in *Illinois Central*.

Field invoked the public trust doctrine to create a market. His view of the public interest was linked to his understanding of the economic significance of Chicago's harbor. The justice observed that "the arrivals and clearings of vessels at the port exceed in number those of New York, and are equal to those of New York and Boston combined"[149] Field noted the port was of "immense value to the people of the state of Illinois, in the facilities it affords to its vast and constantly increasing commerce." Chicago's harbor was so central to the economy, Field concluded, that "the idea that its legislature can deprive the state of control over its bed and waters . . . is a proposition that cannot be defended." In effect, Field proclaimed the harbor public to create an accessible marketplace.[150]

Not only did the volume of the commerce in Chicago's port influence Field's decision to invoke the public trust doctrine, the justice also took the physical size of the grant into consideration. In his decision Field drew comparisons between the one-thousand-plus acre grant and other harbor facilities throughout the world, observing that it was "as large as that embraced by all the merchandise docks along the Thames at London . . . much larger than

that included in the famous docks . . . at Liverpool . . . twice that of the port
of Marseilles, and nearly . . . equal to the pier area along the water front of the
city of New York." The size of the submerged lands grant was of crucial importance in Field's opinion that the grant violated the public trust. Field even
conceded that the state could grant small parcels of the submerged lands to
private parties. He contended "that the control of the state can never be
lost . . . except as to such parcels . . . used in promoting . . . or which do not
substantial impair the public interest." Large grants violated the public trust
by placing too much power into the hands of a company that could limit access to the harbor, whereas small grants might not.[151]

The justices who dissented with Field included the former Pittsburgh corporate attorney George Shiras, the Boston Brahmin and former justice of the
Massachusetts Supreme Judicial Court Horace Gray, and a former admiralty
lawyer, Henry Billings Brown, who frequently opposed government intervention in business.[152] They claimed that Field privileged practical considerations over general policy. Writing for the minority, Shiras remarked that
"The opinion of the majority . . . concedes that a state does possess the power
to grant the rights of property and possession in such lands to private parties,
but the power is stated to be in some way restricted to 'small parcels.'" To
Shiras, however, the scope of the grant was irrelevant. He argued "it is difficult to see how the validity of the exercise of the power, if the power exists,
can depend upon the size of the parcel granted." The larger issue was really
whether or not the state had the power to grant submerged lands. Field's notion of the public interest, Shiras point out, was predicated on subjective ap-
praisals of the size, commercial importance, and location of particular parcels
of land.[153]

Field did not disagree. He argued that the state of Illinois could not relinquish its title to the submerged lands precisely because the legislature needed
to respond to changing economic conditions. "The legislature," Field held,
"could not give away nor sell the discretion of its successors in respect to matters . . . [that] from the very nature of things, must vary with varying circumstances." In this view, Field concurred with his colleague Harlan who had
written the 1888 Circuit Court opinion. Field observed that "The [Circuit]
court, treating the act as a license to the company . . . observed that it was
deemed best . . . for the public interest that the improvement of the harbor
should be effected by the instrumentality of a railroad corporation." In 1873,
however, the state legislature thought otherwise. Rather than seeing the 1873
Lake Front Act repeal as revoking a contract, Field reasoned that the legisla-

ture was merely deciding to carry out its duty to manage the submerged lands for the public in a different way, rather than through the Illinois Central Railroad.[154]

Field's distinctly nineteenth-century view of the corporation also contributed to his view that the 1869 Lake Front Act was invalid. While the twentieth-century corporation derived its rights from legal status as a "natural entity" like a person, the nineteenth-century corporation possessed only the rights and privileges granted by a state government in a charter. The charter functioned as a contract, defining the specific purposes of the corporation as well as how the state could regulate its business practices. The nineteenth-century corporation then, unlike a corporate person, operated within very narrow parameters defined by its creator, the state.[155] Thus, in his *Illinois Central* ruling, Field invoked the principle of *ultra vires*, the doctrine that prohibited a corporation from engaging in business practices not expressly stated in its charter. He noted that the 1869 act could not have been valid because under it, "a corporation created for one purpose, the construction and operation of a railroad between designated points, is . . . converted into a corporation to manage and practically control the harbor of Chicago, not simply for its own purpose as a railroad corporation, but for its own profit generally."[156] There was, Field held, no legal basis for a corporation to enter an entirely different business than the one for which it had been created by the state.

Field's contractual understanding helps explain the distinctions between his rulings in *Illinois Central* and in *Munn*. In Illinois Central, Field invalidated the 1869 submerged lands grant based on the provisions of the charter. Conversely, in *Munn*, Field determined that the state could not impose rate regulations at grain elevators because they were not corporations and no regulations had been agreed to in the terms of a charter. The Illinois state legislature, Field reasoned, could not simply decide to tell a businessman what to charge for access to his private property. Field considered the contract, not the legislative statute, to be the proper instrument of economic regulation.

Field's ruling in *Illinois Central* suggests, moreover, that he did not necessarily consider the goals of the public diametrically opposed to those of the private sector. Field thought public power essential for noncommercial reasons like preserving health, safety, and morals. And, in *Illinois Central* he showed an instrumental understanding of public power. Field recognized that private property was, in some circumstances, injurious to commerce. "The sea and navigable rivers" he observed, "are natural highways, and any obstruction to the common right, or exclusive appropriation of their use, is injurious to commerce and if permitted at the will of the sovereign, would be very likely to end materially crippling, if not destroying it." His assertion of the public interest then was aimed at removing obstacles to commerce. Field recognized a vibrant commercial economy demanded public ownership and regulation of strategically located natural resources. In *Illinois Central*, he invoked public power to provide private parties with access to a crucial space so they could pursue profit.[157]

To this end, Field suggested the city of Chicago construct a harbor. He found Chicago to be the riparian owner of Lake Park. He noted, "The city of Chicago, as riparian owner of the grounds on its east or lake front of the city ... and in virtue of authority conferred by its charter, has the power to construct and keep in repair on the lake front ... public landing places, wharves, docks and levees." This city's rights, moreover, did not interfere with the state's ownership of the submerged lands. Rather, they were "subject ... in the execution of that power, to the authority of the State to prescribe the lines beyond which piers, docks, wharves, and other structures ... may not be extended into the navigable waters of the harbor." Thus, the city could build harbor facilities provided that it did not interfere with the duty of the state to ensure access to navigable waterways.[158]

The Supreme Court's decisions in *Illinois Central v. Illinois* and in *Munn v. Illinois* followed a strikingly similar logic. In both cases, the court created public spaces to promote economic development. By the end of the Civil War, Chicago had become the great commercial crossroads prophesied by its antebellum boosters and canal builders as well as by the French explorers of the seventeenth century. An astonishing volume of commodities flowed through Chicago en route from the continental interior to the eastern seaboard and far-flung points across the globe.

The city's waterfront, in turn, became a bottleneck. By controlling the flow of goods and information, Chicago's grain elevator operators could enrich themselves at the expense of grain farmers, consumers, and traders alike. The Illinois Central Railroad, meanwhile, gained power over another such bottleneck in 1869 when it acquired the title to Chicago's outer harbor. Politicians and some key business leaders quickly mobilized to break the grain elevator operators and the Illinois Central's monopolies on the waterfront. To do so, they passed laws designating what the railroad and elevator operators considered their private property as a type of public space. The Supreme Court upheld these laws in two key rulings that expanded governmental oversight of the economy in order to promote economic development.

The court's *Munn* ruling legitimized what had already become an effective regulatory regime. In keeping with the city's history of public-private partnership, the Board of Trade, the state of Illinois, and Chicago's banks were already working in tandem to curb grain elevator operators' abuses, such as issuing false receipts, recycling old receipts, lying about the quantity or condition of grain stores, and charging exorbitant fees for storage. These regulations were crucial to the functioning of the commodities markets. Traders required accurate market information; bankers needed to have faith in elevator receipts; and farmers did not want to be gouged at the elevator.

The city's grain elevator operators, meantime, saw in *Munn* an opportunity to challenge the regulations that limited their opportunities for plunder. If their lawyer, Jewett, could convince the Supreme Court to invoke the Fourteenth Amendment to overturn rate regulations and declare their private property rights absolute, they could extort farmers and, perhaps, challenge the authority of regulators to enter their private property to peer inside their storage bins. In *Munn*, the court ensured affordable access to the storage bins—and to reliable information about what they contained.

For as long as they stood, Chicago's grain elevators remained sites of commercial exchange, but the city's lakeshore would come to have a very different type of economic value to the city. Justice Field and the Supreme Court's majority had assumed that the city of Chicago would build a great industrial harbor along the downtown lakeshore after deciding *Illinois Central*. Field believed, and rightly so, that the decades of litigation over the submerged lands along Chicago's downtown lakeshore had stymied harbor development.[159] If Field ruled in favor of the Illinois Central, the railroad would have gained monopoly power over the city's outer harbor, determining who could or could not enter, and at what cost. This would potentially limit access, impeding economic development. Field, however, ruled against the railroad, invoking the "public trust doctrine" to establish that the submerged lands beneath Chicago's harbor were so centrally located that they must remain public. Field saw the public trust doctrine as pro-development, reasoning that if he designated the submerged lands as public the city would develop harbor facilities that all economic actors could use. His ruling was intended to be an act of market creation. He assumed the city of Chicago would build a harbor after the ruling.

Field's decision had radically different consequences than he had anticipated. By the 1890s, many of Chicago's business and civic leaders wanted to adorn the downtown lakeshore with parks, museums, and civic monuments instead of a harbor. These recreational facilities would, they believed, have greater value than a downtown industrial harbor. There were, it turned out, good reasons to keep industry away from the city's central business district. Larger ships, industrial pollution, and rising downtown land values all boded for moving water-reliant industry to the banks of the Calumet River on the city's southeast side or to the ports of Northwest Indiana.

Even though the city did not build an industrial harbor on the lakeshore as Field had suggested, it did not, by any means, abandon its role of promoting economic development. Nor did the state or federal government, for that matter. In the 1890s and 1900s, the three branches of government grappled with the question of how to remake the waterfront to respond to seismic shifts in Chicago and the nation's economy: the advent of iron and steel ships on the Great Lakes, the rise of the steel industry, the proliferation of white-collar commercial jobs in the city's downtown business district and the growth of tourism.

CHAPTER 3

The Creative Destruction of the Chicago River Harbor

The Chicago River reached its commercial peak in 1889, when it handled 10,994,036 tons of freight—making Chicago the fourth largest port in the world behind New York, London, and Hamburg.[1] Despite its status as one of the most important industrial harbors on the planet, the river was little more than a small, stinking stream that poured out of Lake Michigan and spilled onto the prairie.

Many of the businesses that made the city a modern metropolis stood on its banks, including the hardware firm Hibbard, Spencer, Bartlett and Company, which in the late 1880s employed the Indiana native and future novelist Theodore Dreiser.[2] In 1898, Dreiser penned an essay about the river that flowed beside his former workplace, dubbing it "the smallest and busiest river in the world." Its banks were crowded with "stock-yards, lumber-yards, railway-yards, stone-yards, coal-yards . . . interspersed with docks, elevators, [and] manufactories" with "belching smokestacks, sooty black . . . in forest-like numbers." Situated within this welter of commerce were such iconic nineteenth-century American businesses as McCormick Harvesting Machine Company and the Illinois Central Railroad.[3]

The riverbanks were also home to Chicago's great lumber industry. Many of the city's 220 lumber dealers crowded along the south branch. In the lumber yards, observed *Harper's Weekly* in 1883, blackened piles of wood stood as tall as buildings. The lumber stacks were punctuated by "long [boat] slips from which [rose] the graceful spars of the lumber schooners." The air resounded with the "hum of the planing-mills, the snorting of . . . busy switch engines . . . and whistling of tugs on the river." Swirling breezes carried chimney smoke and fine sawdust, which often found "snug lodgment in the eyes."[4]

The river's main stem flowed west from Lake Michigan for a mile and a half along the northern border of the city's central business district to Wolf Point, where it split in two. One branch extended to the northwest, and the other, busier branch flowed due south, forming the western boundary of the central business district. At Twelfth Street, the river veered southwest to Ashland Avenue and received Bubbly Creek, a bloodstained rivulet thick with offal from Chicago's Union Stockyards.[5] From Ashland, the river flowed southwest until it reached the ninety-seven-mile-long Illinois and Michigan Canal, which linked the Chicago River to the Illinois and Mississippi Rivers.[6] Together, the three branches of the Chicago River totaled about sixteen miles in length and measured two hundred feet across at their widest points.[7] The waters, slick with combustible oil and gas from nearby refineries, ran up to seventeen feet deep.[8]

On any given day during the seven to eight months of the year when winter relinquished its icy grip on the river, hundreds of ships covered the water's surface, "all out of place and as if they had lost their way in the great city and could no longer find the broad open sea," as Dreiser observed.[9] Sometimes, the river itself was hidden beneath a shroud of smoke under which vessels "quarrel[ed] for the right of way with all the vehemence inherent in gongs and whistles."[10]

Even as Dreiser peered through the smoke and glimpsed the jumble of boats jockeying for position within the port, sweeping technological and economic forces were rendering it obsolete. Driven by economic competition and late nineteenth-century changes in marine technology, Great Lakes shipping lines were purging wooden sailboats from their fleets and replacing them with larger iron and steel-hulled steamships. The upshot was that some of the very harbor infrastructure that had once facilitated travel began to stifle it. Large ships often had difficultly navigating the river channel, which was narrowed by wharves and bulkheads and crisscrossed with bridges and tunnels.

The obsolescence of port infrastructure sparked a debate between businessmen dependent on the river and the Army Corps of Engineers about whether the harbor should be retrofitted to accommodate larger ships. In March 1896, more than 120 businessmen gathered at Chicago's Great Northern Hotel to stop a "murder." At issue was a policy proposal by Major W. L. Marshall, chief of the Army Corps of Engineers' operations in Chicago, who had urged Congress to drive waterborne commerce from the Chicago River to the Calumet River, on the city's southeastern periphery. One of the businessmen, a leading dry goods merchant named John V. Farwell, described the major's proposal: "We have an officer of the United States government report that the harbor that has made this city has got to be closed and that the Congress of the United States must do the murder and he will be the coroner."[11]

Marshall considered the development of the Calumet River Harbor essential for not only the accommodation of large ships, but also as a response to changes in the city's economic geography. Several factors—rising downtown land values, the increasing costs of urban congestion, and the development of the steel industry—were driving manufacturing firms from the banks of the Chicago River. Marshall described the exodus in 1893: "The increasing value of lands . . . near the mouth of the river is causing grain elevators, coal yards, lumber yards and manufacturing establishments, dependent upon marine transportation, either to recede farther and farther from the mouth of the river, or to go elsewhere." According to Marshall, some firms had moved to Milwaukee, Waukegan, or the rapidly growing industrial district along the Calumet River.[12]

He had a point. Economist Joseph Schumpeter famously described capitalism as a process of ceaseless economic and technological innovation, or "creative destruction," and Chicago's harbor absorbed the brunt of that ceaseless process.[13] In 1881, 80 percent of Chicago's manufacturing firms lay within three miles of the intersection of State and Lake in the Loop. Yet, by the 1920s, the city no longer had a single central industrial district. The number of manufacturing companies in the Loop had declined, and the region's heavy industries stretched out from the Loop for forty miles in all directions. Manufacturing firms had created specialized industrial districts on the urban periphery, where they could escape the physical and political constraints of older landscapes.[14]

The businessmen who gathered at the Great Northern Hotel in 1896 tried to plot a response to these forces, and under the auspices of their official organization, the Chicago River Improvement Association, they lobbied Congress for appropriations to save the Chicago River Harbor.[15]

They were waging a hopeless battle, as it turned out. The sinking fortunes of the Chicago River Harbor, and the departure of so many firms from it, were tied to the relentless pace of change in the shipping industry. By the turn of the century, the replacement of wooden sailboats with ever-larger iron and steel steamships had rendered many of the built structures along the river channel obsolete. But that technological transformation did not, in and of itself, destroy the port.

The transition from sail to steam was a fatal blow to an industrial harbor already in decline. The riverside had ceased to be the most desirable location for many water-reliant manufacturing firms. Riverside land values were high, and downtown congestion and pollution caused costly delays. So many stakeholders had conflicting ideas about the proper use of the river, in fact, that it was politically difficult to stem the decline of industrial freight shipping on the Chicago. The tonnage carried on the Chicago River plummeted by nearly 75 percent in the first two decades of the twentieth century.[16]

The destruction of the Chicago River Harbor correlated with the creation of new industrial harbors by businessmen and federal government officials. At the turn of the twentieth century, many manufacturing firms—especially in the growing steel industry—created new industrial districts on the urban periphery, not only on the banks of the Calumet River but also on the shores of Lake Michigan in Northwest Indiana.[17] These firms were assisted by the Army Corps of Engineers, which dredged and widened the Calumet to make it a suitable harbor. In 1906, it finally overtook the Chicago River as the city's principal industrial port.[18]

The Industrialization of Great Lakes Shipping

On a summer day in 1893, a ship named the *Centurion* steamed into the mouth of the Chicago River on its maiden voyage. Soon after entering the Great Lakes' leading port, its captain ordered the crew to turn back. At 379 feet in length, the *Centurion* was simply too big to negotiate the river's narrow bridge spans and avoid scraping its hull on the muddy bottom.[19] That ill-fated voyage signaled the arrival of a gale of creative destruction, which soon rendered obsolete the Chicago River Harbor's infrastructure.

Chicago's experience was not atypical. From the 1870s to the 1910s, port cities on the Atlantic Ocean responded to a process that historian Joseph Konvitz has dubbed the "industrialization of shipping." Merchant marine fleets employed ever-larger vessels with the latest technological improvements in propulsion, hull design, and superstructure engineering to enable them to move larger cargoes at greater speeds and lower unit costs. These developments provoked what Konvitz calls the "crises of Atlantic port cities," as officials responsible for harbor development struggled to accommodate the larger, more technologically sophisticated ships.[20]

From the 1870s to the 1890s, as a combination of economic forces and

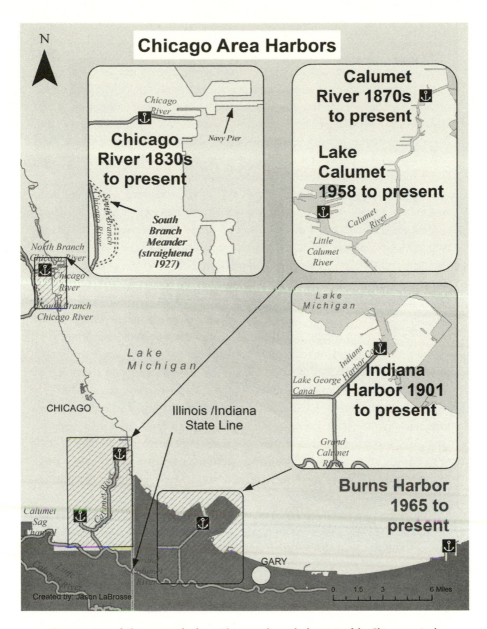

Figure 6. Map of Chicago area harbors. This map shows the location of the Chicago region's main harbors during the nineteenth and twentieth centuries. The Chicago River was the main harbor until 1906 when the Calumet River surpassed it in total annual tonnage. Over the course of the twentieth century the Chicago River's tonnage dwindled. Today, it is mainly used for pleasure boats. The Calumet River and the harbors of Northwest Indiana continue to handle bulk commodities like coal, iron ore, and limestone. Map created by Jason LaBrosse.

federal government policies drove shippers on the Great Lakes to use ever-larger iron and steel steamships, Chicago's port officials were similarly challenged. Prior to 1888, sailboats rather than steamships dominated the Great Lakes trade. Wooden schooners were a critical technology driving the development of the region, but many vessel lines began to commission metal steamships instead of wooden schooners in the 1870s. Initially, the transition from sail to steam was driven by the depression of the 1870s. Shipping rates had fallen, and some vessel lines compensated for the loss of income by using larger metal steamships that could haul greater cargos in fewer days.[21]

After the depression, lake lines continued to replace schooners with steamships to help them contain costs and compete with railroads, which carried goods much faster than ships. The larger ships allowed the lake lines to remain competitive by lowering their rates, since they charged their clients for the amount of freight shipped and paid their crews by the voyage.[22] Moreover, steamers were faster and more reliable than sailboats.[23] Powered by coal, they usually stayed their course no matter how fickle the wind.

The steamships' combination of speed and size was crucial to the sustainability of lake lines, which had to turn a profit before winter ice ground their operations to a halt. Consequently, from the 1870s to the 1900s there was a steady rise in the number of steamships on the Great Lakes and a simultaneous decline in the number of sailboats. This trend is illustrated in Table 2, which charts the number and gross tonnage of steamships and sailboats documented on the Great Lakes at five-year intervals from 1868 to 1906. The table shows that the number of steamships rose consistently from 624 in 1868 to 1,844 in 1906, whereas sailboats declined from 1,855 in 1868 to 519 in 1906.[24] By 1888, the number of steamships (1,342) surpassed the number of sailboats (1,277) on the Great Lakes.[25]

The same economic forces that compelled lake lines to switch from sail to steam also created incentives for lake shippers to use ever-larger steamships. But the demand could be satisfied only as quickly as the Army Corps of Engineers dredged key waterways. In the early 1890s, the corps did just that. Army engineers cut a twenty-foot channel at a critical point between Lake Huron and Lake Eerie. Since the 1850s, the passageway between Huron and Erie—via the St. Clair River, Lake St. Clair, and the Detroit River—had been among the shallowest, and most crucial, on the Great Lakes. The depth of that passageway, in part, governed the size of the vessels that many lake lines employed. So when the Army Corps of Engineers began dredging a twenty-foot channel at a particularly shallow point where Lake St. Clair emptied into

Table 2. Number and Gross Tonnage of Sailing Vessels and Steam Vessels Documented on the Northern Lakes, 1868–1906

Year	Sailing		Steam		Total	
	No.	Tons	No.	Tons	No.	Tons
1868	1,855	293,978	624	144,117	2,479	438,095
1873	1,663	298,002	802	180,250	2,465	478,252
1878	1,546	315,908	918	201,550	2,464	517,458
1883	1,373	310,454	1,149	304,641	2,522	615,095
1888	1,277	314,765	1,342	480,138	2,619	794,903
1893	1,205	317,789	1,731	828,702	2,936	1,146,491
1898	960	333,704	1,764	993,644	2,724	1,327,348
1903	676	315,195	1,796	1,467,992	2,472	1,783,187
1906	519	269,136	1,844	1,841,438	2,363	2,110,574

Source: Chicago Harbor Commission, *Report to the Mayor and Aldermen of the City of Chicago* (Chicago: H. G. Adair, 1909), 272.

the Detroit River, many lake lines placed orders for larger iron and steel steamships.[26]

The combination of Army Corps dredging and these economic incentives inflated the size of the new ships plying the Great Lakes from the 1880s to the 1900s. The figures in Table 3 illustrate this trend. It shows the number and tonnage of new vessels built on the Great Lakes each year from 1888 to 1907. During that period, there was a small decline in the number of ships built on the Great Lakes each year—but a dramatic rise in the average number of tons those new ships were capable of carrying. From 1888 to 1897, the number of new ships built each year averaged 162.2. The average fell to 130.6 new ships per year over the next decade. While the number of ships built each year declined by about 20 percent, the average carrying capacity of new ships more than doubled. Ships built in the years from 1888 to 1897 carried an average of 557.6 tons, while ships built between 1898 and 1907 averaged 1,132.1 tons of carrying capacity.[27]

As the size of ships in the Great Lakes fleet ballooned, so did the size of the ships calling on the Port of Chicago. According to records maintained by the Chicago Department of Public Works, the average ship visiting the

Table 3. Number and Net Tonnage of Vessels Built Each Year on the Great Lakes, 1888–1907

Year	Number of Vessels	Net Tons	Average Tonnage
1888	222	101,103	455
1889	225	107,080	476
1890	191	108,526	568
1891	204	111,856	548
1892	169	45,969	272
1893	175	99,271	567
1894	106	41,985	396
1895	93	36,353	391
1896	117	108,782	929
1897	120	116,937	974
1898	87	54,084	622
1899	122	80,366	658
1900	125	130,611	1,045
1901	175	169,085	966
1902	133	168,873	1,269
1903	123	136,844	1,112
1904	119	159,433	1,339
1905	101	93,123	922
1906	204	265,271	1,300
1907	117	244,291	2,088

Source: Chicago Harbor Commission, Report to the Mayor and Aldermen of the City of Chicago (Chicago: H. G. Adair, 1909), 269.

Chicago River carried 229 tons of freight from 1862 to 1870. In the 1870s, ships carried an average of 302 tons; and in the 1880s, they carried an average of 376 tons. Between 1891 and 1897, just after iron and steel ships came to dominate the lake trade, the figure jumped to 667 tons. At the same time, the ships frequenting the steel mills and grain elevators at the more commodious Calumet River Port carried an average of 1,397 tons.[28]

The cost of shipping goods by lake plummeted as ever-larger ships delivered ever-greater cargos. In 1896, a representative of the grain elevator interests at the Chicago Board of Trade, William H. Harper, testified before Congress about the effects of larger ships on the price of shipping. Harper recalled that, between 1848 and 1860, it had cost an average of 15 cents a bushel to ship grain from Chicago to Buffalo. In the period when steamships overtook sailboats on the Great Lakes, 1885 to 1895, the cost of shipping grain averaged only 8 and 7/10 of a cent per bushel. Harper speculated that rates would continue to fall. He predicted that "the day is not far distant when, with larger boats, grain will be carried from Chicago to New York for 3 cents per bushel." But Harper cautioned that the use of larger boats threatened Chicago's position as a grain port. "If this rate is ever reached," Harper noted, "it will be [because of] . . . larger boats; and for the accommodation of such boats the Chicago River must be deepened."[29]

What Harper proposed—deepening the Chicago River—was not necessarily a simple or wise solution to the problem of bigger boats. Rather, it was the solution favored by the businessmen who had invested millions in riverside property. In 1896, Harper and those businessmen who comprised the Chicago River Improvement Association lobbied Congress to improve the harbor. The members of the River Improvement Association wanted, and even expected, the federal government to insure their investments against the creative destruction of the harbor. Association member A. J. Earling summed up this position. Earling, vice president of the Chicago, Milwaukee, and St. Paul Railway Company, noted that his railroad had "its principal terminals along and on the north branch of the Chicago River, where it serves nearly one hundred industries . . . dependent upon water transportation." If the federal government failed to improve the Chicago River Harbor, Earling concluded, it "would be a great breach of faith . . . of those whose investments have been based on the quasi promise of the Government, to maintain navigable waterways."[30]

What Earling regarded as a breach of faith, Major Marshall of the Army Corps of Engineers considered a strategic response to the industrialization of shipping. Marshall knew that the rapid transformation of the Great Lakes fleet threatened to destabilize the marine commerce that had long supported Chicago's dynamic economy. "It is not a matter of sixty years to develop a port," Marshall cautioned in 1896, "it is now a matter of two or three years to maintain an existing commerce."

The Chicago River could accommodate a ship of only 325 feet in length and 16 feet in draft. But Marshall surmised the city's port needed to handle vessels of over 400 feet in length and 19 feet in draft. "Such vessels," Marshall pointed out, "can only peer into this port from the open lake." Even the Calumet River could not accommodate such a large ship. For Marshall, then, the critical question was not how to save the Chicago River Harbor from destruction, but which port should be improved.[31] For him, the answer seemed clear.

The Rise of the Calumet

Major Marshall reasoned that, in addition to allowing it to accommodate the large new ships of the era, developing the Calumet would help relieve traffic congestion and pollution along the Chicago River, which ran right through the city's central business district.[32] It would also benefit pedestrian and other street traffic. Since the Chicago River encircled the city's busy central business district, large boats calling on the river port forced bridge openings, which ground street traffic to a halt. But when ships called on the more peripheral Calumet River Port, Marshall noted, they did so "without annoyance to the population of the city seeking its business center."[33]

The issue took on special urgency in the 1890s, but efforts to develop the Calumet as a viable, alternative harbor actually stretched back to the years after the Civil War, when tens of thousands of ships began clogging the Chicago River. One of Marshall's predecessors, Army Engineer Major Junius B. Wheeler, proposed transforming the "capacious" Calumet River—located eleven miles to the south of the mouth of the Chicago River—into a harbor.[34] Congress followed Wheeler's recommendation, making a fifty-thousand-dollar appropriation to open the mouth of the Calumet in 1870.[35] Over the next two decades, the Army Corps of Engineers made some additional, piecemeal improvements.

By the late 1880s, the increased size of the Great Lakes fleet, the growth of the steel industry, and the urging of private developers compelled the federal government to make further improvements to the Calumet River Harbor. In 1888, the first year that iron and steel steamers came to outnumber wooden schooners on the lakes, Congress began making routine appropriations to improve it.[36]

In June of the following year, the city of Chicago annexed 125 square miles of territory, which included the Calumet River, which, with sustained federal investment, quickly became the city's most efficient port.[37] In 1888, the Army

Corps of Engineers widened the channel to a uniform two hundred feet and dredged the river to a depth of sixteen feet.[38] As ship sizes increased in the 1890s, the corps further increased the depth to twenty feet.[39] These improvements enabled large, cargo-laden steel and iron steamships ships to navigate the Calumet River with greater ease than they did the Chicago River.

As the Army Corps of Engineers improved the harbor, private land developers transformed it into a vibrant industrial district. The president of the Calumet and Chicago Canal and Dock Company, Colonel James Bowen, took steps to create a framework for economic development on the shores of the river. Bowen advocated for federal appropriations for improvement of the Calumet River, urged railroads to establish connections to the area, as well as subdivided and sold industrial and residential lands.

By 1874, the Calumet and Chicago Canal and Dock Company had established an industrial district that included lumberyards, grain elevators, the Illinois Steam Forge, and the Chicago Iron and Steel Company. The population of the subdivisions laid out by the Calumet and Chicago Canal and Dock Company rose from two thousand in 1880 to sixteen thousand in 1883 to twenty-six thousand in 1890. After 1890, the pace of economic development along the Calumet continued to increase.[40]

Federal Improvement of the Chicago River Harbor

Many of Chicago's elite—particularly those with a vested interest in the fortunes of the Chicago River Harbor—watched this process with dismay and attempted to slow or even reverse it. In 1896, for example, the Chicago River Improvement Association dispatched representatives to Washington, D.C., to urge Congress to reject Marshall's proposal to develop the Calumet River at the expense of the Chicago.[41] The association declared, "We strenuously protest against the policy of improving the Calumet and neglecting the Chicago River for we insist that the Chicago River will be . . . the principal harbor of Chicago, and must eventually be improved to meet the . . . demands of lake navigation."[42] To meet those demands, the association asked Congress for money for improvements. Its demands echoed those of westerners who successfully appealed to the federal government for money to "reclaim" arid lands with massive irrigation projects.[43]

Congress obliged, making a progressive appropriation of seven hundred thousand dollars in 1896 to dredge and widen the channel.[44] This generosity pleased the association, but it failed to stem the decline of industrial freight traffic. Nor did it make up for many years of neglect.

For six decades, though the Chicago River served as the city's key port, the city of Chicago had treated it with contempt. In recognition of this fact, journalist Elliot Flower dubbed the Chicago River the "Cinderella of Navigable Streams." Like Cinderella, Flower explained, the river was a "drudge receiving the most contemptuous treatment from those it served."[45] Chicagoans depended on the river for sewage and shipping, but those uses created nuisances: stinking sewage and black smoke belching from ships that emitted shrill, ear-splitting whistles.[46] Worst of all, boats forced bridges to open, causing delays to harried overland travelers.[47] According to Major Marshall, most Chicagoans considered the river "as a nuisance to be abated."[48] Many city officials agreed. Two mayors, the elder Carter Harrison and Dewitt Cregier, went so far as to propose filling the river in with dirt.[49]

The problem was that improving the Chicago River Harbor was not just a matter of the right technology. It also required political will, which was often impossible to muster, because many residents of Chicago considered river improvements inimical to their economic interests.

The 1897 debate over widening the river to make it more accessible to larger ships is a case in point. Alderman George Duddleston told the city council that his constituents did not want to pay taxes for river improvements that would not directly benefit them.[50] Even when the city council resolved to ask Congress for the money to widen the Chicago River, many businessmen and property owners on the city's north and west sides opposed the improvements, which they feared would necessitate larger bridges that would take longer to open and close.[51] The added delay, they worried, would be a "menace to the property values and business interests of the West Division," which was cut off from the central business district by the river.[52]

Such turf battles, which were common, encouraged the mayors' neglect of marine commerce. As a result, the city of Chicago ceded much of the work of harbor construction and improvement to private property holders.[53] In 1893, Marshall described the river as essentially "a long private slip," without any "public wharves or docks."[54] Riparian property owners shouldered the costs of building docks, wharves, bulkheads, and, often, of dredging the river bottom.[55] As might be expected, those riparian owners usually made improvements suited only to their interests. Consequently, the improvements of riparian owners were uncoordinated and often even harmful to navigation. They dredged the river to different depths and built uneven dock lines that

encroached on the channel. Their efforts caught the attention of urban planner Daniel Burnham, who complained in his 1909 *Plan of Chicago* that "riparian owners have been permitted to encroach on its channel until there are
to be found as many as four lines of docks, each newer one having been built
further into the stream."[56] What Burnham described was the result of official
neglect in the years before 1894.

In the 1890s, the federal government assumed greater responsibility for
improvement of the Chicago River. From the city's inception in the 1830s, the
federal government had made improvements to the mouth of the river and
the lake shoreline, known as the "outer harbor." These infrastructural developments, like the Supreme Court's rulings in *Munn* and *Illinois Central*,
helped create public spaces conducive to commerce. The federal government,
however, did very little to improve the "inner harbor," or the city's busy river
channel, until it changed its policy on river improvement in the 1890s.

In 1889, the state of Illinois created a regional agency, the Sanitary District
of Chicago, to construct a twenty-eight-mile Sanitary and Ship Canal from
the south branch of the Chicago River, near Damen Avenue, to the Des
Plaines River at the town of Lockport. As its name suggests, the canal had
two intended functions, sanitation and shipping. The canal would increase
the flow of water from Lake Michigan through the Chicago River in order to
prevent sewage from back washing into the lake from which Chicagoans
drank. The waterway would also serve as a shipping lane for boats too large
to navigate the older, smaller Illinois and Michigan Canal.[57]

With construction of the Sanitary and Ship Canal under way, in 1892 Congress ordered Marshall to report his views on necessary Chicago River improvements. Marshall issued a report in 1893 that lamented the river was "but a
third class port" and questioned the wisdom of continuing to rely on the Chicago River for either navigation or drainage.[58] Yet, he dutifully drafted a list of
necessary improvements, and, beginning in 1894, Congress paid for the work.
The army dredged the channel to a depth of between sixteen and eighteen feet,
straightened the river's banks, and constructed turning basins at Goose Island,
on the north branch, and at the junction of the south and west forks of the
south branch. The corps also ordered the removal of 106,848 cubic feet of docks
and bulkheads encroaching on the channel at their owners' expense.[59]

These improvements helped clear the channel, but as the size of ships
continued to increase, manufacturing firms continued to migrate to the
urban periphery, and longstanding conflicts over rights of way continued to
exact a toll on river commerce.

Bridges Over Traveled Waters

Chicago's success as a hub for the transshipment of waterborne freight was contingent on city harbor officials' ability to coordinate the flow of traffic through the city. In other words, public sector employees managed the circulation of the goods of private citizens and businesses.

The biggest challenge was reconciling overland and marine travelers' rights of way. Each year, approximately twenty thousand ships hauled cargos into or out of the river port, which wrapped itself around the city's central business district.[60] As they plied the Chicago's waters, those ships forced open some number of the fifty-two bridges that led into and out of the central business district and crisscrossed the north and south branches.[61] With each opening, commuters, teamsters, and trains ground to a halt and waited for the ship's passage with what Dreiser described as "savage impatience."[62] Larger ships often could not pass the bridges moored on piers in the center of the river channel. The city's marine interests urged the city to replace center pier bridges with less obstructive models. Many overland commuters, however, resisted improvements that might bring more ship traffic and costly delays.

The city of Chicago selected several officials to regulate the opening and closing of bridges.[63] The mayor appointed a harbor master, vessel dispatcher, and numerous bridge tenders. An agent of the police department, the harbor master wielded the power to open or close bridges, demand that riparian owners remove obstructions in the channel, and enlist tugs to free entangled boats. The harbor master's subordinates, vessel dispatchers and bridge tenders, managed the flow of ships through the channel.[64] Vessel dispatchers recorded the movement of each ship in and out of the port, and advised bridge tenders on how to manage the traffic in order to reduce delays.[65]

Most often, the decision to open or close a span rested with bridge tenders. For eight months a year, those petty tyrants perched on the center pier, frustrating ship captains and overland commuters alike as they imposed delays on both.[66] When approaching a bridge, a vessel would give three sharp, short sounds of the whistle to signal its desire to pass.[67] When the bridge tender pleased, he sounded a bell and turned his crank to swivel the span around on the pier set in the middle of the river. Journalist Theodore Dreiser described the scene: "The air resounds with the clang of bridge bells announcing to hurrying pedestrians and teamsters that the draw is about to

Figure 7. The Chicago River looking west from the Rush Street Bridge, 1905 ca. The photo shows the Rush Street swing bridge looking west on the main stem of the Chicago River. The swing bridge was moored in the center of the river and swiveled open to permit the passage of ships. The opening and closure of bridges caused delays, frustrating river and overland travelers alike. The bridge cut the river channel in two, making it difficult for the increasingly large steel and iron steamships of the early twentieth century to navigate the river. Many vessel line operators urged the city to replace swing bridges with bascule bridges that were anchored on the riverbank, thereby creating more room in the river channel. This picture was taken circa 1905 by Barnes and Crosby Company. It is housed at and was reproduced by the Chicago History Museum.

open and allow a ship to pass."[68] During the two to ten minutes that the span remained open, crowds, occasionally in excess of two hundred, hovered on the riverbank in anticipation of the moment when the bridge tender raised his red ball or lantern to signal the closing of the span.[69]

Although bridge tenders had a tremendous degree of latitude in deciding when to open or close spans, they were still obliged to follow some rules aimed at preventing long delays. In 1867, when the city had become crowded with nearly three hundred thousand inhabitants, the Chicago City Council enacted a law that prohibited bridge tenders from delaying either river or overland traffic for any longer than ten minutes.[70] Fourteen years later, in 1881, the city council passed additional bridge laws that closed Chicago's spans between 6:00 and 7:00 a.m. and 5:30 and 6:30 p.m. in order to reduce delays as many of the city's half-million residents hurried to and from work.[71] Still, the regulations did not always prevent bridge openings from detaining some laborers who complained that their employers docked them up to half a day's pay for even a few minutes tardiness.[72]

Bridge closures also imposed considerable costs on businesses relying on waterborne commerce. After the passage of the 1881 bridge law, the Escanaba and Lake Michigan Transportation Company sued the city of Chicago. Escanaba, which hauled iron ore from Michigan's Upper Peninsula to the Union Iron and Steel Company works on the south branch of the Chicago River, argued that both the ten-minute ordinance and rush hour bridge closures interfered with navigation and constituted an unlawful taking of property. The circuit court agreed with the Escanaba Company, but in 1883, the city won an appeal in the United States Supreme Court.[73]

Justice Stephen Field issued the majority ruling. Six years after Field's famous dissent in *Munn v. Illinois* (1877), which argued against state authority to regulate rates at the grain elevators on the banks of the Chicago River, the justice ruled in favor of bridge regulations. In *Munn*, Field defined rate regulation as an unlawful taking of private property without the due process afforded by the United States Constitution.[74] Although bridge regulations delayed ships, thereby imposing additional costs on the Escanaba Company, Field did not consider bridge regulations to be a taking of private property. Unlike the grain elevators in *Munn*, government officials were not regulating the use of private property but, rather, the manner in which economic actors moved through public space. In particular, a large number of teamsters hustled about the city, stocking homes and businesses with coal and other goods.[75] As long as river and overland travelers competed for rights of way, Field held, "Some concession must be made on every side for the convenience and the harmonious pursuit of different occupations."[76]

As the Escanaba Company's argument indicated, the ships that ran Chicago's gauntlet of bridges faced numerous delays that ate into their owners' profits, thereby jeopardizing the river's position as a transportation hub.[77] In 1883, Chicago's engineer in charge of the Department of Public Works, Dewitt Cregier, observed that the "growth of Chicago and her immense business interests have reached a point where swing bridges have become a serious check to her further progress."[78] The city did not spend much money to address the problem, and bridge delays continued to take a toll on marine commerce. In 1897, the *Chicago Tribune* reported that there was a "crisis in lake traffic." One boatman told the paper that, due to bridges, vessel owners "cannot afford the time it takes to get in and out of Chicago."[79]

Delays were only one component of the burden that Chicago's bridges imposed on lake lines. Vessel lines often incurred expenses hiring tug boats to guide their large ships past bridge spans spaced closely together. A ship captain with four decades of navigation experience, J. G. Keith, voiced his frustration with the bridge spans in 1909. "The river is not a harbor," Keith observed, "as long as our streets are to be 300 and 400 feet apart, and they come there with an opening which in the largest part of the largest modern bridges is 140 feet [across]." Under these conditions, Keith estimated that sending one of his three-thousand-ton capacity ships to a coal dock on the Chicago River cost him "about twenty four hours' lost time and from $100 to $150 towing charges." When Keith took the same vessel to Manitowoc, Wisconsin, he noted, "I will get my cargo to the dock in less than an hour, unload my cargo, turn around and go out again, and it will not cost me a dollar."[80]

To make the bridge spans easier for large ships to negotiate, the four-thousand-member Chicago Association of Commerce, which had subsumed the Chicago River Improvement Association, petitioned the city council in 1901 to replace the river's center pier bridges with bascule bridges.[81] Based on a medieval design adapted in nineteenth-century London, bascule bridge designers anchored half of the bridge span on each side of the river and raised the two halves of the span skyward when a ship approached. By anchoring the bridge on the shoreline, the bascule's designers eliminated the need for center pier supports in the middle of the river, thereby increasing the space available for ships and water to move through the channel.[82] Not surprisingly, the city of Chicago was slow to act. It stopped building new center pier bridges after 1890, when the secretary of war issued a directive banning their construction.[83] For the next two decades, the city did little to remove the obstructive bridges. In the meantime, the Sanitary District replaced some center pier bridges in order to increase the flow of water through the river channel.[84] The city did not make a concerted effort to get rid of the center pier bridges until 1911, when it issued bonds in the amount of $4,655,000 to build new bascule bridges.[85]

The city's slowness to replace swing bridges added to the difficulties of large ships attempting to navigate the Chicago River. Moreover, bridges were not the only barriers to navigation. The tunnels that ran underneath the river threatened to block the larger draft ships that began plying the waters in the 1890s.

The Chicago River Tunnels

Great Lakes shipping lines urged the city to remove the tunnels, but the city was reluctant to do so because they carried downtown streetcar traffic. The city of Chicago had built the tunnels beneath the river at Washington and LaSalle Streets in 1869 and 1871 to aid pedestrians and teamsters. For a toll, they could travel under the river rather than wait for a bridge. Few people, however, wished to pay for passage through the dank, leaky passageways. By the 1880s, the tunnels had become the subject of neglect. Then they caught the attention of the streetcar magnate Charles Tyson Yerkes.[86]

Yerkes was a banker, womanizer, and convicted white-collar criminal who had come to Chicago in 1881 with an eye to rebuilding the fortune and esteem he had gained and lost in Philadelphia. His nefarious dealings in the bond market had landed him in prison, and his decision to leave his wife and six children for a younger woman had earned him the scorn of his social circle.[87] In Chicago, Yerkes got a fresh start.

Yerkes set his sights on acquiring and improving Chicago's streetcar system. With backing from speculators, Yerkes took over two of the city's three main street railway companies, the North Chicago City Railway Company, and the Chicago West Division Railway. When Yerkes took over, streetcar travel was slow for several reasons, including two related to bridges. Bridge openings frequently brought cars to a standstill while on the way into or out of the central business district. Bridges also forced street railways to use horse-drawn rather than faster cable-drawn cars because there was no way to string cables across spans that were continually opened and closed by their tenders.[88]

Yerkes recognized that the river tunnels could be used to avoid bridge delays. Dreiser describes Yerkes's approach to Chicago's street railways in his novel about the capitalist's life, *The Titan*. Increasing the speed of streetcar travel was, as Dreiser's chapter title indicates, only "A Matter of Tunnels." In that chapter, Yerkes's fictional counterpart Frank Cowperwood notes that "if the street-car traffic were heavy enough, profitable enough . . . one of the problems, which now hampered the growth of the North and West Sides would be obviated."[89] If Yerkes could run his railcars through the tunnels, there would be no need to endure bridge delays. In 1886, Yerkes convinced the city council to pass ordinances granting him a right of way to run his cable cars through the tunnels at Washington and LaSalle Streets. Two years later, the railway magnate secured the council's permission to build another tunnel underneath the south branch of the river at Van Buren Street.[90] When Yerkes gained control of the tunnels, he lowered them from fourteen to seventeen feet below the surface of the Chicago in order to prevent collisions with deep-draft boats. In the late 1880s, seventeen feet sufficed. However, by century's end it proved inadequate. In 1902, the tunnels snared an average of one ship each week during the navigation season.[91]

Although it was a simple engineering feat, lowering the tunnels presented—as with every issue relating to river improvements—several political complications. The fate of the tunnels hinged on a larger political debate about the future of the streetcar system. In 1897, Yerkes tried to secure an extension of the operating franchise that he had acquired from the city council in 1883. Yerkes bribed lawmakers to pass a fifty-year franchise extension bill known as the "Allen Law" through both the Illinois state legislature and Chicago City Council. In 1899, an anticorruption voluntary association called the Municipal Voters League convinced the state legislature to repeal the Allen Law.[92] Subsequently, Yerkes sold his stake in Chicago's traction companies, moved to New York and then to London, where he helped build the Underground, the city's subway system.[93]

Despite Yerkes's departure from Chicago, the traction question remained. Some Chicagoans favored municipalization, or public ownership, of the streetcars. The traction companies favored private ownership and wanted their franchises extended. With unresolved questions over who would control the street railways, neither the streetcar companies nor the city government were willing to spend money to lower the river tunnels. Complicating matters further, the traction companies fell into a court-ordered receivership. Since creditors owned the companies' equipment, it was not even clear if the city or the traction companies had the authority to lower the tunnels.[94] In the meantime, vessel owners and operators had to contend with the obstructed river channel or use other ports like the Calumet River.

Since neither the city nor the traction company would lower the tunnels, several businessmen asked Congress to remove the obstructions. In 1903 and 1904, the Chicago Association of Commerce sent Charles L. Dering to Washington, D.C., to ask that Congress order the city to lower the tunnels. Dering, the Chicago agent for the Delaware, Lackawana and Western Railway Company's coal department, testified that the tunnels harmed his business. Since the tunnels prevented the passage of large ships, Dering noted, his company was hampered by an "inability to get boats" able to transport its annual cargo of two hundred thousand tons of anthracite coal from Buffalo to the railroad's docks on the Chicago River.[95] Dering's testimony was corroborated by the president of the Cleveland-based Lake Carriers Association, William Livingstone. No one, Livingstone reported to Congress, could "afford to build the small type of vessels." Small ships simply could not carry enough cargo to make money. If the tunnels remained, Livingstone predicted, the Chicago River would become "no more or less than a ditch."[96]

The prospect of losing river traffic did not seem to worry city officials. Many city councilmen urged Congress not to order the tunnels lowered because construction would interrupt streetcar traffic. Speaking for the Chicago City Council, Alderman Frank Bennett told Congress that, "The position we take is the transportation of 60 per cent of the population of the city of Chicago is more important than the matter of a little freight."[97] Lowering the tunnels would throw a cog in an already overburdened streetcar system. Moreover, some councilmen, like Milton Foreman, worried that if Congress ordered the tunnels removed, the city would be in an untenable legal position. Either the city would be forced to break its contract to lease the tunnels to the traction companies or refuse to comply with Congress's order.[98] Congress ordered the tunnels removed.[99]

Before the tunnels were lowered, they created an incentive for businessmen to reroute freight traffic from the Chicago to the Calumet River. In his 1904 testimony to Congress, businessman Harvey Carr described the tunnels' influence on grain rates. Carr reported that "shippers paid 2 1/2 cents per bushel on wheat from the south branch to Buffalo, while at the same time shippers at South Chicago [the Calumet], where the largest boats could load to the full depth, were getting all the boats they needed at 1 3/4 cents per bushel." In effect, the tunnels made wheat on the banks of the Chicago River less valuable than the same wheat would have been on the banks of the Calumet.[100]

Sewage and Commerce

Those wheat harvests also traveled along a river that Chicagoans used as a sewer. This use of the river was often at odds, or at least in tension, with its use as a leading world port. One man described a typical experience with the foul river in the summer of 1879. While traveling home from work, he dashed to cross the State Street Bridge, rather than "run the risk of standing so near the deadly stench." He was too slow. The bridge swiveled open, stranding him beside the bridge tenders. As he waited for six boats to pass, the man "hardly dared to draw full breath for fear of inhaling the poisonous miasma."[101]

As the city and businesses like slaughterhouses dumped sewage into the river, the channel clogged. As a result, some large, deep draft ships scraped their hulls across the muck and got stuck. The channel could be cleared if the city and industry stopped polluting the river, but where would the waste go? Alternatively, engineers could increase the current in the Chicago River, flushing the channel more thoroughly. They finally did so in 1900. The faster current helped cleanse a waterway that had long been making people sick. At the same time, it made it dangerous to pilot large ships on the narrow river. As with the tensions between property owners and shippers, it was difficult to reconcile the competing uses of the river channel.

Chicagoans had struggled since the 1850s to harness the region's waters for drinking, sewage, and navigation. Since Chicago sat a mere five feet above the level of Lake Michigan and the Chicago River, it did not drain easily.[102] Pools of filthy, stagnant water often simmered on the streets, making the city fertile ground for terrible diseases. Germs, moreover, traveled to Chicago on new infrastructure. When the Illinois and Michigan Canal opened in 1848 it carried goods, but it also carried cholera.

On April 29, 1849, Captain John Pendleton brought the deadly cargo from New Orleans to Chicago. Within a few hours of Pendleton's arrival on the *John Drew*, the captain died of the scourge. Several of Pendleton's passengers also succumbed, and the disease spread through the city that spring, rapidly killing its victims.[103] The outbreak intensified in the summer heat. Physicians hurried from patient to patient, documenting the cold sweats, cramps, and diarrhea in grim detail for the worried Chicago Common Council.[104] One in ten of the city's residents contracted the disease and 678 died.[105]

Cholera and other waterborne diseases remained part of life in the swampy city. From 1849 to 1854, epidemics of cholera, typhoid fever, and dysentery ravaged Chicago; an outbreak of cholera in 1854 sent more than fifteen-hundred city residents to their graves.[106] Although scientists had not yet identified the *Vibrio Cholerae* bacterium that caused the disease, even casual observers could see that diseases spread due to poor drainage. In 1850, the literary miscellany *Gem of the Prairie* observed that many parts of the city were simply "quagmires, the gutters running with filth at which the very swine turn up their noses." From the "reeking mass of abominations" beneath the planks on the streets, the magazine speculated, "miasmas wafted into the neighboring shops and dwellings, to poison their inmates." The only solution was "a thorough system of drainage."[107]

To address the drainage problems, in 1855 the city hired the renowned Boston engineer Ellis Sylvester Chesbrough. Chesbrough raised Chicago's streets from two to eight feet and built an extensive network of sewers that deposited waste water directly into the river.[108] Although Chesbrough's plan worked, his meddling created new environmental problems. Sewage flooded the river which, in turn, emptied into the source of the city's drinking water, Lake Michigan.[109] Chesbrough therefore reversed the Chicago River in 1871 so that it flowed away from Lake Michigan and into the Illinois and Michigan Canal.

In spite of Chesbrough's efforts, the river sometimes flushed backward into Lake Michigan when inundated with rain or snowmelt. In 1885, for example, a storm washed the city's wastes back into the lake, raising fears of a disease epidemic.[110] After the scare, the city's Drainage and Water Supply Commission determined that it would be necessary to build a waterway larger than the Illinois and Michigan Canal to flush even more water and sewage from the Chicago River. In 1889, the Sanitary District of Chicago was charged with constructing just such a waterway, the Sanitary and Ship Canal, from the south branch of the Chicago to the Des Plaines River.[111] The Sanitary District would ensure that Chicagoans could continue to foul the river and safely drink from Lake Michigan.

By reversing the Chicago River, the city of Chicago had reconciled using the same watershed for both drinking and sewage. Yet, the city's sewage policy pitted polluters against businesses that relied on marine transport. Solid wastes dumped into the Chicago River clogged the channel and blocked the passage of some large ships. In an 1896 congressional hearing, Captain J. S. Dunham of the Chicago River Improvement Association commented that, while "modern vessels draw 20 feet of water . . . the average depth at the mouth of the Chicago is only 16 feet." Dunham urged Congress to provide funds for dredging, noting that without dredging "we [Chicagoans] will lose all our commerce."[112] Dredging, however, was a contentious issue.

Marshall and his boss, Secretary of War Stephen B. Elkins, argued against spending federal dollars for dredging so long as the city used the Chicago River as a sewer.[113] They believed that the city should either stop dumping or regularly dredge the channel itself. "It is necessary," Elkins counseled, "that either . . . the sewers [be] sealed up, or . . . that solid matter . . . placed in the river by the citizens of Chicago shall be removed by them before accumulating to such an extent as to obstruct navigation."[114] Elkins wished to keep the national government out of the position that the city government had put itself in for decades. The city poured sewage into the river to the point where it clogged the channel and then paid for dredging.[115] Congress allocated money for dredging over Elkin's objections, but the filling of the channel had already become costly to shippers.

Freight rates from cities on the eastern seaboard to Chicago reflected the difficulty of bringing large ships into the Chicago River. In 1896, Chicago alderman Martin B. Madden testified to Congress that freight rates from eastern cities to Chicago were up to 25 percent higher than to other cities because vessel lines often had to hire a "large number of tugs" so that deep draft vessels could be "drawn along the bottom of the river."[116] By polluting the river, the city diminished its capacity as a port.

The completion of the Sanitary and Ship Canal in 1900 created a new challenge for Chicago River navigators. The canal—with the aid of large pumps—drew more water out of the Chicago River and, by extension, the river's source, Lake Michigan. This sparked two environmental controversies. First, Great Lakes states sued the city of Chicago, alleging that diversions into the Chicago River were reducing lake levels. The suit resulted in a 1930 Supreme Court ruling that limited Chicago's diversions.[117] Second, vessel operators protested that the greater speed of the current in the river threatened navigation. As a result, the War Department ordered the Sanitary District to limit its diversions. The Sanitary District, therefore, had to divert enough water from Lake Michigan to cleanse the river, but not so much as to create a current that hindered navigation. To do so, it slowed diversions in navigation season and at peak river travel times.[118] Even so, the current remained too swift for some river navigators to steer their large ships through the crowded channel.

Thus, in 1909 ship captain Keith lamented that, "The current has destroyed our river for harbor purposes."[119] Keith exaggerated. The current did not destroy the harbor, but it did contribute to its decline. Given the current, it was common for boat managers to charge more to ship bulk commodities via the Chicago River than via nearby ports like the Calumet.[120]

Chicago's New Industrial Harbor

On January 6, 1908, Republican Mayor Fred Busse addressed the Chicago City Council about the alarming decline in lake commerce on the Chicago River. "It is a notorious fact that the lake commerce of Chicago, once the pride and boast of this city, has been steadily decreasing for a number of years." Busse attributed the decline to the "inadequacy of its harbor facilities."[121] The mayor understood the significance of Chicago's waterborne commerce firsthand. During his teens, Busse inherited a horse and wagon from a friend who committed suicide and used it to start a business hauling coal from Chicago's docks to the local businesses and residences that relied on it for heat. He prospered, entering politics as a state legislator in 1894 and winning election as mayor in 1907. Harbor improvement was a priority of his administration.[122] In 1908, Busse assembled a team of academics and engineers, known as the Chicago Harbor Commission, to determine how to revive Chicago's waterborne commerce.

The Chicago Harbor Commission determined that the river was losing its "industrial" rather than its "commercial" harbor traffic. Commercial traffic consisted of fruits, vegetables, passengers, and individually packaged merchandise. Industrial harbor traffic, on the other hand, consisted of bulk commodities for manufacturing and in-transit freight.[123] The Chicago River's decline as an industrial harbor is illustrated by the figures in Table 4, which show the total tonnage of freight handled on both the Chicago and Calumet Rivers each year from 1886 to 1920. From 1886 to 1898, the Chicago River usually handled between seven and eight million tons per year. After 1898, though, the total tonnage carried on the Chicago River dropped steadily to a low of just over one and a half million tons in 1920. Thus, from its peak in the 1890s to 1920, the Chicago River lost as much as 80 percent of its freight traffic. At the same time, the Calumet River Harbor logged steady gains in tonnage from half a million in 1886 to over ten million in 1920.[124]

By the turn of the twentieth century, it was common for shippers of in-transit freight to avoid using the Chicago River Harbor whenever possible. In 1909 William Johnson, an agent for the Anchor Line of the Erie and Western Transportation Company, observed that crowding and delays on the Chicago led shippers to search for alternative routes when sending goods via rail and lake. According to Johnson, it took "six days longer to get lake and rail traffic through the Chicago gateway than any other port." Given the costliness of delays, "it is not uncommon," Johnson noted, "for shippers to demur when asked to rout traffic, lake and rail, through Chicago when they have an outlet through other ports."[125] It was simply too expensive to send in-transit freight via the congested Chicago River channel.

Another indication of the Chicago River's decline as an industrial harbor was that it never gained any of the region's rapidly growing traffic in iron ore. In 1886 and 1887, the Chicago River handled 466,117 and 356,475 tons of iron ore, slightly more than the Calumet River. After 1887, the Chicago River lost tonnage of iron ore, even as the Calumet gained by the millions (see Tables 5 and 6). The Chicago River—with its crowded banks and narrow, obstructed channel—was just not equipped to serve the region's growing steel industry. Thus, even as the Chicago River carried peak rates of grain, coal, and building materials in the 1890s, it had already lost out on the key industrial commodity of the future, iron ore.[126]

The Chicago River, nonetheless, remained a commercial harbor. From 1886 to 1917, the river handled growing, or consistently large, quantities of unclassified merchandise, a catch-all category for miscellaneous freight. The figures in Table 5 show steady increases in the tonnage of unclassified merchandise until 1902 when the figures topped out at about one million tons per year, where they remained through 1917. Although the nature of these items is unknown, it is most likely that they were not, by and large, bulk commodities—which, if carried in significant numbers, would have been classified.[127]

Though the Chicago River Harbor remained a commercial port longer than it did an industrial harbor, there is still evidence of commercial decline. The figures for classified merchandise offer a case in point. The category of classified merchandise comprised foodstuffs as well as unfinished goods like leather and wool. While the Chicago lost tonnage in bulk commodities around 1900, it posted peak levels of tonnage in classified merchandise of about one million tons from 1901 to 1906. After 1906, the totals of classified merchandise declined sharply. Since there was no attendant increase on the Calumet River, it is likely that the Chicago River lost its traffic in classified merchandise to rail or trucking.[128]

The Calumet River overtook the Chicago River as the city's principal industrial harbor in the early 1900s. The availability of cheap land, connections to the region's railways, and a wide, straight, and deep river channel made the

Table 4. Total Receipts and Shipments at Chicago River and Lakefront Harbor, Calumet River and Lakefront Harbor and for the Port of Chicago, 1886–1920

Year	Receipts and Shipments Chicago River and Harbor (Tons)	Receipts and Shipments Calumet River and Harbor (Tons)	Total Receipts and Shipments Port of Chicago (Tons)
1886	7,292,700	500,735	7,793,435
1887	7,182,062	588,271	7,770,333
1888	7,920,349	491,822	8,412,171
1889	10,994,036	560,952	11,754,988
1890	7,209,514	1,796,401	9,005,915
1891	7,214,765	2,066,751	9,281,516
1892	8,412,992	1,822,907	10,235,899
1893	7,958,963	903,397	8,862,360
1894	7,209,236	1,436,897	8,646,133
1895	7,205,942	2,857,750	10,063,692
1896	6,699,918	2,818,544	9,517,572
1897	7,149,759	3,494,118	10,643,877
1898	7,391,654	4,117,526	11,509,180
1899	6,089,364	3,229,874	12,319,238
1900	5,873,070	3,786,674	9,659,744
1901	6,184,242	3,995,277	10,179,519
1902	5,215,044	4,454,428	9,669,472
1903	6,105,553	4,742,225	10,847,778

Table 4. Total Receipts and Shipments at Chicago River and Lakefront Harbor, Calumet River and Lakefront Harbor and for the Port of Chicago, 1886–1920

Year	Receipts and Shipments Chicago River and Harbor (Tons)	Receipts and Shipments Calumet River and Harbor (Tons)	Total Receipts and Shipments Port of Chicago (Tons)
1904	4,446,071	3,728,261	8,174,332
1905	3,388,986	4,530,394	9,919,380
1906	5,011,786	5,290,326	10,302,112
1907	4,980,123	6,430,347	11,410,470
1908	4,025,170	5,932,153	9,957,323
1909	4,224,655	6,155,104	10,379,759
1910	4,273,304	7,254,317	11,527,621
1911	4,025,576	6,607,996	10,633,572
1912	3,644,745	8,318,838	11,963,583
1913	3,829,442	9,445,878	13,275,320
1914	3,780,509	6,549,576	10,330,085
1915	3,259,170	6,908,660	10,167,830
1916	2,439,381	10,308,735	12,748,116
1917	1,900,687	10,269,304	12,169,991
1918	1,925,633	10,594,123	12,519,756
1919	1,631,620	8,574,542	10,206,162
1920	1,527,265	10,392,490	11,919,755

Source: The data in this table are from the Army Corps of Engineers and the Chicago Harbor Commission, Army Corps of Engineers, *Annual Report of the Chief Engineer* (Chicago District, 1908–1921); Chicago Harbor Commission, *Report to the Mayor and Aldermen of the City of Chicago* (Chicago: H. G. Adair, 1909), 280.

Table 5. Chicago River and Lakefront Harbor Receipts and Shipments of Goods by Tonnage, 1886–1917

Year	Unclassified Merchandise (Tons)[a]	Classified Merchandise (Tons)[b]	Ore and Ore Products (Tons)[c]	Coal (Tons)[d]	Grain (Tons)[e]	Building Materials (Tons)[f]
1886	613,500	356,976	466,117	890,326	1,559,945	3,405,836
1887	759,600	383,547	356,475	941,847	1,303,409	3,437,184
1888	785,200	396,189	166,612	1,247,845	1,726,077	3,571,426
1889	739,600	480,687	162,421	1,230,030	5,561,064	3,312,903
1890	391,772	398,040	162,290	1,323,821	2,115,660	2,973,247
1891	418,522	373,817	164,976	1,246,106	2,226,094	2,785,250
1892	670,707	567,050	217,650	1,368,329	2,544,738	3,044,518
1893	871,590	429,466	149,294	1,351,023	2,405,805	2,751,785
1894	973,557	627,901	165,109	1,214,819	1,742,478	2,485,072
1895	1,091,471	465,254	104,127	1,135,478	1,777,010	2,632,602
1896	547,600	940,848	215,667	1,146,365	2,043,590	1,777,958
1897	536,115	673,639	236,930	1,044,855	2,539,805	2,118,415
1898	619,876	634,920	200,517	1,234,633	2,984,097	1,717,611
1899	621,428	702,301	175,592	1,039,134	1,714,165	1,836,708
1900	462,067	827,677	106,331	856,599	2,104,864	1,515,532
1901	926,668	1,266,304	144,755	877,240	1,278,069	1,691,206
1902	1,014,920	1,346,075	96,188	262,843	911,103	1,583,924
1903	1,000,367	1,160,616	147,852	985,133	1,595,173	1,216,413
1904	777,064	967,850	46,252	762,671	925,645	966,589

Table 5. Chicago River and Lakefront Harbor Receipts and Shipments of Goods by Tonnage, 1886–1917

Year	Unclassified Merchandise (Tons)[a]	Classified Merchandise (Tons)[b]	Ore and Ore Products (Tons)[c]	Coal (Tons)[d]	Grain (Tons)[e]	Building Materials (Tons)[f]
1905	1,112,435	1,155,458	113,721	777,892	1,210,865	1,017,824
1906	1,050,757	991,476	203,254	627,175	1,114,718	1,024,406
1907	1,083,464	789,394	142,076	866,051	1,151,349	947,785
1908	939,556	739,352	21,547	763,509	792,727	768,479
1909	1,077,818	838,504	43,375	662,431	774,846	827,681
1910	1,135,938	577,700	152,144	840,341	844,559	732,622
1911	1,156,438	607,179	69,401	705,044	878,457	609,057
1912	1,086,683	543,309	60,687	688,416	673,722	591,928
1913	1,178,361	500,557	64,080	754,357	822,867	509,220
1914	1,157,635	466,587	34,525	688,186	1,108,993	324,583
1915	1,257,432	378,091	123,989	633,247	589,821	276,590
1916	1,117,505	295,650	10,196	471,774	347,261	196,995
1917	1,006,121	161,669	633	457,225	96,785	178,254

Source: The data in this table are from the Army Corps of Engineers and the Chicago Harbor Commission, Army Corps of Engineers, *Annual Report of the Chief Engineer* (Chicago District, 1908–1921); Chicago Harbor Commission, *Report to the Mayor and Aldermen of the City of Chicago* (Chicago: H. G. Adair, 1909), 276–277.

[a]Unclassified Merchandise = unknown goods; [b]Classified Merchandise = salt, groceries, fish, boots and shoes, sugar, flour, potatoes, cheese, coffee, green fruits, hides and leather, wool and hair, malt, meats and meat products, mill stuffs, oil, oil cake, and glucose; [c]Ore and Ore Products = iron ore, manufactured iron, nails and hardware, steel rails, copper, and sulphur; [d]Coal = hard and soft coal; [e]Grain = wheat, rye, oats, corn, barley, and flaxseed; [f]Building Materials = lumber, shingles, lath, posts, railroad ties, poles, wood in cord, plaster, cement, and asphalt.

Table 6. Calumet River and Lakefront Harbor Receipts and Shipments of Goods by Tonnage, 1886–1917

Year	Unclassified Merchandise (Tons)[a]	Classified Merchandise (Tons)[b]	Ore and Ore Products (Tons)[c]	Coal (Tons)[d]	Grain (Tons)[d]	Building Materials (Tons)[f]
1886	521	35,838	317,452	43,489	17,604	85,831
1887	450	67,944	349,360	41,202	18,757	110,558
1888	1,900	54,665	281,640	88,575	9,075	55,967
1889	1,900	34,294	562,115	99,335	4,456	58,187
1890	20,736	42,390	703,149	98,000	20,326	911,800
1891	41,251	54,216	979,498	113,880	54,815	823,091
1892	50,000	79,906	1,339,933	123,500	82,411	147,157
1893	50,000	56,445	352,962	117,702	213,382	112,906
1894	51,500	87,059	886,568	94,383	203,713	113,674
1895	55,226	199,535	1,920,828	145,837	376,264	160,060
1896	23,665	152,366	1,329,361	213,935	904,485	194,736
1897	19,948	195,414	1,802,632	264,879	1,011,226	200,019
1898	15,563	180,174	2,465,355	334,050	683,369	439,015
1899	8,859	216,651	2,234,951	299,879	330,148	139,386
1900	10,069	212,819	2,334,936	128,645	981,285	115,920
1901	22,335	224,955	2,673,095	185,165	686,008	203,719
1902	47,500	251,992	3,356,209	36,669	569,753	192,305
1903	42,408	100,183	3,138,740	265,482	1,049,451	145,961
1904	63,269	77,536	2,577,089	262,182	637,870	110,315

Table 6. Calumet River and Lakefront Harbor Receipts and Shipments of Goods by Tonnage, 1886–1917

Year	Unclassified Merchandise (Tons)[a]	Classified Merchandise (Tons)[b]	Ore and Ore Products (Tons)[c]	Coal (Tons)[d]	Grain (Tons)[d]	Building Materials (Tons)[f]
1905	104,919	131,978	3,213,626	260,813	643,416	175,642
1906	69,311	171,891	4,085,121	287,386	550,010	126,607
1907	57,005	167,658	4,719,914	642,440	710,184	133,146
1908	33,436	158,642	4,401,639	766,479	502,133	69,824
1909	31,783	287,793	4,705,871	577,855	504,138	47,664
1910	21,304	156,125	5,418,170	741,599	906,163	10,956
1911	86,697	238,409	4,151,261	824,280	1,303,865	3,484
1912	465,702	270,315	5,652,166	1,024,543	898,732	7,380
1913	815,258	69,652	6,253,373	1,254,252	1,049,375	3,969
1914	616,914	73,746	3,458,861	754,391	1,643,724	1,940
1915	533,450	66,842	4,232,951	1,133,193	957,248	44,976
1916	948,853	28,623	7,745,975	1,181,263	399,717	4,304
1917	1,010,586	3,225	8,095,302	978,817	181,574	0

Source: The data in this table are from the Army Corps of Engineers and the Chicago Harbor Commission, Army Corps of Engineers, *Annual Report of the Chief Engineer* (Chicago District, 1908–1921); Chicago Harbor Commission, *Report to the Mayor and Aldermen of the City of Chicago* (Chicago: H. G. Adair, 1909), 278–279.

[a]Unclassified Merchandise = unknown goods; [b]Classified Merchandise = salt, groceries, fish, boots and shoes, sugar, flour, potatoes, cheese, coffee, green fruits, hides and leather, wool and hair, malt, meats and meat products, mill stuffs, oil, oil cake, and glucose; [c]Ore and Ore Products = iron ore, manufactured iron, nails and hardware, steel rails, copper, and sulphur; [d]Coal = hard and soft coal; [e]Grain = wheat, rye, oats, corn, barley, and flaxseed; [f]Building Materials = lumber, shingles, lath, posts, railroad ties, poles, wood in cord, plaster, cement, and asphalt.

Calumet an attractive place to industrialists, who were forging a vast manufacturing district on its banks.

In addition to having superior harbor facilities, land was far cheaper on
the Calumet than along the Chicago River. Between 1905 and 1908, manufacturing sites just south of the central business district near the Chicago River
sold for no less than twenty dollars per square foot, and riverfront land on
the west side of the city ranged from about five to ten dollars per square foot.
But, at the mouth of the Calumet River, land sold for only forty-five cents per
square foot.[129]

In the 1890s and early 1900s, businessmen built numerous manufacturing
facilities and grain elevators along the Calumet. In 1892, a writer for the
American Elevator and Grain Trade magazine took note of grain trader
Charles Counselman's move to the banks of the Calumet. Counselman purchased six hundred feet of riverfront land at Harbor Avenue near Ninety-
second Street and built a 1.25-million-bushel capacity grain elevator and a rail
connection to the Rock Island and Indiana Belt Railroads. The trade magazine regarded Counselman's move as a logical reaction to conditions on the
Chicago River: "The Chicago River and all the avenues of approach to the
grain elevators of this city are so badly crowded, and the houses are on such
valuable land, that it is uneconomical to operate them where they are."[130] Several other grain traders soon followed Counselman, setting up elevators on
the banks of the Calumet.[131] By 1907, sixty grain elevators had been established on the Calumet's banks.[132]

Tonnage statistics demonstrate the Calumet River's increasing significance as a harbor for industrial goods and bulk commodities in the 1890s and
1900s. The figures in Table 6 show the growth of the Calumet's grain trade
from lows of below one hundred thousand tons per year prior to 1893 to between five hundred thousand and over a million tons in all but one of the
years from 1896 to 1915.[133] Coal shipments and receipts showed similar increases from below fifty thousand tons a year in 1886 and 1887 to in excess of
a million tons per year by the 1910s. By the turn of the century, the Calumet
attracted cargoes of bulk commodities, but none more than iron ore.[134]

Steel was king on the Calumet River, which was a crucial resource in the
growing industrial district that stretched from Southeastern Chicago to Gary,
Indiana, U.S. Steel's company town founded in 1906. Thousands of acres of
flat land, rail connections, and a good port adjacent to a water route to the
iron-ore rich Mesabi Range near Duluth, Minnesota, lured steel and iron
manufacturers to Southeast Chicago and Northwest Indiana. In 1880,

officials of the North Chicago Rolling Mill shut down their plant on the north branch of the Chicago and opened a new plant at the mouth of the Calumet River. That plant helped spur the development of the steel industry along the Calumet, which would soon become America's second largest steel-producing center after Pittsburgh.[135] By 1906, there were forty large firms along the Calumet River that manufactured, stored, or sold steel and iron, including the massive Illinois Steel and Iroquois Iron Companies.[136] These firms relied on the Calumet River as a port for large ships laden with iron ore. The figures in Table 6 show enormous yearly increases in iron ore tonnage from lows of several hundred thousand per year in the 1880s to in excess of eight million tons in 1917.

The Calumet River essentially became a steel harbor situated in an industrial region that stretched from Southeast Chicago to Northwest Indiana. The rise of the Calumet River and the decline of the Chicago as an industrial harbor were consequences of creative destruction. The age of metal steamships and steel production required a different built environment than the age of wooden ships and lumber processing. In 1909, the president of the Merchant Marine League C. E. Kremer commented on the relationship between economic dynamism and the built environment: "While . . . the Chicago River, taken by itself, has suffered a great loss in recent years by changing conditions of commerce, it is again the changing conditions of commerce which are bringing back to this metropolitan district a lake commerce greater than it ever had before . . . In the place of lumber there will be iron ore."[137]

Government officials responded to the gales of creative destruction that ruined the Chicago River's lumber trade and led to the rise of iron ore and steel that remade the Midwest. As had been true from Chicago's earliest days, government intervention in the city's economy facilitated rather than inhibited commerce. In the case of the Chicago River Improvement Association's struggle against the rise of the Calumet River as Chicago's primary harbor, in fact, only the federal government—which was responsible for maintaining the navigability of the Chicago River—was solicitous of the concerns of businessmen interested in marine commerce. Congress allocated money for improvements, even as federal officials like Marshall promoted the Calumet as an alternative industrial harbor. Although the goals of these interventions were at odds, both efforts smoothed the way for commerce. And, ultimately, government intervention proved crucial to the reinvention and repurposing of the Chicago River and even the entire lakeshore.

With industry migrating from the city's central business district to the

Calumet and Northwest Indiana, and a rising tide of class conflict, many of Chicago's business leaders and politicians were eager to reinvent the downtown waterfront. No longer would it serve as an industrial corridor. Rather, it would become a thing of beauty to be admired by the city's restive working class and the increasing number of shoppers, tourists, and white-collar workers who filled the Loop each day.

This way of thinking about the waterfront—as a site for nature, beauty, and civic celebration—had its roots in reform movements of the mid-nineteenth century, when park advocates like Olmsted and sanitarians such as Dr. John Rauch argued for bringing "natural" spaces into polluted industrial cities to promote public health, morality, and, especially, to quell the city's increasingly virulent class conflicts. Their efforts culminated in the Progressive Era's City Beautiful Movement, led by Chicago's famous architect and planner Burnham, who in 1909 would author the City Beautiful Movement's iconic text, the *Plan of Chicago*.

It marked the symbolic end of one distinctive era in Chicago's industrial history—an era in which the Chicago River was the city's critical economic artery, facilitating its rapid transformation from a desolate swamp into an international engine of economic growth. Burnham's plan offered a bold blueprint for moving forward and transforming the chaotic industrial city into a beautiful, orderly Paris on the prairie.[138] No landscape would be as crucial to the plan, and to its civilizing mission, as the one with the greatest potential for beauty and connection to nature: the waterfront.

CHAPTER 4

Beauty and the Crisis of Commercial Civilization

Chicago's waterfront took center stage in a crucial discussion about the relationship between the economy and America's experiment with democracy. The pivotal moment happened in July 1893, when Chicago hosted the World's Columbian Exposition to commemorate the four-hundredth anniversary of Christopher Columbus's discovery of the New World, and a young historian from Portage, Wisconsin, explained how the United States had so successfully cultivated, even perfected, its own democratic brand of Western Civilization.

Speaking at the newly built Art Institute of Chicago, Frederick Jackson Turner declared that Americans had forged their egalitarian, individualistic, and democratic national character on the rugged frontier that lay just beyond the advancing line of civilization. The harsh conditions of life on the frontier had forced American settlers to shed their European cultural baggage and create a distinctive American society based on their experiences transforming the frontier into civilization.[1]

Turner's thesis reflected how many people understood Chicago's growth. A promoter of the Columbian Exposition, Thomas B. Bryan told Congress in 1889 that "The marvelous growth of Chicago from a frontier camp to the active city of more than a million souls . . . can best typify the giant young nation whose discovery the projected fair is to commemorate."[2] But even as Chicago's growth inspired pride, it raised pressing questions about the nation's present and future. Turner instructed his audience that settlement had claimed the last of America's frontier as of the 1890 census.[3] "Now," he proclaimed, "the frontier has gone, and with its going has closed the first period of American history."[4] An uneasy question followed. If American democracy was born on the frontier, could it survive in the city?

That uncertainty likely resonated with Chicagoans who had witnessed some of the most violent, deadly clashes between workers and capitalists in U.S. history.[5] The flash of a bomb hurled by an unknown culprit into the ranks of policemen in the city's Haymarket Square on May 4, 1886, had, for instance, seemed to threaten the very destruction of the republic. The anarchists who had rallied that evening to support striking workers at the McCormick Harvesting Machine Company had abandoned civil discourse for chants of "dynamite." With their incendiary rhetoric and often foreign names, anarchists became a target of state prosecutors, fearful capitalists, and the mainstream press alike. A jury quickly convicted eight anarchists of the bombing despite a lack of evidence, and the state sent four men to the gallows before Illinois's governor issued a controversial pardon in 1893. The "Haymarket Affair" showed just how quickly class conflict could lead to the breakdown of civil government and social order.[6]

As Chicagoans considered the breakdown of civil order, they also struggled with the unseemly aspects of urban life on a daily basis: the stench of dead animals, urine, and feces, the smoky air, and the earsplitting din of steam whistles, trains, streetcars, people, and wagons. The city's violent class conflict and dismal sanitary conditions stood in stark contrast to the egalitarianism, democratic self-governance, and pristine wilderness found on Turner's frontier.[7]

The threats of disorder and pollution compelled the city's large-scale proprietary and corporate capitalists to take action. Burnham, the Chicago architect and urban planner, led the effort. Burnham was a powerful character whose work straddled the private and public spheres. He urged civic-minded businessmen to take charge of beautifying the city. Burnham, for instance, addressed the Chicago Commercial Club in 1897, using his speech as an occasion to reimagine the downtown lakeshore. He envisioned the waterfront not as a grimy industrial port, but as a place for parks, recreation, and beauty. The planner boldly told the room full of corporate leaders, "Beauty pays better than any other commodity."[8]

Beauty's dividends would come in two forms. Most directly, public parks and civic monuments would spur a market for tourism and make the city more livable. At the same time, Burnham argued, those public spaces filled with natural beauty would have a healthful, moralizing influence on the city's workers, thereby forestalling the social unrest that threatened to tear the city apart.

Members of the Commercial Club worked with planners like Burnham to change not just the physical characteristics of the city but also its economic and social future. Their efforts would make Chicago into a more beautiful whole, and counterbalance what they saw as the morally harmful effects of economic progress and commercial civilization. Exposure to nature would promote physical and moral health, while neoclassical civic monuments would provide common cultural reference points for native-born Americans and European immigrants. In essence, the urban landscape would become a key social safety valve, defusing the very tensions that, Turner claimed, the frontier had once erased from American life.[9]

The Metropolis's Nature

Burnham's ideas about the benefits of beauty found their fullest expressions in the neoclassical architecture of Chicago's 1893 Columbian Exposition and the grand parks laid out in the 1909 *Plan of Chicago*. These moments in urban design, in turn, marked the culmination of an older park movement. Beginning in the 1850s, middle-class Protestant reformers like Olmsted urged political leaders to adorn the nation's growing industrial cities with parks, which would bring nature into the metropolis with welcome social and economic effects. Through parks, city-dwellers would find connection to the healthy, bucolic nature that seemed to be receding from American life as the nation shifted from agriculture to industry.

Leaders of the parks movement like Olmsted operated under the assumption that manmade cities were fundamentally distinct from the natural countryside. This view was, moreover, consistent with a belief in a stage theory of economic development, which held that rural, agricultural societies were a forerunner of commercial cities. Economic development in Chicago, however, did not follow such linear stages. As historian Cronon has shown in *Nature's Metropolis*, the development of rural agricultural landscapes went hand-in-hand with the rise of commercial hubs like Chicago.[10] Urban and rural spaces were a joint development, even if Olmsted and many of his contemporaries saw the two as quite distinct.

As a young man, Olmsted had himself had bounced back and forth between the city and the countryside. The son of a successful dry goods merchant in Hartford, Connecticut, he enjoyed significant educational and economic opportunities. In his youth, he studied with a topographical engineer and sat in on lectures with his brother at Yale. He also worked at a

French importing house, a job that afforded him the opportunity to travel to China in 1843 and 1844. After his return, Olmsted decided to become a farmer, and he prevailed upon his father to buy him a farm in Connecticut. The farm failed, but Olmsted's father bought him another one on Staten Island where the future landscape architect busied himself studying horticulture. Olmsted showed little enthusiasm for the daily toils of farming, though, and in 1850, he traveled to England where he studied agricultural techniques while missing the planting, growing, and harvest seasons on his own farm. On his return, he published a chronicle of his trip titled *Walks and Talks of an American Farmer in England*. In 1857, Olmsted took a position as the superintendent of New York's Central Park. The following year, he and the architect Calvert Vaux collaborated on "Greensward," a successful design for New York's Central Park. Having earned great fame for his design for Central Park, Olmsted spent the rest of his career working as a landscape architect, creating pastoral landscapes in great American cities like New York and Chicago.[11]

Olmsted regarded population density as a grave health risk and believed that parks and tree-lined boulevards helped negate the negative physiological and psychological effects of city living. He recognized that communicable diseases spread rapidly among people living close together, as they had in old European commercial cities. Thus, he regarded more diffuse contemporary cities as much healthier environments. Olmsted attributed nineteenth-century improvements in health to the "abandonment of the old-fashioned compact way of building towns, and the gradual adoption of a custom of laying them out with much larger spaces open to the sun-light and fresh air."[12] Even so, Olmsted saw drawbacks to living in contemporary cities, because the more spread out cities became, the further people had to travel to reach the countryside for fresh air, recreation, and respite from the "intense intellectual activity which prevails . . . in the . . . work shop, and the counting-room."[13] To bring city-dwellers closer to the countryside, Olmsted advocated building parks and boulevards modeled on rural, pastoral landscapes.[14]

Olmsted's design for Central Park in particular inspired Chicagoans to build parks in their city. Chicago landscape architect H. W. S. Cleveland noted that Olmsted's Central Park made all other cities "conscious of their deficiencies," moving them to "adorn themselves in like manner."[15] One of the leading advocates of park construction in Chicago, William Bross also attributed his interest in the topic to Olmsted. Born in New Jersey in 1813, Bross worked in his father's lumber business as a teen before going away to Williams College. He taught school for a decade after college before heading west to Chicago where he cofounded the *Democratic Press* newspaper. Bross joined the Republican Party in 1854 and became a staunch supporter of Lincoln, whose support helped him become lieutenant governor of Illinois in 1865. That same year, Bross visited California, where he encountered Frederick Law Olmsted. Bross recalled that he "met Fred Olmsted on top of the Sierra Nevada" and that "we discussed nothing so much . . . as the Central Park of New York . . . and Olmsted agreed with me that nothing was needed to make Chicago the principal city of the Union but a great public improvement of a similarly gigantic character." In the spring of 1866, Olmsted sent Bross a copy of his San Francisco park report. Bross replied that he hoped to convince Chicagoans to adorn their city with parks.[16]

Bross and other leading citizens of Chicago regarded parks as essential components of a refined, prosperous city. Thus, even as parks recalled agrarian life, bringing "nature" into the city, they were also distinctly urban landscapes, accoutrements of urban, commercial civilization. Park builders, notes historian Daniel Bluestone, sought to "meet a national and international standard of cosmopolitanism . . . and to realize the progressive possibilities of urban culture."[17] Beauty and refinement justified the crass accumulation of material wealth through commerce. "If Chicago is to be anything better than a hive or a rookery, where men buy and sell and get and gain," Bross maintained, "we must have parks."[18] His argument that the city must be something more than just a moneymaking industrial landscape anticipated Daniel Burnham's 1909 *Plan of Chicago*.[19]

Before Burnham, the Chicago lawyer Ezra B. McCagg took a leading role in securing parks for the city.[20] McCagg had been instrumental in acquiring land and handling the litigation necessary for creating Chicago's Lincoln Park, which was established on the city's north shore in 1865.[21] In 1867, McCagg, Bross, and other park advocates allied with real estate developers to press the state legislature to pass a bill that would create a South Park District on Chicago's South Side and nearby suburbs. One of those suburbs included Hyde Park, the three-hundred-acre railroad suburb founded in 1856 by lawyer and real estate developer Paul Cornell.

Cornell advocated for a park bill in hopes of creating demand for land in Hyde Park. The state legislature passed a bill providing for the establishment of a park system in Chicago's far South Side and suburbs, but the bill was subject to voter approval. Suburban voters generally supported the measure, but Chicagoans voted against it by a heavy margin, often citing concerns that the new parks would be too far from the city's population center.[22] The measure failed. The state legislature would revisit the issue of establishing a system of parks at its 1869 session.

In the meantime, scientists like Rauch made powerful arguments about how parks would foster public health. Rauch, a University of Pennsylvania trained physician, played a leading role in the American sanitarian movement by highlighting the connections between environmental conditions and human health. Rauch had nurtured his fascination with environmental conditions early in his career in Iowa, where he had studied the region's medical botany and collaborated with the famous biology professor Louis Agassiz on a study of the Upper Mississippi River. In 1857, Rauch had moved to Chicago to take a post as professor of medical botany at Rush Medical College. During the 1850s and 1860s, the doctor urged city leaders to dig up and relocate the bodies interred in the Northside Lakefront Cemetery. Decaying bodies stuck in sandy, low-lying graves along the shoreline, Rauch argued, were contaminating the water supply, leading to outbreaks of cholera. In 1864, the city moved the graves, joining the old cemetery grounds with a lakeside park that had been established in 1860. After the assassination of the president in 1865, the city dedicated the area Lincoln Park. Rauch continued in the role of one of Chicago's leading park and sanitation advocates until his death in 1894.

Rauch's scientific rationale for park construction was rooted in the prevailing stage theory of economic development. Parks were a mark of advancement to commercial civilization. In a paper presented to the Chicago Academy of Science in 1868, Rauch argued that parks "may be regarded as an unerring index of the advance of people in civilization and refinement."[23] Citing the examples of Egyptian and Jewish civilizations, the doctor held that, "From the earliest period of history, a love of nature and landscape gardening has been fostered and encouraged in the same ratio as civilization has advanced."[24] Chicago had now reached that stage in its development when the city should no longer be just a "place for business, but also one in which we can live."[25]

Making the city livable would require some work. Rauch considered nature and the nonhuman world harmonious, while cities, with their large concentrations of people, were "unnatural and artificial."[26] In order to mitigate the "ill effects" of living in cities, including the spread of disease and moral depravity, Rauch believed that it was essential to "resort to artificial means [such as building parks and sanitation systems] to equalize the disturbing agencies." Referring to "artificial means," Rauch demonstrated that he grasped the irony of his position that parks constituted an "artificial" form of nature. The doctor concluded, like Olmsted, that bringing nature, even in the form of "artificial" man-made parks, into the presumably more artificial city would help cut rates of disease and ameliorate the negative psychological and moral effects of urban life. He suggested that in a park, "Man is brought in contact with nature,—is taken away from the artificial conditions in which he lives in cities; and such associations exercise a vast influence for good."[27] By "good," Rauch meant moral. Like some of the progressive reformers who would shape turn-of-the-century Chicago, including Burnham, Rauch considered beautiful, natural surroundings morally uplifting, a contention he supported by citing low incidents of crime in New York's Central Park.[28]

A coalition including Rauch, civic boosters Bross and McCagg, and the real estate speculator Cornell urged the 1869 Illinois General Assembly to pass a park bill.[29] For these men, parks served a broader public interest by making the city prettier and healthier. Parks also enhanced real estate values, a point not lost on the developer Cornell. Nor was it lost on the landless citizens of Chicago. The city's landless protested that the bills would introduce new taxes to build parks that would primarily benefit Chicago's real estate interests and property holders.[30] Their protest echoed the idea that taxation was fairest when the city only billed those who benefitted from a public service. Of course, men like Rauch, Bross, and McCagg held that parks did benefit the whole public, especially the landless poor who opposed the bill.

Urged on by these powerful men, the Illinois legislature passed a bill that created three independent park commissions. The Lincoln Park Commission oversaw Chicago's Lincoln Park on the north shore. The West Park Commissioners managed the parks on the city's West Side and the South Park Commissioners controlled the parks, including a large area of the lakefront, south of the mouth of the Chicago River. Each commission had the power to buy and condemn land, collect taxes for park purposes, and borrow money. As the park bill's opponents predicted, parks helped buoy real estate values. They also provided recreation grounds and sanctuary from noise and pollution.[31]

To construct those sanctuaries, the park commissions hired some of the city and nation's leading landscape architects, including Olmsted and Vaux. In 1868, the two men had worked on designs for the garden suburb of Riverside, nine miles from Chicago. During that time, Olmsted stayed with lawyer and park advocate McCagg, who tried his utmost to convince the landscape architect to design plans for Lincoln Park. Due to some ongoing litigation over part of the parkland, however, Olmsted declined. When the 1869 parks bill passed the Illinois state legislature, Rauch tried to secure the services of Olmsted and Vaux to design the city's entire park system, but the various park commissions rejected that proposal.

Each park commission hired its own landscape architect. The Lincoln Park Commission hired Chicago landscape architect Swain Nelson. The West Park Commission employed William LeBaron Jenney, a Civil War engineer who had assisted Olmsted in designs for Riverside. Jenney would later play a seminal role in the development of the steel-framed skyscraper and would train many notable architects, including Burnham. The South Park Commission retained the services of Olmsted in 1871 to craft plans for some of the very tracts of lakefront land on which he and Burnham would create the grounds for the 1893 Chicago World's Fair.

In order to turn the South Side parks into sanctuaries from urban life, Olmsted believed that they must command views of the most, if not the only, aesthetically pleasing natural feature in Chicago, Lake Michigan. The Chicago region's flat, monotonous prairie landscape often dulled the senses of those accustomed to hills and mountains. Olmsted, who grew up in hilly New England, was no exception. He stewed over how to beautify the three tracts of brush-covered land that comprised the South Park system. One tract, which would later be named Jackson Park, sat on the shore of Lake Michigan between Fifty-Sixth and Sixty-Seventh Streets, about six miles south of the central business district. Another, later to be dubbed Washington Park, was located about a mile and a half west of the lakeshore and was bounded by Cottage Grove Avenue on the east and Kankakee Avenue on the west between Fifty-First and Sixtieth Streets. A six-hundred-foot-wide strip of land called the Midway Plaissance connected the two.[32]

After examining these flat stretches of land, Olmsted determined that there is but "one object of scenery near Chicago of special grandeur or sublimity . . . the lake."[33] Given that the lake provided the only grand, beautiful natural feature, Olmsted concluded that it "should be as closely as possible associated with . . . the Park and be made to appear, as much as possible, part and parcel of the Park."[34]

Olmsted devised elaborate plans to construct small lakes, several lagoons, and a boardwalk that highlighted the park's proximity to, and connection with, Lake Michigan. The South Park Commission, however, was reluctant to spend the money to implement Olmsted's elaborate designs.[35] Instead, it hired landscape architect Cleveland to complete Washington Park.[36] Olmsted would make his mark on Jackson Park and the Chicago lakeshore two decades later, when he and Burnham collaborated on a design for the 1893 World's Fair grounds.

In the grounds of the World's Columbian Exposition, Chicago's capitalists would sketch their vision of the future, a future that did not look at all like the real Chicago—that is, a dark and dirty, hog-butchering, steel-forging industrial site where people of want and plenty lived side-by-side. Rather, it would be a "White City," as the fairgrounds came to be known, where all people—regardless of ethnicity or class—would enjoy beauty, cultural refinement, and material progress.[37]

The White City on the Waterfront

Olmsted thrust himself directly into a debate over the site of the fair, raising central questions about whether the lakeshore had greater commercial or aesthetic value. In the summer of 1890, he traveled to Chicago, where he surveyed seven proposed fair sites. As he surveyed the flat Midwestern metropolis, he came to the same conclusion about Chicago that he had reached during a visit two decades earlier: It lacked the natural beauty of eastern cities like Boston, New York, and Philadelphia.[38] Writing in 1890, Olmsted noted that "there is at Chicago but one natural . . . object of much grandeur, beauty, or interest. This is the lake."[39] The landscape architect believed that the 1893 World's Fair should be held on the lakeshore.

Lake Michigan's commercial significance was just as essential to his calculations as its beauty. He predicted that "Chicago itself is . . . to be . . . perhaps the most interesting, of all the exhibits of the Exposition." Thus, Olmsted believed that fairgoers would not only want to see the serene expanse of blue water, but the fleet of steamships that were the lifeblood of the city's great economy. "What," Olmsted asked, "would have been its history, what its commerce, what its interest to the world if Chicago were without this lake?"[40] The landscape architect was right. To understand Chicago, fairgoers would have to appreciate the lake as the great, beautiful thoroughfare that made Chicago's economic growth possible.

Olmsted identified a central tension that would divide lakefront planners for the coming decades, a variation on the tension over the city's water resources that had bedeviled Chicago's leaders from almost the very beginning:

The lakeshore held value both as a port and as one of the city's few beautiful, natural landscapes for civic events like the fair.

This tension influenced the course of debate over selection of the site for the fair. The Columbian Exposition's board of directors rejected Olmsted's recommendation to hold the fair on the north lakeshore because that site lacked railroad service.[41] Although they had rejected Olmsted's first choice, the exposition's directors did respect the landscape architect's aesthetic arguments for a lakefront site. Many of the fair's directors believed that the Columbian Exposition should be held in Lake Park, a strip of land in downtown Chicago situated between Michigan Avenue and the Illinois Central tracks. Its dimensions had been enlarged considerably in 1871 when Chicagoans heaped debris from the fire into the water beside the Illinois Central tracks, making dry land. Situated as it was, Lake Park was very easy to reach. As a result of its proximity to the central business district, Chicago's downtown merchants believed that if the fair were held in Lake Park, they would grow rich from the throngs of people passing their storefronts going to and from the festivities. Moreover, many of the fair's directors believed that in the aftermath of the fair, the City of Chicago could use the fairgrounds as a permanent, downtown park and civic center.[42]

Still, there were numerous drawbacks to using Lake Park as the site of the World's Fair. Most notably, Lake Park was too small. In order to accommodate the massive exposition, engineers would have to fill Lake Michigan with dirt and debris to make an additional 150 acres of land. This was technically possible, but the fair's engineers and directors worried that the project would take far too long to complete.[43]

The challenge of filling Lake Michigan was not even the biggest drawback to using Lake Park. The legal status of the lakeshore was still undetermined. It was not yet clear whether the submerged lands beside the lakeshore belonged to the city of Chicago, the state of Illinois, or the Illinois Central Railroad. Since nobody could definitely say who owned the submerged lands, it was also unclear whether those lands would be used as a park and civic grounds or as a railroad depot and harbor.

Exposition authorities nonetheless attempted to broker a solution to the lakefront controversy that had been dragging through the legislature and the courts since 1869. They advanced several proposals to solve, even if just temporarily, the lakefront controversy. One proposal would have had the Illinois Central relinquish its riparian rights and sink and cover its tracks in return for the right to build a great passenger station on the newly made land opposite Washington and Madison Streets.[44] Approaching a hearing before the United States Supreme Court, the Illinois Central Railroad refused to make any concessions that might be construed as a tacit admission that the city of Chicago or the state of Illinois had any legal claim to the tremendously valuable submerged lands.[45] It was left to Justice Stephen Field and his colleagues on the Supreme Court, not the directors of the World's Fair, to decide the fate of the submerged lands.[46]

Even though the fair's board of directors could not arrange to fill additional lands, the board clung to the idea of using Lake Park. In September of 1891, it voted to proceed with plans to use two fair sites, one in Lake Park and the other in Jackson Park, on the city's southern shore.[47] In the winter of 1891, the fair's directors abandoned the dual site idea when it became clear that it would be tremendously expensive to make the necessary improvements to Lake Park.[48] The Columbian Exposition would be held in Jackson Park, on the lakeshore south of the city's central business district.

In the years and months leading up to the summer of 1893, Olmsted collaborated with Burnham to transform Jackson Park into the White City, which embodied the themes of the World's Fair. Exposition authorities had named Burnham as director of the fair's works just after Congress chose Chicago to host the World's Columbian Exposition in 1890. Burnham's personal ambition and background made him an ideal candidate for the job. In 1890, he ranked among Chicago's foremost architects. Born in 1846 in Henderson, New York, he had come to Chicago with his parents in the 1850s and grown up with the city. His parents had schooled him in Swedenborgian Christianity, one of the religious movements that swept across New York's "burned over" district during the 1830s and 1840s. Burnham's parents instilled in him a belief that "all religion has relation to life, and the life of religion is to do good."[49] Burnham's civic actions bore this view out. He would later spend two years working on the 1909 *Plan of Chicago* without accepting any compensation for his services.

Burnham had demonstrated an interest in public life long before he had achieved success as an architect and urban planner. After failed attempts to gain admission to Yale and Harvard, a young Burnham had gone west to a Nevada mining camp where he made an ill-fated attempt to launch a career in politics. Having failed at scholarship and politics, he returned to Chicago, where he took a post in the office of architect Peter Wright in the 1870s and began to learn the architect's craft. It was in Wright's studio that Burnham met John Root, an academically inclined southern gentleman. The charis-

matic Burnham and the studious Root subsequently built their own architectural practice and, over an eighteen-year period, designed over forty million
dollars of residences, office buildings, railroad stations, churches, and
schools.[50]

From 1890 to the summer of 1893, Burnham and Root (until he died of
pneumonia in 1891) devoted themselves to designing the World's Fair
grounds, a monumental task. In less than three years, they designed buildings to house a massive fair that would host over twenty million visitors who
would come to gawk at the technological wonders of the age, hear the latest
ideas of great intellectuals, and examine artifacts and people from civilizations across the world.[51] To complete the project, Burnham and Root brought
together some of the nation's foremost architects, including Charles McKim,
Henry Ives Cobb, William LeBaron Jenney, Dankmar Adler, and Louis
Sullivan.

The team designed two hundred white buildings, which dotted the six-
hundred-acre fair grounds encompassing Jackson Park and the Midway
Plaissance. The mostly temporary neoclassical-style structures were arranged
symmetrically and lit with electric light; their presence boldly proclaimed
that Chicago now carried the torch of Western Civilization. Where Columbus and the pioneers who followed him had found a wilderness, there now
stood a beautiful White City containing all the material wonders of the age.[52]

If the White City symbolized the triumph of Western Civilization in
North America, the circumstances surrounding the destruction of the fairgrounds symbolized the forces that threatened civil society, at least according
to elite Chicagoans. Railroad car magnate George Pullman, for instance,
worried deeply about the prospect of cataclysmic class war.

Pullman had tried to manage class conflict through social engineering,
building a model company town, named Pullman, south of Chicago in the
1880s. Unlike workers in Chicago's crowded tenements, those in Pullman
lived, played, and worshipped in their boss's cleaner, more spacious community. The industrialist reasoned that by providing a hospitable working and
living environment, he could avoid the violent clashes between capital and
labor that had marked late nineteenth-century America.

He was wrong. Pullman became the site of one of the fiercest strikes in
American history. Hurt by the depression that had begun in 1893, George
Pullman imposed wage cuts at his Pullman Palace Car Company. Although he
had cut wages, Pullman did not lower rents in the company town. In May
1894, Pullman employees struck in protest of the wage cuts. Acting in support

of the strikers, members of the American Railway Union led by Eugene Debs refused to switch Pullman cars on tracks throughout Chicago and the nation, thereby bringing rail traffic to a halt. Stepping in on behalf of Pullman and the railroads, President Grover Cleveland ordered the United States Army to crush the strike on the grounds that it interfered with the movement of the United States mail, in violation federal law. The federal government stopped the strike, but it did not solve the underlying class tensions.[53] Amid the strike, fire had scorched the abandoned, already-decaying buildings of the Columbian Exposition. Strikers and strike sympathizers had set several other fires across the South Side of Chicago. It is possible, though not certain, that they were also responsible for burning down the World's Fair grounds. Even though most of the buildings of the fairgrounds had perished, the visions of its architects seemed more critical to the city's future than ever.[54]

The City Beautiful Movement on the Chicago Lakefront

In the aftermath of the 1893 World's Fair, Chicago's large-scale proprietary and corporate capitalists launched a movement to realize their vision of civic unity on the city's most beautiful and inspiring landscape, the lakefront. They believed that by decorating the city with civic spaces, monuments, and buildings reminiscent of classical Greek and Roman architecture, they could help to uplift, inspire, enrich, and, above all, unite warring classes of Chicagoans. This was a bold and lofty goal, a point underscored by science fiction writer H. G. Wells's 1905 description of the city: "Chicago burns bituminous coal, it has a reek that outdoes London, and right and left of the [Pennsylvania Limited Express train] line rise vast chimneys, huge blackened grain-elevators, flame-crowned furnaces and gauntly ugly and filthy factory buildings, [and] monstrous mounds of refuse." The prairie had been utterly destroyed in what Wells called a "nineteenth century nightmare."[55]

Even some spaces supposedly reserved for greenery lacked beauty. Lake Park was a site of filth and vice in the 1890s. The mail order store magnate Aaron Montgomery Ward descried the park as an eyesore and a den of vice particularly for the working class. From his new office tower on Michigan Avenue, Ward recoiled at the site of the garbage, horse stables, squatters' shacks, abandoned freight cars and wagons. Several disheveled buildings cluttered the park too, the ruins of an old exposition hall, railroad sheds, a firehouse, and an armory sometimes rented out for prize fights, wrestling matches, and masquerade balls where, as one brothel madam observed, "joy reigned unrefined."[56]

Ward filed a lawsuit against the city of Chicago on October 16, 1890, to force it to "clear the lakefront . . . of unsightly wooden shanties, structures, garbage, paving blocks and other refuse piled thereon." As the basis for his petition, he cited the 1836 decree by the canal commissioners that the grounds abutting the lake remain "Public Ground—Forever Open, Clear and Free of any Buildings, or Other Obstruction Whatever." The Illinois Supreme Court ruled in Ward's favor in 1897, mandating that the city remove all the structures in Lake Park, except two, the Chicago Public Library, built in 1893 at the corner of Michigan Avenue and Randolph in the place of Dearborn Park, and the beautiful art institute whose construction Ward had not challenged.[57] Ward's 1890 lawsuit was the first in a series that would not be resolved until 1910. Ward's vision of a park unfettered by buildings clashed with the prevailing wisdom of Chicago's corporate elite. They wanted to make the lakeshore in the image of the White City, a landscape covered with neoclassical buildings and civic monuments.

As Ward fought his suit to clear Lake Park of buildings and debris, the United States Supreme Court's 1892 ruling in *Illinois Central v. Illinois* empowered the city to develop the lakeshore. Justice Field confirmed the city's title to Lake Park. By declaring the shoreline "public" property, Justice Field believed he was empowering the city to build a harbor accessible to all commercial interests.[58]

Leading Chicago businessmen, however, developed different ideas about how to best use public space. Members of the Chicago Commercial Club became acolytes of the City Beautiful Movement, advocating urban beautification as a means to foster civic unity and promote moral uplift.[59] These goals were largely an extension of those of the older, mid-nineteenth-century parks movement. Planners like Burnham echoed Olmsted, Bross, and Rauch, claiming that beauty would promote health, morality, and moneymaking.

One of the exposition's directors, a fruit merchant and real estate speculator named Washington Porter, led the charge to materially and culturally enrich the city by bringing parts of the White City to the lakefront. A portly man with a handlebar mustache and a top hat, Porter wanted to disassemble the fair's Manufactures Building in Jackson Park and rebuild it on the lakefront where it could be used as a "People's Palace," or a civic and commercial convention center.[60]

Porter's plan highlighted a central tension in the movement to transform the lakefront into a civic center. On the one hand, the plan attempted to promote community and civic unity over competitive individualism. A supporter of the plan, Reverend H. W. Thomas noted that individualism had overwhelmed Chicagoan's sense of collective identity. Thomas regarded a civic center as an ideal way to foster unity, noting that "Such a building . . . with lodge halls, concert and lecture rooms . . . quarters where all the labor organizations can have permanent homes, is just the thing needed to concentrate all interests."[61]

On the other hand, Porter hoped his plan would stimulate the very commercial forces that reduced people to individual market actors. Porter bragged that, "The Manufactures Building on the Lake-Front will mean millions of dollars yearly to the people of Chicago. You can take 80,000 pairs of boots and hang them up in it and the people will come to see the show."[62]

Like Porter and Reverend Thomas, Alderman James L. Campbell believed that the park could be made to serve both economic and civic interests. In 1895, Campbell advocated filling in the lakeshore east of the Illinois Central tracks along Lake Park and building a park and exposition center. Alderman Campbell reasoned that if his plan were enacted, Chicago "will have the most beautiful park of any city on earth and the greatest world market to boot."[63] Campbell and Porter's plans ultimately failed for legal and financial reasons. But several other political and business leaders attempted to transform Chicago by bringing parts of the White City to the lakefront.[64]

Republican Chicago Alderman Martin B. Madden, like Porter, took the White City as his inspiration for an even grander lakefront development plan that, he believed, would promote social harmony. Madden moved to Chicago from England in 1869. He graduated from Bryant and Stratton Business College in 1873 and worked in mining and banking. He won election to the city council in 1889. Alderman Madden proposed filling Lake Michigan with dirt dug out of the Sanitary and Ship Canal that the Sanitary District was building. On that soil, Madden wished to build a granite or marble replica of the World's Fair ground's Court of Honor to celebrate the rise of the nation in the place of the frontier. The monument would foster unity even as it celebrated the nation's ethnic diversity. Classical-style buildings as well as portraits and busts of distinguished businessmen, professionals, and artists would invoke a sense of common, Western intellectual and civic traditions. Yet, Madden also intended to transform the lakefront into a showcase for world cultures in order to demonstrate "their progress in civilization and their methods of religious worship." Madden believed that even as the replicated Court of Honor stood as a paean to American civilization, it would also help "to obliterate the denominational lines and stamp out bigotry and prejudice."[65]

Madden's attack on the forces of bigotry stemmed less from a concern for the rights of individuals than from a pragmatic belief that it was necessary to cultivate civic harmony in a city divided along ethnic and class lines.[66] In the 1860s, more than 50 percent of the city's population had been born abroad. That figure had dropped by 1910, a year after Burnham published his *Plan of Chicago*, but still, 35.7 percent of the city's 2.1 million residents were foreign-born.[67]

The city was, moreover, separated along class lines. The large-scale proprietary and corporate capitalists who ran the city's banks, meatpacking houses, steel mills, department stores, and railroads tended to be Anglo-Americans, have ties to the East Coast, and oftentimes had attended college. They lived in the mansions of Prairie Avenue and joined organizations like the Chicago Commercial Club. Their factories and packinghouses were sites of toil for Chicago's poor, foreign-born, uneducated laborers. These immigrant workers filled slum districts like Chicago's near West Side where social reformer Jane Addams and other upper-middle-class professional women offered wholesome recreation, education, and relief at Hull House.[68] A larger number of Chicagoans, however, did not fall within the ranks of the destitute or the fabulously wealthy. The city was filled with craft workers including bricklayers, carpenters, plumbers, sailors, butchers, barbers, and teamsters who came from both "old" German and Irish and "new" southern and eastern European waves of immigrants. They worked in small firms where the lines between worker and boss were fluid.[69]

Architects like Burnham worked for the capitalist elite, and they were solicitous of their concerns about class conflict and a lack of ethnic homogeneity. Taking the White City as their model, they sought to tame the city with beauty and culture. In October 1894, members of the Illinois chapter of the American Institute of Architects, including Normand S. Patton and Burnham's mentor Peter B. Wright, launched the Chicago Municipal Improvement League to ensure the design of public buildings and monuments to stimulate "an appreciation of art and give to the city a fit expression of greatness."[70]

The league first began work on a plan for lakefront development. Like Madden, Patton took the Court of Honor as a starting point for planning the layout of the lakefront.[71] Ultimately, Patton's plan called for establishing a large public parade and event space flanked by massive public buildings including an armory, exposition center, and amphitheater. The park would also contain numerous promenades, a police station, a new city hall, buildings for the Crear Library, and the Field Columbian Museum that retailer Marshall Field promised to build for the city. Numerous lagoons and a boat landing would line the lakeshore and several boulevards would link the park to the North, South, and West Sides of the city.[72] Many of these features were also central elements of a plan advanced by the Chicago Architectural Club in 1896.[73]

Porter likewise devised a lakefront development scheme that contained elements of the Municipal Improvement League plan, including a museum and a civic center. Porter, moreover, sought to build a grand boulevard along the lakeshore stretching from the downtown park to Jackson Park and abutted by beautiful greenery, lagoons, and a canal.[74] Though none of the lakefront development plans was implemented to the letter, many of their features—such as a boulevard connecting Lake and Jackson Parks, lagoons, and classical civic buildings arranged on the lakeshore—were incorporated as central elements in Burnham's *Plan of Chicago*. What distinguished Burnham's 1909 plan from earlier lakeshore development plans was its endorsement by the Chicago Commercial Club, which consisted of the city's leading businessmen, professionals, and politicians. Before the Commercial Club threw its tremendous political and economic capital into Burnham's 1909 plan, though, several of the city's aldermen took steps to clear the physical and legal barriers to lakefront development.[75] Private citizens like Burnham and voluntary associations like the Chicago Commercial Club may have led the charge to build parks and civic monuments on the lakefront, but their success was contingent on the actions of city and state policymakers.

Public Policy in Advance of Private Philanthropy

Chicago's Republican Mayor George Swift began negotiations with the Illinois Central Railroad to make the lakefront more easily accessible in the summer of 1895. Swift had served as the city's commissioner of public works and an alderman for two terms. Swift became mayor pro tem in 1893 when a disgruntled office seeker shot Mayor Carter Harrison to death. Swift lost reelection later that year, but regained the office in 1895, and he soon became agitated with the Illinois Central for cutting off downtown Chicago from the lakeshore.

That summer, a steamship loaded with passengers landed at the foot of
Van Buren Street to let the people off. But an Illinois Central official had removed the steps over the railroad tracks leading to the viaduct. The passengers could not disembark and were stranded aboard until Swift arranged
means for their passage.[76] The incident showed that, in spite of Field's 1892
ruling in *Illinois Central v. Illinois*, the railroad maintained practical control
of access to the lakefront.[77] Swift determined that he had to take measures to
ensure safe, easy, routine access to the lakeshore, if the city was going to build
a park east of the tracks.

Mayor Swift and President Stuyvesant Fish of the Illinois Central hashed
out an agreement to provide Chicagoans access to the lakeshore. The city gave
the railroad about eight acres of land along the lakeshore near Monroe Street
and at the foot of Eldridge Court. It also granted the railroad permission to
erect small buildings along its right-of-way and to build a station at the foot of
Van Buren Street. The Illinois Central Railroad, in turn, agreed to hand over
approximately eight acres of recently filled shoreline adjacent to Peck Court
and Harrison Street and to depress its tracks; it also agreed to build four viaducts between Randolph Street and the south end of Lake Park to provide
Chicagoans with access to the lakeshore and the park land that the city intended to create east of the tracks. To expedite park construction, the railroad
agreed to construct a seawall east of the tracks to prevent the lake currents
from washing away the landfill that the city would heap into the water to expand the park.[78]

The Chicago City Council had to ratify their agreement by making it law.
Madden urged his colleagues to approve it so that the city of Chicago could
transform the lakeshore into a fabulous park.[79] Despite protests from residents of the West Side, who opposed spending money on improvements for
another section of the city, the city council passed an ordinance approving
Swift and Fish's agreement.[80] With the passage of this ordinance, the long
controversy over the lakefront came full circle, ending much like it had begun
in the 1850s. The Illinois Central agreed to build a breakwater for the cash-
strapped city government in return for use of the lakefront.[81]

The city of Chicago, meanwhile, began creating new land east of the railroad tracks. In the spring of 1896, the Department of Public Works began
filling in the lake between Randolph and Twelfth Streets. Each day, teamsters
hauled an average of one hundred carloads of debris and waste from various
corners of the city to the viaduct at Van Buren Street, where they dumped
their cargo into Lake Michigan. Hundreds of bystanders watched it swallow

up Chicago's refuse. Light-weight garbage floated on the water's surface. As the *Chicago Tribune* described it, "Cabbage leaves and lettuce predominate, while an occasional tomato contributes a speck of red to the otherwise sea of green."[82]

As the city of Chicago undertook the work of filling in the lake, Mayor Swift put plans in motion to cede Lake Park to the South Park Commission. The South Park Commission was the institution best suited to building the park. The state had endowed it with the authority to build and improve parks as well as to levy taxes for park purposes. In October of 1896, the South Park Commission formally accepted an ordinance from the city council granting it control over the portion of Lake Park that lie south of Jackson Street.[83]

For the time being, the city of Chicago held on to the north part of Lake Park, home to several civic buildings including the art institute at the foot of Adams Street, two armories between Monroe and Madison Streets, and a temporary post office at Washington Street. In 1903, the city granted the northern section of the park—since renamed Grant Park—as well as the art institute to the South Park Commission.[84]

Even before the South Park Commissioners received the south portion of Lake Park, they began contemplating how to make it beautiful. The president of the South Park Commission's board of directors, James W. Ellsworth, hosted a dinner at his residence on October 10, 1896, to discuss plans for the lakefront with civic luminaries, including the evening's keynote speaker, Daniel Burnham, who regaled Ellsworth's dinner guests with his ideas about lakefront development.

The Plan of Chicago

Burnham had devised plans well before that evening's meal. A year earlier, he and fellow architect Charles B. Atwood had presented a plan for the lakefront that, like many of the plans devised by other citizens, was modeled on the White City. Its centerpiece was the Columbian Museum that retail magnate Marshall Field wanted to build for the city. Never one to be accused of self-effacement, Burnham planned to design the museum himself.[85]

At Ellsworth's dinner, Burnham outlined a plan similar to the one he and Atwood had created, featuring civic spaces on the lakefront, including a museum, military building, parade ground, and lakeshore drive that would link

the North Side's Lakeshore Boulevard—built by the Lincoln Park Commission—
to Lake Park and Jackson Park. In 1909, these features would find their way into
Burnham's larger, more ambitious *Plan of Chicago*.[86] More importantly, Burnham began to formulate the intellectual rationale for his 1909 masterwork at
Ellsworth's residence that evening. His ideas were not particularly original, but
he expressed them in an eloquent, captivating manner, drawing implicitly on
the stage theory of economic development by invoking parallels between Chicago and Pericles's Athens.

Burnham saw in ancient Athens a city that had reached an advanced
stage of commerce and had funneled its wealth into the greatest of human
pursuits: the creation of beauty. In Burnham's view, this was the inevitable
result of having reached the highest form of development, commercial society. "The great flowers of . . . art," Burnham proclaimed, "are born on the
stalk of commerce." Commercial competition "arouses longings for lovely
surroundings," he continued. Cities like Chicago and ancient Athens had
reached the most advanced stage of commercial state of civilization and possessed the resources necessary to create beauty. Burnham noted that "The
works of Pericles' day were the direct result of conditions brought about by
the intensity of Athenian commercial activity and the World's Fair in 1893
would not have been thought of or built by any other country except our
own."[87]

Burnham suggested that great commercial cities like Athens and Chicago
needed to create beautiful, inspiring physical surroundings to help deal with
immigration. Burnham believed that the tide of immigrants that had flocked
to Athens and Chicago needed to be assimilated. Burnham argued that Chicago reaped benefits from immigration just as Athens had. Each newcomer
brought "some special knowledge and skill . . . from his home and which was
unknown to Athens." These benefits, though, came at a cost to the city's cultural unity. Burnham therefore recommended that Chicago imitate Athens,
which "opened her arms and took . . . [immigrants] in and assimilated them."
Assimilation, Burnham predicted, could occur in shared cultural and civic
spaces.[88]

Burnham also took great pains to convince Chicago's business elite that
beauty was good for business. He believed that the ancient Athenian tradition of civic republicanism could be reconciled with the economic imperatives of a modern, capitalist city. Burnham considered promoting civic unity
entirely consistent with the individual pursuit of profit. Beautiful civic
grounds, the planner reasoned, would make Chicago a more attractive place

to do business. In the 1897 New Year's edition of the *Chicago Tribune*, Burnham noted that if the city were beautified, the merchant "who given the same quotations from other towns, will invariably come here to trade . . . because of the attractiveness of the city apart from mere business."[89] Beauty would also help the city retain capital, "By making Chicago so delightful that our wealthy people will leave it reluctantly and only when necessity calls them away."[90]

It is likely that Burnham emphasized the economic benefits of lakefront beautification, in part, because he knew that his plan to transform Chicago would require the support of the city's most powerful businessmen. No doubt, Burnham's success with the 1909 *Plan of Chicago* had less to do with the originality of its ideas than with the position of those who supported them.[91] Burnham gained the backing of two of the city's leading business associations, the Commercial Club and the Merchants Club.

Founded in 1877 by thirty-nine of the city's leading businessmen, the Chicago Commercial Club became one of the most powerful voluntary associations in the city. It threw its financial, social, and political capital at addressing a range of issues, including taxation and trade policy reforms, public school reform, and eradicating corruption in city government.[92] The Merchants Club, which was founded in 1896, likewise consisted of well-to-do Chicago businessmen, many of whom were under forty-five years of age, a requirement for membership in the Commercial Club. Much like the Commercial Club, the Merchants Club contemplated matters of civic importance, hosting lectures on current events, including one by Jacob Riis on the playground movement and another by Booker T. Washington on "The Negro Problem in the South."[93] Most members of the clubs were Protestant Republicans who worked in the central business district and lived on Prairie Avenue or in the Gold Coast neighborhood near Lincoln Park. The members had much in common with Burnham who, having achieved the "conspicuous success" necessary for membership, joined the ranks of the Commercial Club himself in 1901.[94]

In that same year, the Commercial Club first entertained the possibility of developing a comprehensive plan for Chicago. It had long supported enacting a more limited plan to beautify the lakeshore. In December 1894, one hundred of the Commercial Club's leading members, including retail magnate Marshall Field, Pullman Palace Car Company owner George Pullman, and wholesale grocer Franklin MacVeagh, sat around a horseshoe table at the Grand Pacific Hotel and contemplated the beautification of the lakefront.[95]

Again in 1897 the Commercial Club held a dinner—this time at the Hotel Metropole—to consider the prospects of building a lakefront park. Serving as the evening's keynote speaker, Burnham argued that beautifying the lakeshore would spur economic development because it would draw businessmen and tourists to the city. His appeal elicited no immediate reaction, but it helped build momentum to beautify Chicago.[96]

In 1901, MacVeagh, the wholesale grocer and one-time president of the Commercial Club, proposed that Burnham and the club work together to devise a grand plan to beautify the entire city, not just the lakefront. This proposal resulted in little immediate action. Burnham was busy preparing plans for other major cities, including Washington, D.C., Manila, Cleveland, and San Francisco.

Burnham continued conferring with Chicago's businessmen. In 1903, for instance, he delivered an address to the Merchants Club titled "The Lake Front."[97] But Burnham did not turn his full attentions on the beautification of Chicago until 1906, when Merchants Club members urged him to complete a major plan for the city. A fateful meeting took place that year on a train somewhere between San Francisco and Chicago. On April 18, 1906, a terrible earthquake and fire had leveled much of San Francisco. In the wake of that catastrophe, Burnham traveled west to urge city officials to adopt his plans for the rebuilding of the city by the bay. On his return, as Burnham's train rolled eastward from San Francisco to Chicago, the planner talked with one of the train's other passengers, the publisher of the *Chicago Tribune* and a Merchants Club member, Joseph Medill McCormick. McCormick spoke with Burnham about the possibility of completing a comprehensive plan for the city of Chicago in conjunction with the Merchants Club. After McCormick arrived in Chicago, he wrote a letter to fellow Merchants Club member Charles Norton advising him to speak with Burnham about devising a plan for the city.[98]

Norton and his Merchants Club colleague Fredrick Delano took the lead in pushing for the creation of a plan for Chicago. As was the case with all Merchants Club members, the two men had lucrative jobs and powerful social and political contacts. Delano served as president of the Wabash Railroad. He was also the uncle of future president Franklin Delano Roosevelt. Norton held a position as a life insurance company executive.

In 1903, Delano and Norton had attempted to convince Burnham and the Chicago Merchants Club to devise a comprehensive plan for Chicago. Their fellow Merchants Club members agreed to host a dinner to honor Burnham for his work on a plan for Washington, D.C., and to generate support for similar work in Chicago. But Burnham was embroiled in tenuous negotiations over the implementation of his plan for Washington, D.C., and did not wish to celebrate his accomplishments prematurely.[99]

Having failed in their initial attempts to court Burnham, Norton and Delano jumped at the chance to talk with him in 1906, when they learned that he was receptive to the idea of drafting a plan for Chicago. Burnham agreed to work with the Merchants Club, but only after making sure that MacVeagh and his Commercial Club colleagues did not feel slighted, since they had asked him to work on a plan years earlier. MacVeagh endorsed the project.[100] Having secured MacVeagh's blessing, Burnham agreed to work with the Merchants Club. Now, Norton had to get his fellow club members to agree to work with Burnham.

Norton drew on the language of civic republicanism and on ideas about the modern business corporation. In a letter to his Merchants Club colleagues, Norton developed an appeal for the plan that might be characterized as corporate republicanism. He viewed the city as a unified entity created to advance both pecuniary and cultural goals for its citizen-shareholders, and he employed a republican language in lauding the civic value of the plan, insisting that, "The project is a noble one. It appeals to the good sense and pride of every citizen." Norton linked the idea of common purpose to a business plan, adding that, "we are only suggesting for the municipal corporation what most large corporations have found to be wise, namely, laying down in advance a comprehensive scheme of development."[101] Merchants Club members agreed and voted in favor of taking on the project. In the following year, 1907, the Merchants Club merged with the Commercial Club—taking the latter's name—to gain broad support for the plan from the city's financial and political elite.[102]

The Commercial Club created a plan committee headed by Norton, who enlisted the assistance of Delano and Charles H. Wacker, a former director of the Columbian Exposition. The Commercial Club sold subscriptions to the plan to raise money for its completion. Just as Norton had noted in his appeal for the support of his club members, the Commercial Club's message to subscribers appealed to Chicagoans as citizen-shareholders. One letter to subscribers explained the rationale for the Chicago plan: "In the same way that every great corporation finds it economical to prepare a plan or scheme for its future growth, so it was thought a corporation like the city of Chicago, which spends annually about $50,000,000, much of it for permanent improvements like Parks, Schools, etc., should prepare a plan or scheme for its future growth and development."[103]

Having secured funding, Burnham began drafting the plan in 1907 from his offices on the fourteenth floor of the Railway Exchange Building overlooking Grant Park and Lake Michigan. The planner enlisted the help of his assistant, Edward Bennett, and numerous Commercial Club members, who formed committees to help pave the way for the implementation of particular aspects of the plan. For instance, the lakefront committee, consisting of Edward B. Butler, Leslie Carter, Victor F. Lawson, Charles G. Dawes, John V. Farwell Jr., and Harold McCormick, worked to secure legislation to permit the city of Chicago to extend a great boulevard along the lakefront from downtown to Jackson Park.[104] The Commercial Club asked the state legislature for a law permitting the South Park Commission to acquire the riparian rights from the shore owners. By May 1907, the governor signed a bill allowing the park district to acquire riparian lands. An existing statute passed in 1903 enabled the South Park district to fill in the lakeshore, provided that it intended to use the new lands for park purposes.[105] Having secured the power to purchase and fill in the lakeshore, the South Park Commission was poised to implement the recommendations that Burnham would make for the lakefront in the 1909 *Plan of Chicago*.

The Commercial Club published the *Plan of Chicago* on July, 4 1909. That date, argues historian Carl Smith, signified Chicago's emancipation from the chaotic urban growth that threatened to squelch the city's commercial fortunes and divide its population along class and ethnic lines.[106] Burnham's plan promised to inculcate in Chicagoans a sense of civic unity and pride, promote the efficient circulation of rail and automobile traffic, and make Chicago a visually attractive tourist and business destination befitting the city's official motto, *urbs in horto*, or "city in a garden."

These claims were both promises and appeals. Burnham and the Commercial Club had no formal political power at their disposal to enact any of the *Plan's* recommendations. To do so, they had to convince the city's inhabitants and political leaders to demolish and refashion large chunks of their mighty metropolis.

The *Plan of Chicago* was as much a technical blueprint for the city as a promotional catalog. Acutely aware of the need to sell the plan, Burnham and Bennett enlisted seven artists to adorn its pages with beautiful colorful drawings. The *Plan of Chicago*'s leading illustrators included Jules Guerin and Fernand Janin. A Saint Louis-born painter, illustrator, and muralist, Guerin's work could be found on the pages of some of the nation's leading magazines and, in later years, on the walls of New York's Penn Station. Janin was a Parisian artist who Bennett had met during his studies at the École des Beaux-Arts, where many of the City Beautiful Movement's leading architects and designers were trained in traditional, classical Western styles. Janin and Guerin's bird's-eye-view drawings provided sweeping images, not of the dirty, crowded, vertical city that was, but of a clean, spacious, low-rise idealized city. Burnham and his Commercial Club colleagues made certain that political power-players received copies of the illustrated *Plan of Chicago*. Upon its publication on Independence Day, 1909, the Commercial Club distributed 1,650 copies of the plan, beginning with Chicago's mayor and aldermen.[107]

Burnham invoked historical parallels between Chicago and other great cities to help sell readers on the ideas in his *Plan of Chicago*. To lend legitimacy to the enterprise of planning, Burnham drew from both ancient and recent history for examples of city planning. He noted in the *Plan of Chicago* that, "Chicago, in common with other great cities, realizes that the time has come to bring order out of the chaos incident to rapid growth, and especially the influx of people of many nationalities without common traditions of habits of life."[108] Chicago, Burnham reasoned, had reached an advanced stage of commercial development; it had become necessary to give order to the landscape, lest uncontrolled growth destroy the city as a cancer.

Burnham also argued that planning was not a new phenomenon. Rather it was a process undertaken by all great commercial cities, dating back to ancient Athens and Rome. More recently, Burnham found inspiration in Paris. Four years after the 1848 revolution, Napoleon III hired Baron Georges-Eugène Haussmann to modernize the French capital. While Haussmann worked to provide better housing and sanitary conditions, the most crucial element of his work was the construction of a massive boulevard system throughout Paris, which served tourists and shoppers, as well as the soldiers who sometimes moved about the city to put down homegrown rebellions like the revolutionary, socialist Paris Commune that briefly took power in 1871.[109] As the *Plan of Chicago* noted, "The task which Haussmann accomplished for Paris corresponds with the work which must be done for Chicago."[110]

Burnham drew directly on the logic of the nineteenth-century parks movement in his plans for Chicago. In the pages of the plan, the planner recalled that in the 1860s, the city of Chicago sought to put the city back into the garden. Flowers and prairie grasses had once surrounded Chicago, the *urbs in horto*. By the 1860s, the city stretched so far that it seemed distant from the garden. By building a system of parks and boulevards around the city, the leaders of Chicago's park movement restored the city's place in the garden.

As the city's population grew, the percentage of park space per inhabitant dropped precipitously. Burnham and many of his contemporaries grew concerned, and in 1905, a Special Park Commission issued a report to the city council detailing the problem.[111] Burnham, in turn, cited this report in the *Plan* as evidence of a critical shortage of park space, noting that in Chicago there were "590 persons for each acre of park" and that for "health and good order there should be one acre of park area for each hundred people."[112] Burnham believed that park space was essential to civic harmony. "Density of population beyond a certain point," Burnham warned, "results in disorder, vice, and disease, and thereby becomes the greatest menace to the well-being of the city itself. As a measure of precaution, therefore, the establishment of adequate park area is necessary."[113]

The development of Chicago's most beautiful landscape, the lakefront, was one of the most important components of the *Plan of Chicago*. Burnham believed that, on the lakefront, the city's masses could commune with nature. "The Lake front," Burnham contended, "belongs to the people." Standing on the lakefront and gazing out at the expansive, unobstructed view of the horizon, Burnham believed, would "beget calm thoughts and feelings, and afford escape from the petty things of life." Solace could be found, not in the city, but looking away from it toward nature and Lake Michigan's "living water."[114] For he who "habitually comes in close contact with nature develops saner methods of thought than . . . when one is habitually shut up within the walls of a city."[115]

Burnham suggested that men would have to fashion a landscape conducive to communion with nature. He recommended the construction of lakefront parks with a chain of lagoons, beaches, yacht harbors, sports fields, greenery, and a boulevard along the length of Chicago's shoreline.[116] In addition to giving the masses an unfettered view of the lake, Burnham suggested that lakefront parks would be an ideal location for the establishment of the city's civic and cultural centers. In particular, he sought to transform Grant Park into a public center and garden complete with civic statuary and neoclassical buildings, including the art institute, the proposed Crear Library, and the Field Columbian Museum, modeled after the World's Fair. If constructed, the museum would contain "the records of civilization culled from every portion of the globe, and representing man's struggle through the ages for advancement."[117]

In addition to their value as natural, civic, and leisure spaces, Burnham considered the lakefront, as well as the city's riverfront, essential to the

Figure 8. View of the Chicago lakefront from the *Plan of Chicago*, 1909. Jules Guerin painted this image of the Chicago lakefront for Daniel Burnham's 1909 *Plan of Chicago*. It shows Burnham's vision for the lakefront looking southwest. Instead of being a site of industry, Burnham conceived of the downtown lakefront as a place for leisure, civic life, and beauty. There are two great piers flanking a pleasure boat harbor. Grant Park and downtown Chicago are situated on the shoreline to the right. Burnham envisioned the park as a site for greenery and cultural institutions like museums and libraries. Reproduced from the 1909 *Plan of Chicago* by the Chicago History Museum

circulation of people and goods. Burnham lamented that the Chicago River, "which gave to the city its location and fostered its commerce," had become a "dumping spot and a cesspool." He proposed lining the river in the central business district with expansive boulevards extending from the mouth of the river to North Avenue on the North Side and Halsted on the South Side. Burnham believed that the riverbanks did have some utility for docks and shipping terminals, but he predicted the eventual gentrification of the downtown waterfront, noting that: "It has been the experience of European cities that the banks of a river, although at first devoted only to commercial purposes, sooner or later are transformed into places which combine business uses with drives and promenades for traffic and for the pleasure of the people."[118]

Figure 9. View of the Chicago River from the *Plan of Chicago*, 1909. This drawing from
Burnham's 1909 *Plan of Chicago* shows the South Branch of the Chicago River looking
northward toward the confluence of the river's three branches. Burnham envisioned creating
multilevel boulevards along the river. One level, closest to the water, would be for handling
freight. The second, higher level would be for overland travelers, shoppers, tourists, and
businessmen who wished to be separated from the grittier functions of the port and enjoy
views of the river. The city of Chicago built a similar boulevard. In 1926, it completed
Wacker Drive, a double decker road that replaced South Water Street and River Street
along the south side of the main stem and east side of the South Branch of the Chicago
River. Reproduced from the 1909 *Plan of Chicago* by the Chicago History Museum.

In order to relieve commercial boat congestion on the Chicago River and
hasten the transformation of the downtown riverfront into pleasure grounds,
Burnham suggested that the city extend two large piers out into the lake, one
jutting from the southern part of Grant Park, the other from the north side of
the mouth of the Chicago River. These piers would enable ships to avoid entering the river and causing bridge openings that would bring overland traffic
to a halt. Moreover, the piers would provide civic pleasure grounds, as well as
freight and passenger terminals.[119]

The *Plan of Chicago* had broad support among the city's business community, but the elite was not entirely unified. Mail order merchant Ward challenged Burnham's vision of a waterfront filled with cultural institutions. Ward did not want Burnham and the city of Chicago to build any structures in Grant Park. He took aim at the plans to construct the Field Museum. Ward's rival, department store owner Marshall Field, had died in 1906, leaving eight million dollars for construction of the museum with the provision that the city furnish a site, for free, within six years of his death. The city and Burnham wanted to place the Field Museum in Grant Park. Ward fought it in court, citing the canal commissioners' decree that the land remain free and clear of buildings. In 1910, the Illinois Supreme Court concurred with Ward, blocking construction in Grant Park.[120]

Even so, the South Park Commission and Marshall Field's nephew Stanley realized Burnham's vision of a waterfront dominated by public cultural institutions. They built the museum just south of Grant Park on lands gifted by the Illinois Central Railroad. In 1925, Stanley Field convinced John G. Shedd, then president of Marshall Field's department store, to give three million dollars for an aquarium to be built next to the museum. A few years later, Max Adler of Sears, Roebuck, and Company donated seven hundred thousand dollars for a planetarium. Meanwhile, in 1924 the city opened Municipal Grant Park Stadium, which it soon renamed Soldier Field. Part of the Lake Michigan shoreline thus became a site of learning, tourism, and leisure.[121]

Burnham's plan notwithstanding, it was not a foregone conclusion that most of lakeshore would become parkland. His vision of a leisure and tourism-centered waterfront was at odds with its uses as a harbor. He had recognized the tension—between beauty and commerce—as soon as he had begun drafting the *Plan of Chicago*. In a 1907 letter to plan subscribers, for instance, he complained that he was unsure whether the city's southern lakeshore between Twelfth Street and Jackson Boulevard "was to be dedicated to Commerce or to Park purposes."[122]

At the same time that Burnham and the Commercial Club crafted the *Plan of Chicago*, city officials were contemplating their options: should the city of Chicago usher in a new era of leisure and tourism-centered capitalism on its waterfront, or should it cling to its role as a center for commodity transshipment? Was there a middle ground? Could the dirty, commercial uses of the waterfront be reconciled with its "civilizing" function, and its beauty? These concerns informed the construction of a defining feature of Chicago's lakeshore, Municipal (Navy) Pier.

CHAPTER 5

A Public Pier for Pleasure and Profit

In the winter of 1908, Chicago Mayor Fred Busse took direct aim at Daniel Burnham's plans for the lakeshore. Alarmed that the Illinois legislature had recently passed a law that granted Chicago's South Park Commissioners the power to implement the *Plan of Chicago* by taking possession of the entire lakefront between Grant and Jackson Parks, Busse wrote to Secretary of War William Howard Taft and implored him to invoke his general powers over interstate navigation to delay park construction.[1] Though not opposed to parks in principle, Busse was concerned that beautification of the lakeshore would contribute to the decline of the very waterborne commerce that had made Chicago an economic powerhouse. As Busse put it in an address to the Chicago City Council on January 6, 1908, in an unsubtle jab at Burnham, "No city . . . can thrive on beautification alone."[2]

That speech actually set in motion a chain of events that resulted in the construction of one of the city's principal lakefront recreational facilities and tourist attractions, Municipal Pier (renamed Navy Pier in 1927). Busse, with the city council's consent, assembled a team of experts on harbors, the Chicago Harbor Commission, to determine whether beautifying the lakeshore would harm the shipping industry and to determine how the city could stimulate waterborne commerce. The Chicago Harbor Commission included John Ewen, an engineer and former employee of the architectural firm Burnham and Root; Chicago alderman and distinguished University of Chicago political scientist Charles E. Merriam; businessman and civic leader Charles H. Wacker; and Sanitary District engineer Isham Randolph.[3] After conducting an extensive study of Chicago's port, and those of cities throughout the United States and Europe, the Harbor Commission urged the city to construct a series of piers extending into Lake Michigan, north of the mouth of the Chicago River. The proposed piers would be publicly owned and operated.

Like Morrison Waite and Stephen Field before them, the Harbor Commission was convinced that public property was essential to the functioning of the city's economy. It argued that public piers would help solve spatial problems hindering waterborne commerce in Chicago, since large boats would not be forced to attempt to navigate the river's narrow, crooked channel, pass over its tunnels, or squeeze by its center pier bridges. Further, municipal piers would foster waterborne commerce and promote competition. Railroad companies often prevented lake shipping lines from gaining access to docks by buying waterfront lands, but no railroad could deny vessel owners access to publicly owned piers. Finally, the public piers would help reconcile Burnham's idea of a beautiful waterfront with Busse's vision of a bustling port. If the city built shipping facilities on piers extending out into Lake Michigan, there would be room for public parks and civic grounds along the lakeshore.

The idea of building piers to stimulate waterborne commerce served as a sort of bridge between two different visions for Chicago's lakefront. One believed its potential could best be tapped by developing it as a harbor. The other believed that it should be cultivated as a "moralizing" civic space, in the tradition of the White City.

During the 1910s, Chicago merged Burnham and Busse's visions of the waterfront—combining commerce and pleasure—by constructing a massive pier just north of the mouth of the Chicago River. The process involved multiple actors with distinct, sometimes conflicting, interests. Railroads and lake shippers competed for business and for access to waterfront space. Political and business leaders from the Calumet and downtown Chicago struggled over resources for port development. Engineers and architects grappled with the aesthetic challenges of making a pier both functional and beautiful. In all of this, public officials collaborated with private economic actors to maintain and enhance Chicago's lakeshore—and the city more broadly—as a safe harbor for capitalism. The pier, they reasoned, would help maintain the city's competitive shipping advantages by staving off railroad monopolies. It would also bring beauty to the dirty metropolis. The public spaces of the pier, in other words, would bring Chicagoans both profit and pleasure.

In the end, Burnham's vision prevailed. Opened in 1916, Municipal Pier failed to stem the loss of waterborne commerce to other ports, railroads, and trucks. Instead of becoming a center of industry, it became a centerpiece of the city's leisure economy, drawing millions of visitors each year for dances, concerts, and breezy pleasure cruises.[4]

Beauty Versus Commerce on the Waterfront

In the 1900s, advocates for developing the lakefront as a harbor still had reasons to be optimistic about waterborne commerce and Chicago's key role in national and transnational shipping. While noting the sharp decline in shipping, the Harbor Commission report also suggested that Chicago might profit from several key waterway improvements in Central and North America.[5] The improvement of the Erie Canal, in particular, boded well for the city of Chicago.

Originally completed in 1825, the canal had been crucial to Chicago's initial commercial success, since the route linked the city to consumers of Midwestern food as well as raw materials in New York City and the Eastern Seaboard. In 1905, the state of New York began a project to expand the Erie Canal to accommodate barges. Businessmen in cities like Chicago stood to profit if they could ship larger volumes of goods through the canal at a greater speed.[6]

The improvement of the Erie Canal was not the only cause for optimism. The impending completion of the Lakes-to-the-Gulf Waterway led the Harbor Commission to believe that the city would soon be inundated with a flood of southern commodities. In 1882, the state of Illinois attempted to cede the Illinois and Michigan Canal to the federal government in the hopes that it would spearhead a project to build a large canal, the Lakes-to-the-Gulf Waterway, through the Illinois and Mississippi River systems. That waterway would permit larger, modern ships and barges to transport goods through the nation's midsection. The federal government initially rejected the proposal, but in 1887 businessmen from Chicago revived the plan and convinced both Illinois and federal government officials to make improvements toward the completion of the waterway, in hopes that Chicago would extend its reach far beyond the wheat fields of the Midwest to the sugar and fruit plantations of the Caribbean.[7]

Some observers of Chicago's economy expected that the construction of the Panama Canal would also buoy the city's commercial fortunes. In a report to the Chicago Harbor Commission, J. Paul Goode, a University of Chicago professor of economic geography, surmised that the construction of the Panama Canal would "open the markets of the Orient" to the city.[8] The prospect of Chicagoans conducting a fruitful maritime trade with Asia was not far-fetched. Less than a century earlier, after all, New England merchants like

John Murray Forbes had poured their profits from the China trade into the development of the Midwest and Chicago.[9]

To stem the loss of marine commerce and someday reap these potential harvests, though, Chicago would have to go to great lengths to reconfigure the city's harbors. For approximately forty years, businessmen, engineers, and Chicago politicians had assumed that upon settlement of *Illinois Central v. Illinois*, the winner of the case, the city of Chicago, the state, or Illinois Central Railroad would build a large harbor on the lakeshore south of the Chicago River's mouth.[10] Astute observers like the Major W. L. Marshall believed that Chicagoans could avoid the bridge delays, congestion, noise, smoke, narrows, and shallow water that their river brought through their city's central business district simply by moving the harbor from the river to the lakefront.[11]

But as the Illinois Central case dragged through the courts for decades and the lakefront's potential as a harbor remained unrealized, businesses dependent upon a water route set up their manufacturing and retail facilities along the Chicago River, the Calumet River, the Sanitary and Ship Canal, and the Indiana lakeshore. By 1909, when Mayor Busse and the Chicago Harbor Commission contemplated the idea of building a harbor to handle bulk commodities such as grain, timber, and iron ore on the Chicago lakefront, many of the city's civic and business leaders opposed it for environmental and spatial-economic reasons.[12]

Mayor Busse and the Chicago Harbor Commission considered building a harbor on the land between Grant and Jackson Parks. Yet, the Harbor Commission soon discovered that the city's engineers and key members of its business community had misgivings about its potential effect on water quality. As one editorialist put it, a lakefront harbor would "become a cesspool of filth, fouling the air with impurity . . . [and] eventually pollute to a lesser or greater extent our water supply."[13]

For nearly half a century, the city of Chicago had struggled to prevent the polluted waters of the Chicago River from contaminating Lake Michigan, the source of the city's drinking water. In 1871, the city's engineer, Ellis Chesbrough, reversed the flow of the Chicago River, drawing pollution away from the drinking water in Lake Michigan. Even so, the river sometimes backwashed into the lake, leeching sewage into the city's water supply and causing sickness.[14] At the turn of the twentieth century, the Sanitary District completed the Sanitary and Ship Canal, which siphoned water out of the Chicago River, causing sewage to flow with stronger force away from Lake Michigan

and making it safe from contamination. Engineers who had constructed the
Sanitary Canal, including Lyman Cooley and Isham Randolph, feared the
water quality would be destroyed by a harbor. A big lakeshore harbor flanked
by dirty industrial enterprises would produce pollution. That pollution
might, the engineers surmised, seep into the city's drinking water intake tunnels submerged beneath the surface of Lake Michigan.[15]

The chairman of the Chicago Commercial Associations' Rivers and Harbors Committee, Charles C. Dering, expressed concern that a harbor would
bring a sort of social pollution to the lakeshore. "If you move the harbor to
the Lake Front," Dering cautioned, "you must move the labor with it. This is
inevitable as dock wallopers cannot pay car fare and would not if they could.
They must live close to the docks, and this would turn the fine residence districts of the Lake Front and Michigan Avenue and Twenty-second street,
where the proposed harbors are to be situated, into labor colonies."[16]

Political economist George Tunell counseled against building a lakeshore
harbor for spatial reasons. A harbor located on the shoreline, Tunell wrote,
would be "wholly out of touch with and unrelated to the commercial and industrial life of the city."[17] The city's numerous railroads could not reach the
new harbor without securing rights of way, condemning buildings, and
bursting through established neighborhoods to reach the lakefront harbor. If
railroad connections could not be secured, shippers would have to pay substantial lighterage charges to shuttle goods from the port to the railheads already established along the Chicago River.[18]

The cost of relocating to expensive lakefront land would also hurt many
businesses. An official speaking on behalf of the Edward Hines Lumber
Company described the possible effects that a lakeshore harbor might have
on his company. It would mean "the destruction of the lumber business by
water to this Chicago Harbor," he explained, "because of the fact that we
would be obliged to move from our present quarters and . . . to purchase land
on that outer harbor at such a high price, to provide docks . . . or lighter lumber from outer harbor to our present docks, the expense of which would be
prohibitive in competition with southern woods."[19] These expenses would be
as applicable to dealers of other commodities as they would lumber companies. It would behoove many businesses to remain on the banks of the Chicago or, if they left the riverbank, to relocate to cheap lands adjacent to
railheads along the Calumet River or in Northwest Indiana.[20]

The economic, spatial, and environmental arguments against developing a new industrial harbor augured for Burnham's vision of lakeshore

beautification. So too did the Sanitary District's feats of engineering. After Cooley, Randolph, and the Sanitary District constructed the Sanitary and Ship Canal in 1900, the Chicago River no longer regurgitated sewage into Lake Michigan. Lake Michigan water tasted better. It also looked and smelled better.[21] The improvement in water quality likely enhanced the appeal of carrying out Burnham's plans to build parks, bathing beaches, and yacht harbors on the lakefront.

The environmental and economic forces at play boded well for Burnham's vision of the waterfront, as members of Chicago's political and economic elite increasingly came around to Burnham's position that beauty was good for business.[22] In an article dated January 10, 1908, and titled "Lake Harbor or Lake Park," the *Chicago Daily News* concluded that "Chicago must be good to live in or it will not continue to be good to make money in."[23] It was not, though, the logic of this argument that was the most compelling case for beautification. Rather, there were so many environmental reasons not to build a big lakefront harbor that beautification seemed, more and more, like the city's best way to capitalize on the lakefront.

The Chicago Harbor Commission, though, refused to choose between beauty and commerce, maintaining that there is "no real conflict between the harbor and the park interests of Chicago." The Harbor Commission's recommendations suggest, however, that it was simply indecisive. It recommended tabling the question of constructing a lakefront harbor south of Grant Park, noting that it was not "unmindful of the fact that harbor facilities on the Lake Front will cause pollution of our lake water which we have been spending millions to purify." Meantime, it suggested constructing several municipally owned piers along the lakeshore to handle some of the city's boat passengers and so-called "package freight," or small consumer items like textiles or fruit. The Harbor Commission considered these piers a means to test the demand for bigger lakeshore harbor facilities. The piers would "throw light on the question of the need and desirability for lake front harbor development south of Grant Park."[24]

The Harbor Commission's recommendation to build lakeshore piers was consistent with Burnham's proposals. The *Plan of Chicago* called for two massive lakeshore piers. It is even possible that the commission got the idea from Burnham before the publication of his plan. The Chicago Commercial Club's subcommittee on the *Plan of Chicago* had written the Chicago Harbor Commission on January 7, 1909, to suggest the city "take advantage of our greatest water front asset—viz., the fact that the waters of Lake Michigan are shallow for a long distance from the present shore line. Long and ample harbors can be created for Chicago by extending piers straight into the lake."[25]

The Harbor Commission found piers appealing for many spatial and economic reasons.[26] Ships could visit the city without running the river's gauntlet of bridges, jagged edges, shallows, and congestion, saving both time and money, and because piers would cater primarily to the vessel lines engaged in carrying passengers and consumer goods, they would not create as much pollution as a harbor that handled bulk commodities like grain, timber, and iron ore and was abutted by large manufacturing plants.[27]

From the Harbor Commission's viewpoint, though, the single most important feature of the piers would be their status as publicly owned and operated.

A World of Public Ports

The Chicago City Council's decision to build municipal piers took place in the context of debates over the ownership and regulation of "public utilities," a relatively new concept in the early twentieth century. In the 1890s, the *Chicago Tribune* first began using the term "public utility" in the singular sense of a company supplying a public utility, and Chicagoans used the term in connection with the streetcar controversy that had delayed the removal of the tunnels blocking the passage of large ships. When streetcar magnate Yerkes tried to renew his franchises, he met opposition from advocates of "municipalization," who argued that streetcars were a public utility and, as such, ought to be controlled by the city.[28] The idea that certain services were "public utilities," too vital to entrust to private parties without substantial regulation, formed one of the basic assumptions of the movement for public ownership and governmental regulation of harbors.[29]

When the Chicago City Council's Committee on Harbors, Wharves, and Bridges contemplated building municipal piers in 1910, it considered the relative importance of the port to other public utilities. The Committee on Harbors noted that, "Both public sentiment and expert opinion are divided as to the wisdom of public ownership and operation of such utilities as street railways, lighting plants, and telephone systems. With water works systems, however . . . the case is quite different. It is generally conceded that plants for furnishing water should be publicly owned." The Committee believed that water and, to a lesser degree, docks merited public ownership because of their significance for public health and the economy. It noted, "Docks . . . do not bear the relation to public health that the water system does, but they do affect in a peculiarly vital manner the commercial life of the community."[30] Thus, the Committee on Harbors implicitly suggested that the harbor had greater importance for the city's economy than other public utilities like telephone or electricity. In Chicago, the idea that certain, crucial services constituted "public utilities" led the city council's Committee on Harbors to back the Harbor Commission's recommendation to build municipal piers.

The Chicago City Council was not unique. Policymakers in port cities throughout the world were asserting greater public control over their harbors, on the grounds that public ownership and regulation facilitated waterborne commerce, whereas private ownership of ports dampened economic activity.

Chicago city councilmen learned this through sustained academic research. In 1908, University of Chicago economic geography professor J. Paul Goode made a report to the Harbor Commission on the conditions and administration of ports in North America and Northwestern Europe.[31] Two years later, the Chicago City Council's Committee on Harbors, Wharves and Bridges compiled a similar study of North American and European ports. Chaired by former commission member Alderman Charles Foell, it sought to gain an international perspective on the harbor question as it considered the recommendations of the Harbor Commission's report.

The committee's research showed that policymakers all around the world were repudiating private port management in favor of public control, and that public ownership of port facilities was essential for stimulating economic development. Private companies that managed ports, they found, often refused to spend money on necessary improvements.

In the 1890s, for example, New Orleanians watched their city's port deteriorate because a private management company refused to make improvements. In 1891, the state of Louisiana had leased the waterfront to a private company for a period of ten years. The drawbacks of private management quickly became evident. The company had no incentive to make substantial, costly improvements to a port that it did not own. In 1896, with the port of New Orleans corroding, the state of Louisiana created a board of commissioners to operate the harbor, though it was prevented from taking full control of the port of New Orleans until the company's lease expired in 1901.[32]

As in New Orleans, public officials seized control over the privately managed harbor in Rotterdam, Netherlands, in 1882, and the city of Antwerp,

Belgium, assumed control over its port in 1890 after sixteen years of private management.[33]

New York City, too, struggled to reclaim its port from private parties in the late nineteenth and early twentieth centuries. New York's early charters granted the city title to the harbor's submerged lands. Yet, over the course of many years, the city granted, leased, and sold those valuable lands to numerous private individuals and businesses. With so many different owners, port development was completely uncoordinated. By the 1860s, many city officials, journalists, and businessmen complained that the port's uneven, uncoordinated development interfered with commerce. In 1870, the New York state legislature passed a law creating a system of municipal dock ownership. Throughout the remainder of the century, the city of New York paid large sums of money to regain control over lands it had relinquished. For example, the city rented waterfront lots in lower Manhattan to the fur and real estate mogul John Jacob Astor for a sum of $356.91 per year before his death in 1848. In 1892, the city paid Astor's heirs $520,709.49 to relinquish the family's wharfage rights to that same property.[34]

Officials in other American cities also wrested their ports from private control. Railroads owned substantial portions of Baltimore's port before a 1904 blaze destroyed much of the waterfront. In the wake of the fire, the city's Burnt District Commission recommended that the Department of Public Improvements build a public port in the place of the railroad-owned docks that had burned. Acting upon the commission's recommendation, the Department of Public Improvements created a Harbor Board to purchase and regulate port facilities.[35] Philadelphians also instituted public port ownership in their city. The Philadelphia and Reading Railroad owned and operated numerous shipping facilities, often to the exclusion of some would-be port users. As a result, the city's Maritime Exchange, a business association, lobbied for a public port. In 1907, the Pennsylvania state legislature passed a law creating a Department of Wharves, Docks, and Ferries to purchase and operate harbor facilities on behalf of the public.[36]

The state of Washington attempted to take control of its harbors at the State Constitutional Convention in 1889. When Washington joined the Union, the state assumed control of the tidelands, or the land between low and high tide. Many of the tidelands had been developed by businessmen long before statehood. After a prolonged dispute, the convention added an article to the state's constitution that declared public ownership of the tidelands. The convention also mandated that the new state government set up the state Harbor Line Commission to delineate the boundaries of those public lands and manage them in the public interest.

The convention's decision to call for public ownership and regulation of the tidelands elicited legal challenges from individuals who had built docks on tidelands prior to statehood. One of those individuals, Henry Yesler, was a prominent Seattle businessman who had built docks on the tidelands abutting Elliott Bay. When Washington was admitted to the union in 1889, the state government assumed ownership of those lands beneath the Yesler docks. Yesler's heirs challenged the state's claim to the tidelands in court, and in *Yesler v. The Harbor Line Commission* (1892), the family's attorneys argued that the Constitutional Convention's decision amounted to a taking of private property without due process in violation of the Fourteenth Amendment. In December of 1892, just two weeks after the court had issued its verdict in *Illinois Central v. Illinois*, Chief Justice Fuller wrote a majority opinion ruling against Yesler's heirs.[37] In the wake of the decision, the Washington State Harbor Line Commission expressed relief that the state of Washington would not suffer from private control of their harbors. Referring to *Illinois Central v. Illinois*, the Washington Harbor Line Commission noted that the "State of Illinois and other states of the Union . . . have gotten themselves into serious difficulties . . . by undertaking to sell, grant, and otherwise dispose of, in fee simple, the lands they own under their navigable waters."[38]

Ironically, the Harbor Line Commission eventually brought about the very type of private control that it was designed to prevent. Upon the expiration of the Harbor Line commissioners' first terms, the state legislature named new commissioners who were sympathetic to the interests of the individuals and businesses that had already built on the state's tidelands. The new commission did not faithfully execute the wishes of the Constitutional Convention. It drew harbor lines far out into the water beyond the end of the docks and sold numerous tidelands in Tacoma and Seattle to various businesses, especially railroads. Observing the situation in Washington in 1910, Foell's Committee on Harbors concluded that the people of the state had been denied revenue that might have been afforded by public ownership of the tidelands. Moreover, Foell's committee believed that railroads had gained such a complete monopoly over the docks of Tacoma that they could manipulate freight rates by denying competitors access to a water connection.[39]

With these examples in mind, both Foell's committee report and the Chicago Harbor Commission's report concluded that public ownership and administration of docks had several key advantages that would help stimulate port development. Public ownership ensured that all vessel operators would have access to harbor facilities. Unlike private property owners, the city of Chicago would not turn vessels away from public docks. Thus, vessel lines without dock space in Chicago could still do business at the city's port. Public ownership also helped some vessel operators lower their fixed costs. Rather than maintain docks year-round, vessel owners could simply pay to use them when it was necessary. Finally, public ownership of dock facilities often led to centralization of authority over the port. It was much easier to coordinate economic development in a port run by a single administrator as opposed to one in which numerous private property owners used their segments of the harbor in disparate ways.

This last argument for public ownership was particularly compelling, because there was strong evidence that a crucial world port, London, had begun to lose commerce because of a lack of coordinated administration. In 1908, London was home to over seven million people. Even so, the city's port handled less tonnage than the ports of smaller cities like New York, Antwerp, and Hamburg. According to Goode, during the nineteenth century, London suffered because no single authority managed its growth. In his report to the Harbor Commission, Goode commented that "London, like most of our American ports, is like Topsy in 'Uncle Tom's Cabin,' who 'jest growed.' "[40]

No fewer than four major agencies managed various aspects of that growth. Governmental boards including the Thames Conservancy and the Trinity House of Deptford Strond monitored navigation on the river and managed pilotage, lighting, and buoying from London Bridge seaward. The City Corporation policed the port and regulated sanitation from Teddington Lock seawards while the Watermen's and Lightermen's Company, a medieval-style guild, operated lighterage and barges. The lack of coordinated development took a toll on the port, which began to lose commerce by the dawn of the twentieth century. In 1901 and 1902, a Royal Commission conducted a study of London's port and concluded that the city could stop the commercial exodus by establishing a harbor trust—a powerful nonprofit independent monopoly composed of elected and appointed officials—to manage the port in the public interest.[41] Between the 1850s and 1880s, port cities including Liverpool, Manchester, and Glasgow had established harbor trusts in order to coordinate economic growth.[42] London established a harbor trust in 1908. Both Goode and the Committee on Harbors viewed London's decision as a signal that Chicago might also benefit from such an arrangement. Goode commented, "It is most significant for us in Chicago that the best brains in

Britain, after years of exhaustive study, have adopted the policy of having one powerful independent monopoly in charge of the business of the port."[43]

The Committee on Harbors observed that "the principal ports of Europe are either publicly owned or are managed by harbor trusts on lines that bear much more similarity to public than to private ownership."[44] Yet, it worried that there were few American precedents to support the harbor trust plan. The Council Committee on Harbors recalled the failed efforts of Chicago's Mayor Edward F. Dunne and Cleveland's Mayor Tom Johnson to vest control of their city's streetcars in boards of trustees. If plans to turn the streetcar systems over to trustees did not succeed, the Committee on Harbors reasoned, "there seems little likelihood of its [a harbor trust] receiving serious consideration in this country," which left "public ownership as the only alternative to the various forms of private ownership."[45]

The argument for building publicly managed piers gained additional force and urgency from the very legitimate fear that railroad ownership of docks was diminishing competition among shippers.[46] By the early twentieth century, railroads had bought up docks and waterfront lands in the key Great Lakes ports of Duluth, Cleveland, Buffalo, and Milwaukee. In Chicago, too, railroads had bought substantial tracts of waterfront land. Railroads tried to force vessel lines out of business by denying lake shippers access to docks and refusing to accept cargo transfers from boats. If railroads drove lake lines out of business, they could raise their own rates to and from cities on the Great Lakes.[47] To prevent railroads from driving their competitors out of business, the Harbor Commission and the Committee on Harbors advocated building public piers that would be open to all users for a small fee. When water and rail carriers competed for business, Chicago reaped the benefits of cheap freight rates. Farmers, manufacturers, and retailers did business in Chicago, in part, because of attractive freight rates.[48]

Given Chicago's position as a hub in east-west transshipment, it had everything to gain from continued rail and water competition. Yet, the city could not necessarily guarantee continued competition through its harbor policies, since it was just one of many cities in a vast transportation network. Railroads could, and did, leverage their geographic and economic positions in faraway cities to manipulate freight rates to and from Chicago.

The Economic Geography of Great Lakes Shipping

The Chicago Harbor Commission recruited George C. Sikes, a printer and editorial writer for the *Chicago Record*, to conduct a study to determine what obstacles impeded the continued development of Chicago's harbor. Sikes had performed similar duties while serving on Chicago's Street Railway Commission and its successor, the Council Committee on Local Transportation. In the summer of 1907, he investigated harbor conditions for New York's Bureau of Municipal Research.[49] The following year, when he turned his attention to Chicago's port, Sikes concluded that by controlling docks in Chicago and especially in Buffalo—the gateway to the Eastern Seaboard—railroads were steadily driving independent lake shipping lines out of business. Consequently, freight rates from Chicago to Buffalo were on the rise.

In the early twentieth century, a large portion of Chicago's waterborne commerce came to be dominated by railroads. Lake trade with Buffalo was exceedingly important to the city of Chicago and its businessmen. Boats carried grain and package freight, or retail consumer items, to Buffalo and returned with commodities like coal. In Buffalo, most of the grain and package freight from Chicago was loaded onto Erie Canal boats or railcars and taken to New York City, to other East Coast seaports, or to Europe. Several railroads dominated the package freight trade by setting up their own boat lines, buying up dock space in Buffalo and manipulating rates between New York and Chicago. As of 1908, the primary lake lines operating between Chicago and Buffalo were either owned by or had exclusive service agreements with railroads (Tables 7 and 8).

These lake lines would carry package freight from Chicago to railroad-owned docks in Buffalo where the freight could be loaded onto trains. When

Table 7. Railroad Ownership of Lake Vessel Lines, 1908

Lake Line	Railroad Owner
Erie and Western Transportation Company (Anchor line)	Pennsylvania Railroad
Western Transit Company	New York Central Railroad
Lehigh Valley Transportation Company	Lehigh Valley Railroad
Union Steamboat Company	Erie Railroad

Table 8. Railroad Affiliation with Lake Vessel Lines, 1908

Lake Line	Railroad Affiliation
The Western Transit Company	Delaware, Lackawanna, and Western
The Union Steamboat Company	Baltimore and Ohio Railroad

independent boat lines brought freight to Buffalo to transfer to a railroad line, the railroads often denied the independent lines use of their docks. Thus, independent lines were forced to find other dock space and arrange to haul their cargo to the train station by wagon. This costly process made it difficult for independent boat lines to compete with railroad-owned or railroad-affiliated lake lines.[50]

To make matters worse for independent lake lines, the railroads also manipulated the cost of transshipment between Chicago and New York, devising rate structures that encouraged customers to hire railroad-owned lake lines or to send their freight entirely by rail. The railroads set high rates to ship goods from Buffalo to New York City. Thus, when an independent lake line delivered cargo to Buffalo, the cost of shipping that freight on to New York would be exorbitant. At the same time, however, the railroads offered relatively inexpensive through-rates from New York to Chicago for customers who agreed to use railroad-owned lake lines to send their goods to a railhead in Buffalo. Writing in the *Annals of the American Academy of Political and Social Science*, Walter Thayer, the eastern manager of the Pennsylvania Railroad's Erie and Western Transportation Company, corroborated this point. Thayer explained that "pro-rating arrangements have been made only between the lake lines and their rail owners."[51] The railroads gained control over the Erie Canal trade by making exclusive agreements with canal boat operators. Railroad-owned boat lines also offered through-rates, via lake and canal, to customers in Chicago. Thus, independent lake lines could not offer attractive rates to customers who wished to send package freight beyond Buffalo.

As the railroads came to dominate lake shipping, they consistently raised the cost of water transshipment in order to entice customers to send their freight by rail. For the twenty years preceding 1908, the rates for shipping one hundred pounds of freight via railroad from New York to Chicago remained relatively constant (Table 9).

Prior to the railroads' domination of the lake shipping in 1901, the water-and-rail rates for sending one hundred pounds of freight from New York to Chicago were substantially lower than the all-rail rates (Table 10).

In 1901, the various railroad-owned lake lines began inching their water-and-rail rates higher. By 1908, railroads and their lake lines had increased the cost of sending one hundred pounds of freight from New York to Chicago via water-and-rail (Table 11).

From 1901 to 1908, railroads raised their first class water-and-rail rate from New York to Chicago. In 1901, a customer paid 21 cents less per one hundred pounds by sending their freight via lake and rail than they would have paid if they sent their freight only on the train. By 1908, that same customer would only pay 13 cents less than the all rail rate. This trend continued in subsequent years.[52] In 1910, the railroad-owned lake lines raised rates an additional 5 cents, making the difference between the all-rail and water-and-rail rates a mere 7 cents.[53]

Railroad-owned boat lines also raised canal-and-lake rates from New York City to Chicago in order to squeeze independent lake lines out of the package freight business. For the canal-and-lake rates for sending one hundred pounds of freight in 1892, see Table 12.

Table 9. Freight Rates via Railroad from New York to Chicago per 100 Pounds, 1888–1908

Class	1	2	3	4	5	6
Cents	75	65	50	35	30	25

Table 10. Freight Rates via Water and Rail from New York to Chicago per 100 Pounds, 1900

Class	1	2	3	4	5	6
Cents	54	47	37	27	23	20

Table 11. Freight Rates from New York to Chicago via Water and Rail per 100 Pounds, 1908

Class	1	2	3	4	5	6
Cents	62	54	41	30	25	21

Table 12. Freight Rates from New York to Chicago via Canal and Lake per 100 Pounds, 1892

Class	1	2	3	4	5	6
Cents	30	25	20	18	16	14

Table 13. Freight Rates from New York to Chicago via Canal and Lake per 100 pounds, 1908

Class	1	2	3	4	5	6
Cents	42	36	29	23	21	18

By 1908, railroad-owned boat lines had raised their canal-and-lake rates as well (Table 13).

As the discrepancy between water and all-rail rates diminished, it became more likely that customers would opt to pay slightly more to send their goods entirely by train than by water and rail or lake and canal. Without a substantial discount, there was little incentive for customers to use slower water routes. Not only was the all-rail option quicker, it also involved less risk because freight would not need to be transferred from boat to train at Buffalo, decreasing the likelihood of damaging the goods.[54] Taking note of these rate trends, the *Chicago Daily News* surmised that railroads had stepped up their efforts to stifle water shipping before the state of New York completed the improvement of the Erie Canal. The paper noted that, "Obviously the advance in rail-and-lake-rates is made in the interest of the railroads that control the vessel lines, one purpose being doubtless to discredit water transportation in advance of the time when the enlarged Erie Canal shall be ready for use."[55]

After manipulating rates and waterfront space to dominate the package freight trade, the railroads employed similar tactics in an attempt to consolidate Chicago's grain traffic. In order to entice shippers to send grain via rail and, further, to discriminate against independent lake lines, railroads raised rates from Buffalo to the East Coast. Moreover, they hiked their through lake-and-rail rates from Chicago to New York, Philadelphia, and Boston.[56] This trend worried the Chicago Board of Trade's transportation manager W. M. Hopkins. In 1908, Hopkins warned of a "deliberate plan on the part of the railways to so adjust their rates as to drive the independent lake carriers out of business and force the movement of grain all-rail, controlling to themselves at the same time the handling of package freight through vessels owned by them."[57] In the years between 1908 and 1916, the Chicago Board of Trade, Buffalo Chamber of Commerce, and the Corn Exchange of Buffalo lobbied the Interstate Commerce Commission to reduce or cap the water-and-lake and all-rail grain shipment rates from Buffalo to the East Coast. The railroads successfully defended themselves by pointing out that, in spite of rate hikes, water-and-lake charges remained lower than those for all-rail transshipment.[58]

The city of Chicago could do little to defend itself from the railroads' domination of the port of Buffalo, or from the rate structure that drove up the price of shipping freight to and from the Midwest. In his report to the Harbor Commission, Sikes noted that "providing better facilities is not the whole of Chicago's interest in lake transportation. The eastern gateway must be kept open as well, if this community and others on the lake are to derive the full benefit of their location with reference to water transportation."[59] Chicago's position on the western shores of the Great Lakes had made it a hub for east-west shipment, but it also placed the city at the mercy of those who controlled the port of Buffalo. Chicago city leaders and the Board of Trade could only hope that the Interstate Commerce Commission would intercede on their behalf. In the meantime, the city enacted policies to thwart railroad domination of its own port.

Several Chicago city officials and businessmen advocated for construction of municipal piers in order to prevent railroads, as well as other private property owners, from controlling access to the waterfront. In 1907, the city of Chicago's assistant statistician Frederic Rex figured that private owners owned the majority of the riverfront land in Chicago. Rex observed that "the only property along the Chicago and Calumet Rivers which is public property are the street stub ends along the river front . . . The large number of other docks along these rivers are owned by private parties, there being approximately forty-five miles of private dock on the Chicago River and ten miles of private docks on the Calumet."[60] The implications of Rex's observations were clear. Private property owners could determine who could use the city's harbor. That power allowed private parties to exert significant control over the shipping market. To ensure a free market for shipping, it would be necessary to create publicly owned dock facilities.

Seeking to encourage competition in the shipping business, the Chicago Association of Commerce lobbied the city and the federal government to build public harbors. In 1911, association representative E. S. Conway told the

Chicago City Council Ways and Means Committee that "it is absolutely essential, if we are going to hold our place as a great commercial and industrial center ... that we have absolutely free dockage or open public dockage at every port on our lake."[61] The association believed that public dock facilities would help independent steamship lines compete and, in so doing, drive down the cost of shipping. In a 1913 letter to the army engineer in charge of the Chicago District, the association reiterated its faith in the possibilities of public ownership, noting that "a public dock would encourage independent transportation lines which would reduce the cost of transportation."[62] A reduction in the price of shipping goods to and from Chicago would benefit nearly the entire business community—save the railroads. Accordingly, many Chicago businessmen supported the Chicago Harbor Commission's recommendation, corroborated by Foell's City Council Committee on Harbors, that the city should build municipal piers to stimulate waterborne commerce. Although many businessmen, city officials, and experts agreed on the merits of public piers, it proved very difficult to implement the plans. Political and economic rivalries within Chicago complicated efforts to pass the legislation necessary to build municipal piers.

The Political and Economic Geography
of Port Development

On the night of April 18, 1911, a special train rumbled across the dark, flat fields that separated Illinois's great metropolis from its capital. Aboard the train, seventy Chicago businessmen and officials equipped, as one newspaper put it, with both "olive branches" and "war clubs" readied themselves for the next day's business in Springfield.

The able lot of men included Foell; the legendarily corrupt ruler of Chicago's first ward "Bathhouse" John Coughlin; Sanitary District Chief Engineer G. M. Wisner; businessmen F. B. Montgomery of International Harvester; and W. R. Humphrey and H. C. Barlow from the Chicago Association of Commerce. Many representatives of Chicago's leading retailers also joined the delegation, including C. H. Thorne of Montgomery Ward & Co., James Simpson of Marshall Field & Co, and J. T. Pirie of Carson, Pirie, Scott & Co.

These politicos and businessmen all wanted the legislature to pass a bill permitting the city of Chicago to build municipal piers to provide dock space for the city's package freight and boat passengers. The city needed legislative permission because, in accord with Field's ruling in *Illinois Central v. Illinois*, the state of Illinois held title to the lands beneath the waters of Lake Michigan. The piers would be constructed on those state-owned submerged lands just north of the mouth of the Chicago River.[63]

One man stood in the delegation's way: Benton F. Kleeman. A lawyer, state legislator, and acting chairman of the House Committee on Drainage and Waterways, Kleeman hailed from a district on Chicago's far South Side.[64] One of the most striking geographic features of Kleeman's district was Lake Calumet, located four miles west of Lake Michigan. The lake consisted of about twenty-four hundred acres of shallow water surrounded by soft, swampy land used mostly for hunting and fishing, but Kleeman had grander visions for it, hoping to spur economic development in his district by making the lake into an industrial harbor.[65] To realize this vision, he introduced a bill that required the Sanitary District to dredge a five-hundred-acre portion of Lake Calumet to a depth of twenty-one feet. The bill also required the Sanitary District to use the dredgings to fill in part of the lake and construct docks on the landfill. Additionally, the bill directed the Sanitary District to link the Lake Calumet harbor to Lake Michigan via the Calumet River.

To ensure his bill's passage, Kleeman put a parliamentary stranglehold on the city of Chicago's plans to build municipal piers. Kleeman used his power as the chairman of the Committee on Drainage and Waterways to stall two important bills in his committee. The O'Connor Bill authorized the city of Chicago to construct piers extending out into Lake Michigan. The Juul Bill permitted the Sanitary District to develop the very same piers in the likely event that the city, due to its chronic lack of funds, failed to build the piers. Although both bills had broad support, Kleeman used his parliamentary power to detain the bills in committee until the Senate passed his measure mandating that the Sanitary District build a harbor on Lake Calumet.[66]

Critics charged that the Kleeman Bill was a real estate boondoggle. Sanitary District chief engineer G. M. Wisner, a member of the delegation to Springfield, suggested that Kleeman's plans for a Calumet harbor were totally impractical at the time. Wisner pointed out that the harbor would create some of the very same problems on the Calumet River that hindered navigation on the Chicago River. If the Sanitary District developed Lake Calumet, numerous railroads would have to extend their lines to the harbor, crisscrossing their tracks over the Calumet River in a move that would add substantially to the number of bridge delays. Wisner also expressed concern over the plan's exorbitant cost, which he estimated at a minimum of thirteen million dollars. Wisner contended that the Kleeman Bill called for "spending in a wildly extravagant manner the money of the [Sanitary] [D]istrict for a harbor improvement that it does not want, and which would be impractical and which would attract no shipping."[67]

Citing Wisner's opinion that the Kleeman Bill would be impractical, the *Chicago Tribune* accused Kleeman of trying to force tax payers to support a project that would benefit only a few wealthy businessmen and corporations. The paper alleged that Kleeman had business ties to the Calumet and Chicago Canal and Dock Company, which had substantial land holdings on the north shore of Lake Calumet. If Kleeman's bill became law, that company stood to gain enormous sums from the rising value of its Calumet lakeshore holdings. So, too, would several others, including ice salesmen E. A. and C. B. Shedd, banker and meatpacker Nelson Morris, J. P. Morgan's U.S. Steel Company, and the Pullman Palace Car Company. Although it seemed quite likely that these businessmen and companies stood to profit, Kleeman's plan did have a public interest rationale as well.[68]

Kleeman insisted that his Lake Calumet plan was consistent with a similar public interest rationale that motivated advocates of the municipal pier project, noting that his bill provided for municipal ownership of the harbor. Under his plan, the city of Chicago would own and operate a massive, two-thousand-acre industrial center linked to railroads and bodies of water.[69] With public ownership, there would be less likelihood of one or a few companies controlling the flow of goods through that crucial industrial region. Further, the city of Chicago, Kleeman noted, would generate substantial tax revenue from leasing the docks. Kleeman also pointed out that his bill would help Chicago lure industry that might otherwise go to Northwest Indiana because of the availability of lakeshore land. In Chicago, the park districts owned most of the lakeshore. In Indiana, however, private industry held large portions of the lakeshore. The Indiana state legislature permitted private interests to fill-in and build on the shoreline for a fee of twenty-five dollars per acre. This policy, combined with its strategic location at a point where railroads and water commerce met, encouraged many manufacturers to build plants in Northwest Indiana. To entice industry to Chicago, Kleeman reasoned, the city needed to provide accessible, high-quality infrastructure.[70]

Kleeman worked hard to enact his plan to develop a Lake Calumet harbor, but it ultimately proved untenable. The Harbor Commission had already called for industrial development on Lake Calumet. In 1909, the Chicago Harbor Commission recommended "creating an inland harbor on Lake

Calumet . . . as seems feasible after detailed study of the legal, engineering and financial problems involved."[71] Yet, Kleeman must have suspected that developing Lake Calumet was not a high priority, since he resorted to using strong-arm tactics to push his bill through the legislature, while also holding hostage in committee the Juul Bill, which granted the Sanitary District authority to develop lakefront piers. In an attempt to win the support for his measure, Kleeman's agent Henry W. Lee allegedly sent a message that the legislator would support an increase in Sanitary District officials' salaries if they withdrew their opposition to his bill. In the meantime, the O'Connor Bill, which granted the city of Chicago power to build municipal piers, slipped out of Kleeman's clutches, passed both Houses, and went to Governor Charles S. Deneen for approval, along with the Kleeman Bill.[72]

Deneen signed the former but vetoed Kleeman's measure on the grounds that Kleeman had tried to force the expensive project on the Sanitary District. The governor worried that the project would cost far too much; estimates ran between seven and eighteen million dollars. Deneen also feared that forcing the Sanitary District to take on the harbor project would delay other crucial work in the region. The Sanitary District had begun the process of reversing the Calumet River by digging a channel, the Cal-Sag, from the Little Calumet River to the Sanitary and Ship Canal. It aimed to prevent the Calumet River's increasingly toxic waters from flowing into Lake Michigan, the source of the city's drinking water. Furthermore, the Cal-Sag Channel would provide a waterway for boats traveling between the Calumet River and the Sanitary and Ship Canal. Deneen feared that the Kleeman Bill's provisions might overburden the Sanitary District and thereby delay the Cal-Sag project for years.[73] Even without the enormous task of building a harbor on Lake Calumet, it took the Sanitary District and its successor organization, the Metropolitan Sewage District, eleven years, 1911 to 1922, to finish the Cal-Sag Channel.[74]

In the meantime, the city of Chicago struggled to overcome financial and legal obstacles that hindered construction of municipal piers on the lakeshore. Chicago's coffers were empty. Initially, the city council had planned to create a harbor commission to handle the project. However, in an effort to save money, Mayor Carter Harrison charged one commission with handling both the outer harbor construction and the daunting project of constructing subways in Chicago.[75] Led by the former chief engineer of the Columbian Exposition Edward Shankland, the Harbor and Subway Commission took charge of the city's harbor, which, for administrative purposes, it divided into five districts.

The first district consisted of the area immediately north of the Chicago River's mouth. In that area, the city planned to build a series of five municipal piers. The Harbor and Subway Commission planned to build two of the five piers initially and add the others as demand for dock space increased. In keeping with Burnham's plan, one of the piers was designated to handle passenger travel and provide some recreational facilities, while the other would only handle freight. To finance pier construction, the city issued bonds.[76] The city of Chicago also convinced Congress to spend 1.5 million dollars constructing a breakwater to protect the pier from storms.[77]

In the summer of 1912, Mayor Harrison stopped all the work on the piers when he finally caught on to one of Kleeman's legislative tricks. Toward the end of the 1911 legislative session, Kleeman had added an amendment to the O'Connor Bill that prohibited the city of Chicago from paying companies or individuals who claimed the shoreline lands from which the city hoped to extend its piers. The amendment, Kleeman claimed, was aimed at preventing the "taxpayer from having to pay for property already belonging to the state."[78] The Chicago Canal and Dock Company owned the shoreline on which the city wanted to build. The company had leased the land for a period of ninety-nine years to James Pugh of the Pugh Terminal Warehouse Company, which handled lake cargo. Due to Kleeman's amendment, the city of Chicago had no legal grounds to pay Pugh and the Chicago Canal and Dock Company for either use of or title to the shoreline. This seemingly innocuous provision forced the city of Chicago to go back to the legislature for an entirely new bill.[79] In the 1913 legislative session, Senator O'Connor resubmitted his bill with a provision that stated that the courts could review private parties' land titles before the city purchased shoreline. As in 1911, Kleeman reintroduced his bill mandating that the Sanitary District build a harbor on Lake Calumet. Rumor spread throughout Springfield and Chicago that Kleeman would delay Senator O'Connor's bill in his committee until the Senate voted in favor of his bill.[80] For some reason, however, Kleeman defied expectations. He reported the O'Connor Bill to the house and urged its passage.[81]

After this unexpected turn, the *Chicago Tribune* suggested that Kleeman had traded his support for the O'Connor Bill in return for the governor's approval of his Lake Calumet Harbor bill.[82] Illinois Governor Edward F. Dunne signed the O'Connor Bill, thereby permitting the city to buy the shoreline north of the Chicago River on which it wanted to build the pier.[83] Dunne, a former mayor of Chicago, had championed public control of the city's streetcar system. Thus, it is not surprising that he supported a project, partly influenced by the city's streetcar policy, to place the city's harbors under municipal authority. Dunne did not, however, sign the Kleeman Bill. The *Chicago Tribune* had either been mistaken about why Kleeman threw his support behind the O'Connor Bill—or the governor betrayed the legislator. Dunne rejected the Kleeman Bill on the grounds that it imposed too great a burden on taxpayers already shelling out money for the Cal-Sag Channel.[84]

Though Dunne's veto spelled an end to the Kleeman Bill, the city did build a harbor on Lake Calumet. In 1921, it acquired the title to Lake Calumet from the state of Illinois. In that same year, the Chicago City Council adopted the Van Vlissengen Plan.[85] Created by a former supporter of Kleeman's, it called for dredging a deep harbor in portions of the lake and filling in other portions in order to provide solid ground for terminals and manufacturing facilities. The city did very little to advance the plan. For years the project stood at a standstill or proceeded at a crawl. In 1935, the federal government began dredging a 21-foot-deep, 3,200-foot-long, and 670-foot-wide basin and building a steel dock wall. During World War II, the Pullman-Standard Car Manufacturing Company set up a shipyard on the south end of the lake where it built small navy craft.

Save during wartime, the harbor did not make a significant impact on the city's economy until the 1950s, when political and geographic conditions increased demand for the Lake Calumet harbor. An autonomous agency charged with the region's port development, the Regional Port District (later called the Illinois International Port District) developed the harbor in 1955. The impending completion of the Saint Lawrence Seaway, a system of canals that permitted oceangoing vessels to travel from the Atlantic to the Great Lakes, finally made Lake Calumet harbor development a priority.

After a bond issue, the Port District began construction on more than a mile of wharves, several fireproof transit sheds, a warehouse, and two immense grain elevators. These improvements helped the city of Chicago handle the waterborne commerce that entered from the Saint Lawrence Seaway after it opened in 1959.[86] After more than forty years of planning and legal wrangling, Kleeman's vision of a Lake Calumet harbor had come to fruition.

In the meantime, the city of Chicago's plans to revive lake shipping by building several municipal piers failed to reverse the decline of waterborne commerce on the downtown waterfront.

A Public Pleasure Pier

The city of Chicago's decision to create public piers on the waterfront was motivated largely by economics.[87] Like Justice Field in his *Illinois Central* ruling, the Harbor Commission and the City Council's Committee on Harbors, Wharves and Bridges believed that the city could spur commerce by providing accessible public harbors. They used the word "public" to describe a physical place where businessmen enjoyed equal access to harbor infrastructure without the fear that private property owners might limit it. Yet, the public pier they created ceased to have great value of shipping, as cars, trucks, and railroads drove lake lines out of the passenger transport and package freight businesses. Municipal Pier became, instead, one of the city's most famous and enduring tourist and entertainment destinations.[88]

In 1913, the Chicago Subway and Harbor Commission chose Massachusetts Institute of Technology-trained architect Charles Sumner Frost to design Municipal Pier. Frost was influenced by the City Beautiful Movement. After long stints working alone and in partnership with Henry Ives Cobb, in 1898 Frost teamed up with French-trained architect Alfred Granger who had studied at the world-renowned École des Beaux-Arts in Paris. Founded during the reign of Louis XIV, the school instilled in its students an appreciation for neoclassical buildings that recalled a mixture of ancient Roman, Greek, and Renaissance-era styles that were the hallmarks of the 1893 World's Fair and the City Beautiful Movement. Together, Granger and Frost designed numerous railway stations across the Midwest that bore the markers of classical European architectural styles.[89]

Much like Burnham's designs for the Columbian Exposition and his 1909 *Plan of Chicago*, Frost's Municipal Pier invoked the beaux-art fashion to express the grandeur, permanence, and power of the city. The Harbor and Subway Commission had originally planned to build a series of five piers north of the river's mouth.[90] To begin, the city commissioned Frost to design one large pier that combined both recreational facilities and passenger and cargo docks. Like Burnham's *Plan of Chicago*, Frost's plans for Municipal Pier had to facilitate the circulation of goods and people and inspire a sense of civic unity and beauty.

Frost drafted plans for a monumental structure at the base of Chicago Avenue. The 292-foot-wide pier, completed in the spring of 1916, extended from the city street for three thousand feet into the blue waters of Lake

Michigan. The structure sat atop over twenty-thousand pilings of Oregon timber. On each end of the pier, Frost planted large steel-framed structures adorned with red brick. The classically inspired structures stood as markers of Chicago's civic grandeur and its place in Western Civilization. Decorative ornamentation in the red brick, including the city's seal, a sheaf of wheat, and a Native American, recalled the city's frontier history and illustrated its importance as a hub for the region's grain.

The head house at the foot of Grand Avenue served as the entryway for pedestrians and contained the offices of pier officials and the harbormaster. On each side of the head house stood a tower that held a sixty-thousand-gallon gravity tank to provide water for firefighting. Just east of the head house, the passenger and freight buildings stretched 2,340 feet along the pier. The building had two floors and two separate wings dissected by an eighty-foot-wide road with a trolley track for moving cargo and passengers to and from the docks. On each side of the road sat two-story, one-hundred-foot-wide sheds for handling freight and steamship passengers. A board-walk sat atop each shed so that pedestrians could stroll to or from the terminal building situated to the east of the passenger and cargo sheds. The terminal building measured 245 feet by 30 feet and housed information offices, restrooms, a first aid station, a restaurant, and a rooftop garden. Just to the east of the terminal building, there stood an 80 by 220 foot, two-story-high open-air shelter. That shelter provided a covered passageway to the easternmost building on the pier, the concert hall. The hall was comprised of a 150 by 138 foot half-shell with a one-hundred-foot-tall domed ceiling. It sat up to four thousand people and was flanked on each side by a 165-foot-tall observation tower that treated visitors to sweeping views of the city and its lakefront.[91]

Frost's Municipal Pier, like Burnham's *Plan of Chicago*, sought to address recreational, civic, aesthetic, and economic concerns all at once. In keeping with a central tenet of the City Beautiful Movement, Frost designed the pier with the assumption that beauty was good for business. He was partially right. The recreational and civic, monumental aspects of Municipal Pier did serve some of the city's businessmen. But, the business community was not a unitary group with a single agenda. Some businessmen had conflicting interests in lakefront development.

In congressional hearings in December of 1914, as the Harbor and Subway Commission oversaw the construction of Municipal Pier, tensions within the city's business class began to surface. In a hearing held by the

Figure 10. Municipal Pier, 1920 ca. This photograph shows a bird's eye view of Municipal
Pier looking southwest. The mouth of the Chicago River and downtown Chicago are in the
background. The pier is lined with freight storage sheds. The end of the pier is the site of two
lookout towers and a large auditorium. People are gathered on the end of the pier for boat
cruises and for sightseeing. The recreational uses of the pier were far more important than its
uses for commercial shipping. The photograph was taken by an unknown person in the early
1920s. It is housed in the collection of and was reproduced by the Chicago History Museum.

House Committee, Chicago attorney Edward T. Cahill asked Congress to refuse a $574,000 appropriation for a breakwater crucial for the protection of
Municipal Pier. Cahill, a representative of the Chicago River and Harbor Association, protested that the Municipal Pier privileged recreation over the
demands of commerce. Congress should not, Cahill contended, spend tax
dollars to assist in the construction of a Municipal Pier if it was to be used for
purposes other than navigation. Congress bore responsibility for interstate
commerce, but not for recreation grounds. Cahill believed that the city abandoned the commercial interests in favor of the erection of a recreational park.
He insinuated that the city's motive for putting recreational facilities on the
pier had as much to do with the city council's loyalty to Chicago's railroads as
with a desire to carry out provisions of the Burnham plan. Even so, Cahill

stopped short of alleging out-and-out collusion. He simply remarked to the congressional committee that "the railroads have always done everything they can to prevent navigation on the Lakes." Cahill also commented that he could not disclose the identities of his of his clients because the city's railroad interests might make punitive reprisals against them.[92]

When Congress challenged Cahill to support his claims with evidence, the attorney could do nothing but note that the original plan for Harbor District No. 1 called for the construction of five piers. Chicago's assistant corporation counsel James G. Skinner countered, the "city of Chicago has always considered that [the original plan] as merely showing possibilities. No person officially connected with the city of Chicago . . . deemed that the city intended to go into the matter of harbor development and build at once five piers, for the reason that we want to see how the first pier will be taken up by the steamboat companies and used."[93] Although Congress did not ask Skinner to provide documentation to corroborate his testimony, it was readily available. Two years earlier, the Harbor and Subway Commission sent a report to the city council announcing that it had plans for the "gradual development" of the outer harbor.[94] Congress dismissed Cahill's allegations and opened the federal government's coffers to fund the breakwater.

Although Cahill could not muster compelling evidence to substantiate his charge that the railroads had forced their agenda on the city, his charges were not implausible. After all, the railroads did have a motive to stamp out waterborne commerce. Moreover, several railroads had devised rate structures aimed at smiting their competitors on the lakes. Given the recent history of the Illinois Central Railroad litigation, it would not have been a far stretch to assume that a legislative body conspired with the railroads to shape the course of Chicago's lakefront development. Cahill's testimony shows too that the suspicion of the power of the railroads, so common in the rhetoric of contemporary farmers and laborers, carried over to segments of Chicago's business class. Chicago's businessmen were divided on the best uses for Municipal Pier. There is, however, no evidence to suggest that railroad corporations took action to make the pier into a pleasure park. Nonetheless, the fears of Cahill's clients were confirmed. The city of Chicago never carried out its plans to build additional piers. Demand for shipping facilities at the pier never warranted further harbor development.[95]

Municipal Pier became far more valuable to the city as a leisure grounds than it ever was as a freight terminal. In 1917, the organization charged with the administration of the pier, the Department of Public Works, noted in its annual report that boat traffic at the pier fell short of what city officials had expected.[96] Several factors likely contributed to this condition. Adequate rail connections between the pier and points in the city's central business district were lacking. Shippers had to either truck their cargo off the pier or use the Chicago and Northwestern Railroad, the only railroad well-positioned to handle freight going to or from the pier. The rise of the trucking industry led to a decline in the number of goods and, in particular, the amount of package freight that businessmen sent via ship.[97] Further, railroads continued to attract much of the package freight business. Lake boats bound for the Chicago region mainly carried bulk industrial and agricultural commodities to industrial complexes along the banks of the Calumet, in Gary, and Indiana Harbor. During each of the first ten years after the pier opened, the Chicago region's ports handled between eleven and twenty million tons of cargo. Yet in the middle 1920s, Municipal Pier attracted only a tiny fraction of the total.[98] For the pier cargo totals in 1926 and 1927, see Table 14.

Although the Chicago Harbor Commission and Foell's Committee on Harbors suggested that municipal piers would revive the city's waterborne commerce, their theories never bore fruit. Their logic was not wrong. Public piers could make harbor access routine and inexpensive. Technological, economic, and environmental transformations, however, ultimately undermined their basic assumptions. Competition from railroads continued to squeeze lake shipping lines. More importantly, cars and trucks were increasingly used to transport passengers and consumer items that might be sold in Chicago's department stores. Lake lines, in contrast, were primarily used to ship very heavy bulk commodities like iron ore and concrete, which Municipal Pier was not designed to handle.

The city of Chicago, moreover, never built a substantial, new industrial harbor. Instead, the Calumet River and the harbors of Northwest Indiana became, and remain, the Chicago region's key industrial ports.

The Harbor Commission and Foell's Committee on Harbors were not mis-

Table 14. Freight, Passengers, and Cars Handled on Navy Pier, 1926–1927

Year	Freight in Tons	Passengers	Cars
1926	309,177	472,251	19,546
1927	346,319	393,012	17,470

Source: Chicago Department of Public Works, 1927 Annual Report, 245–247.

taken about the economic value of a public pier. It did stimulate commerce—
but not the type of commerce that the City Council and the Harbor
Commission had anticipated. Instead, it advanced the goals that Burnham
and the Chicago Commercial Club had outlined for the waterfront—a site of
beauty, tourism, and leisure. In 1917, an estimated 3.5 million people visited the
pier, mostly to sightsee, dance, listen to music, watch theatre, eat, take a pleasure boat ride, enjoy lake views, or attend a festival.[99]

The city of Chicago argued that Municipal Pier created a sort of cultural
safe harbor for the family, a port without drunken, carousing sailors. It was
part of a larger project—conceived and carried out through collaboration between the public and private sectors—that stretched back to the park movement of the 1860s, the Columbian Exposition of 1893 and Burnham's 1909
Plan of Chicago. It aimed to use public works both to promote economic development and dampen class conflict. As such, the pier was a tool designed to
influence behavior. A 1918 tourist pamphlet, titled "Spend Your Vacation on
the $5,000,000 Municipal Pier," boasted that the Municipal Pier "is shaping
the tastes of the multitudes and teaching many how to spend their leisure
profitably."

By advertising the "profitable" uses of leisure time, the pamphlet implied
that the pier would divert people's attentions from supposedly less construc-
tive pastimes like drinking in ethnic saloons.[100] In a city where more than a
third of its residents had been born abroad, it could also promote unity.[101] As
the pamphlet put it, the pier's "beauty of situation and holiday attraction
draw thousands of citizens in the making. Men, women, and children, old
persons alike, everybody and anybody are welcome at the Municipal Pier."[102]

The popularity of Municipal Pier highlighted the broader transformation
of the downtown lakeshore and riverfront from a site of industry to one of
tourism and leisure. It was just as Burnham had suggested. Beauty had an
economic utility. This was especially true in the case of Chicago's downtown
waterfront in the early twentieth century. Even though Chicago was, at the
time, a vibrant industrial city, there were few other ways to profit from that
landscape than to decorate it with beautiful public spaces and to hope that
tourists would come. As it turned out, that strategy devised by Burnham
would have particular relevance to the business and political leaders of dein-
dustrialized cities one hundred years later.

A Waterscape for the New Millennium

In 2005, the *Chicago Tribune* reported that the city's lakefront was experiencing something called the "Bilbao effect." The newspaper's Pulitzer Prize–winning architecture critic, Blair Kamin, noted that the phrase gained currency after 1997, when renowned architect Frank Gehry unveiled his Guggenheim Museum building in the old industrial city of Bilbao, Spain. The term, Kamin explained, describes how "a dazzling avant-garde work of architecture could instantly warm a city's artistic and business climates, attract tourists by the plane load and turn a forgotten industrial . . . [landscape] into a world cultural mecca." By 2005, Kamin suggested, a similar transformation had occurred in Chicago, a "Millennium Park effect." In the place of an unsightly rail yard that once flanked tracks leading to grain elevators perched at the mouth of the Chicago River, the city had created a "joyful postindustrial playground" that stands as a "sparkling example . . . of how big cities can get big things done." [1]

The park, though, was not as novel as Kamin suggested. It was a recent iteration of an older strategy—making public and private investments in infrastructure and parks to spur economic development.

Nearly a century before Millennium Park, urban planner Daniel Burnham convinced Chicagoans to accept a central tenet of his 1909 *Plan of Chicago*: "Beauty pays better than any other commodity." [2] Beautiful landscapes, the planner reasoned, would bring tourists to Chicago and make it a pleasant place to live and do business. Powerful Chicagoans concurred. In just a few decades after 1909, city leaders adorned Chicago's waterfront with a grand boulevard, known as Wacker Drive; a beautiful string of lakeshore parks, lagoons, and pleasure-boat harbors; a stunning museum campus containing the Field Museum, Shedd Aquarium, and Adler Planetarium; the colossal Soldier Field; scenic Lake Shore Drive; and the massive Navy Pier.

One hundred years later, Burnham's call to beautify the lakeshore still echoed in the Chicago of Mayor Richard M. Daley (1989–2011), who banked on beauty as a replacement for the last vestige of nineteenth-century industry on the downtown waterfront.

In the 1990s, the Illinois Central Railroad still clung to a prime piece of land that it had supposedly purchased from the city in the mid-nineteenth century. The Illinois Central had long used the space at the corner of Michigan Avenue and Randolph Street as a train yard, but by the 1990s it was a parking lot. Vexed by the eyesore wedged between beautiful Grant Park and the wall of soaring towers lining Michigan Avenue, Mayor Daley ordered his staff to see if the city could acquire the land. In 1996, Chicago Park District counsel Randy Mehrberg discovered that the city had not relinquished title to the land in the nineteenth century, only granted the railroad an easement to use it for "railroad purposes." Mehrberg pressed the Illinois Central into ceding its claims to the property in 1997. Daley soon announced his intention to build Millennium Park.[3]

Millennium Park signaled Daley's commitment to what might be called green-space economic development. It involved transforming public spaces into sites of natural beauty, ecological sustainability, and leisure. Daley's logic was strikingly similar to that of the nineteenth-century park builder Frederick Law Olmsted and leaders of the early twentieth-century City Beautiful Movement like Burnham. The economy had changed, though. Olmsted and Burnham saw beauty as a means to mitigate the harsh social and environmental effects of the Industrial Revolution. Mayor Daley saw beauty and leisure as an economic strategy for a postindustrial city.

When Daley became mayor in the 1980s, Chicago was losing industry. The city's locational advantages—along railroads and waterways—were being steadily undermined by new technologies and economic policies. Transportation had become easier with the advent of containerized shipping, flight, interstate highways, and gushers of cheap oil. Communications had become faster with faxes, email, and the Internet. Political leaders like President Bill Clinton, meanwhile, dismantled tariffs and other barriers to global trade. By the end of the century, manufacturers could, and largely did, produce goods from the lowest-cost, least regulated corners of globe.[4]

Many companies shuttered their Chicagoland plants during the 1980s and 1990s, sometimes abandoning locations on the city's waterways. U.S. Steel's South Works offers a case in point. The facility that became the South Works originated on the north branch of the Chicago River in 1857 as the

North Chicago Rolling Mill Company. The company shifted production to a new plant along the Calumet River during the 1880s, and U.S. Steel took that plant over in 1901. U.S. Steel developed that plant—the South Works—over the first two thirds of the century. By the 1970s, the massive steel mill occupied 575 acres at the mouth of the Calumet where it received boatloads of ore, coke, and limestone destined for its blast furnaces. Ten thousand workers labored in the plant, producing steel and iron for bridges and skyscrapers including Chicago's Sears Tower. Over the 1980s and 1990s, though, U.S. Steel reduced the workforce at the South Works to just seven hundred before closing the plant in 1992.[5] Sadly, the story of South Works was not unique.

Chicago bled manufacturing jobs throughout the 1980s, sparking an economic crisis and raising questions about the city's future. Iconic companies shut plants, including Nabisco, Campbell Soup Company, Beatrice Foods, Schwinn & Co., Sunbeam, General Mills, and Swift & Co. The job losses were staggering. In 1979, there were slightly under a million manufacturing jobs in the metropolitan region; within just seven years it lost 37 percent of those jobs.[6] The *Chicago Tribune* lamented in a May 1981 editorial that the city "is losing the industry that was its original reason for existing and has found nothing to replace it." Chicago was, the paper announced in a front-page headline, a "City on the Brink."[7]

The decline of manufacturing in Chicago and other cities that once touted their locational advantages raised doubts about the significance of place in the global economy. As more and more corporations began to operate across ever-greater distances, some economic pundits concluded that physical space no longer mattered. Frances Cairncross of the *Economist* declared "the death of distance," and Thomas Friedman of the *New York Times* claimed "you can innovate without having to emigrate."[8]

If space no longer mattered for manufacturing, it nonetheless remained crucial to Daley's strategy for responding to Chicago's industrial decline. The mayor invested little in resurrecting industry, but, instead, tried to promote Chicago as a center of tourism, corporate services, finance, and real estate. To achieve this goal, he sought to create urban spaces that were easily accessible and beautiful. Daley prioritized green space and transportation. Air traffic clogged terminals and runways at O'Hare International Airport in the 1990s, just as boat congestion had stymied travel on the Chicago River in the 1890s. In 2001, Daley launched an ambitious airport expansion and modernization project. Meanwhile, the mayor was already cultivating beauty in public spaces. His administration created a rooftop garden on City Hall; built or restored fifty-five school parks between 1997 and 1999; planted approximately three hundred thousand trees from 1989 to 2002; lined city streets with shrubs and flowers; and constructed sixty-three miles of new median plantings by 2003. In the middle of one night in March 2003, Daley's workers secretly bulldozed the runway of a small airport, Meigs Field, located on Northerly Island. The mayor had decided to convert the island into a ninety-one-acre nature park.[9]

Daley, like Burnham, focused on making a tourist attraction out of the city's greatest natural resource—its lakeshore. In 1995, the city of Chicago renovated Navy Pier. The redesign garnered little critical acclaim, but it nonetheless attracted millions of tourists. Thus, in 2006, the *Economist* quipped that the "excruciatingly humdrum collection of attractions" should offer other postindustrial cities great hope. "If a ferris wheel and a putting green on stilts can draw twice as many visitors each year as the Grand Canyon," the magazine continued, "the possibilities for Detroit should be boundless."[10]

In 2004, Daley replaced the abandoned Illinois Central railyard with the stunning Millennium Park. The mayor paid for the park as much of the city's infrastructure had been developed—with funding from taxpayers and private investors alike. To entice private donors to pick up part of the $490 million price tag, Daley promised to emblazon their family names and brands on the park.[11] Millennium Park thus features the McCormick Tribune Ice-Rink and Park Grill; Wrigley Square; the BP Pedestrian bridge; the Lurie Gardens; the towering, electronic Crown Fountain; a stunning metal sculpture called *Cloud Gate,* which sits amid AT&T Plaza; and star architect Gehry's futuristic contribution to the Chicago lakefront, the Jay Pritzker Pavilion.[12]

The grand park built, in part, with corporate dollars reflected Chicago's centripetal position in the global economy at the dawn of the millennium. Chicago had lost its industry, but its location, infrastructure, and green spaces still mattered for business. Daley's Chicago—with its airports, lakeshore convention center, and beautiful shoreline parks—had become a critical site for tourism, futures and options trading, and management consulting. Underscoring the city's economic centrality, in 2001 Boeing moved its corporate headquarters from Seattle to a skyscraper along the Chicago River. Chicago had not withered; it was, in the words of a 2006 feature in the *Economist*, "buzzing with life, humming with prosperity, sparkling with new buildings, new sculptures, new parks, and generally exuding vitality."[13]

Chicago had gained a position at the top of an emerging hierarchy of global cities. Even as pundits like Cairncross and Friedman had argued that place would cease to matter in the age of the Internet, the population of a se-lect number of urban mega-regions swelled. A famous 2008 study by sociol-ogist Richard Florida showed, moreover, that just a handful of cities produced the vast majority of wealth and innovation in the world. According to Florida and another leading urban sociologist, Saskia Sassen, Chicago ranked among that elite group of "global cities" where educated people, money, and innova-tors clustered.[14] People did have to emigrate to innovate, it turned out.[15]

Mayor Daley had shrewdly invested in the urban landscape, recognizing that investment in infrastructure and green space would spark economic de-velopment. Not all Chicagoans benefitted from his projects, though. While Daley lavished attention and resources on downtown Chicago, terrible vio-lence and economic desperation devastated many neighborhoods whose economic fortunes had once been buoyed by the manufacturing sector. Daley could have invested heavily in those struggling neighborhoods, but he did not. Critics charged that this was not an oversight, and that the mayor's poli-cies were largely tailored for the elite.[16] Capital and privileged people could go anywhere in the world. Daley, it seems, wagered that landscapes with beauty, leisure, and culture would make them come to Chicago. In this way, government investment in public space and infrastructure were critical to the urban economy at the start of the new millennium.

The construction of Millennium Park mimicked a much older economic development strategy. Since Chicago's founding in the 1830s, politicians and private investors have collaborated to create new infrastructure and public space on the waterfront to facilitate profit-making. In so doing, they trans-formed Chicago's waterscape from a disease-infested swamp into an asset for moneymaking—into a form of liquid capital.

From the beginning of the city's history, public officials and private inves-tors collaborated to engineer a waterscape conducive to economic develop-ment. Antebellum politicians recognized the commercial potential of the Chicago portage that had been used by Indians and French explorers for cen-turies. The keys to tapping the site's commercial potential were making the Chicago River into a viable harbor and building a canal to connect the Great Lakes and Mississippi River watersheds. Who would pay for expensive canal and harbor infrastructure at the site of a tiny settlement, though? This ques-tion was the subject of a broader national debate over whether the states or the federal government had authority and the responsibility to pay for inter-nal improvements. The debate echoed through the streets of Chicago during July of 1847 when the city hosted the Chicago River and Harbor Convention.

Whig delegates like newspaperman Horace Greeley called for generous federal appropriations to transform western waterways, opening them up to
new commercial possibilities, in cities like Chicago. Jacksonian Democrats
like the powerful New York attorney David Dudley Field, meanwhile, opposed federal spending that took money from one region and spent it in
another.

Even as many Chicagoans cheered Greeley's call for federal funding for
river and harbor improvements, they hesitated to redistribute tax dollars just
across town. Consequently, state and city politicians crafted hybrid public-
private funding schemes to build new infrastructure. The state of Illinois sold
canal lands and issued bonds to New York investors to finance the Illinois
and Michigan Canal. The city of Chicago, in turn, raised money for improvements by levying special tax assessments on the people whose property
abutted improvements, and by leasing riverfront spaces to those who would
develop wharves. The Army Corps of Engineers, meanwhile, spent federal
tax dollars on dredging the sandbar at the mouth of the Chicago River.
Through their collaborations, these governmental leaders and private investors built a viable harbor and constructed a canal connecting Chicago to the
Atlantic Ocean and the Gulf of Mexico. These feats of engineering created
amazing new commercial possibilities for the city; but, they also created new,
unforeseen problems, including the erosion of the valuable Chicago
lakeshore.

After the Army Corps of Engineers dredged a channel through the sandbar at the mouth of the Chicago River in the 1830s, Lake Michigan's currents
began to hit the shoreline more directly and with greater velocity. Those currents eroded the city's lakefront south of the river's mouth, threatening many
homes of the city's elite. City officials, in turn, collaborated with private investors to address the challenge of shoreline erosion. The Illinois Central Railroad agreed to build an expensive, protective breakwater in exchange for a
right of way along Chicago's lakefront. The railroad soon expanded its claims
on the lakeshore. In 1869, the Illinois Central secured a grant from the state
legislature to take ownership of the downtown lakefront.

As Chicago became an increasingly significant port, some politicians and
business leaders grew wary of private ownership of the waterfront. The Illinois
Central Railroad had a virtual monopoly on the city's lakefront. The riverbanks, meanwhile, had come under the control of a cartel of grain elevator operators who fixed storage rates and harbored secret and valuable information
about grain supplies. To break these monopolies, state legislators worked with

farmers and businessmen at Chicago's Board of Trade to pass laws designating critical waterfront spaces "public"—and thus accessible to anyone who relied on them to make money. The Illinois Central Railroad and Chicago's grain elevator operators, in turn, challenged the state's designation of the lakeshore and riverside elevators as "public" property in two landmark Supreme Court cases, *Munn v. Illinois* (1877) and *Illinois Central v. Illinois* (1892). In both cases, the court held that certain, strategically located harbor lands and infrastructure must be publicly owned and regulated to ensure that everyone could gain access to the waterfront to make a profit.[17]

Government leaders also promoted economic development by managing the day-to-day spatial, environmental, and economic conflicts over the use of the Chicago River. By the 1870s, the river had become one of the world's busiest harbors. Each year, tens of thousands of ships clogged its channel, shuttling cargoes to and from the businesses that lined the Chicago's banks and sparking conflict. Overland and river travelers competed for rights of way over and under bridges. Business leaders and citizens who wished to fill the river channel with waste angered vessel operators who wanted to keep the channel clear for navigation. The city of Chicago eased these tensions by regulating bridge openings, dredging the river, and building underground tunnels for passengers and streetcars.

City leaders, however, could not manage the spatial conflicts arising from the increasing use of iron and steel steamships on the Great Lakes during the 1880s and 1890s. Larger ships could barely squeeze past the city's bridges. Their hulls got stuck in the waste that collected on the bottom of the river, and they got caught on the tops of streetcar tunnels. City officials could not remove these barriers to shipping without angering polluters, bridge users, and streetcar companies.

Federal officials, though, stepped in to orchestrate a solution. With appropriations from Congress, the Army Corps of Engineers helped establish a new, industrial harbor along the Calumet River on Chicago's southeast side, which became a new center of the growing steel and iron industry. By 1906, the Calumet River handled greater tonnage than the Chicago, signaling the movement of industrial shipping from the city center to its periphery and creating new possibilities for a leisure-centered waterfront.

At the turn of the twentieth century, business leaders collaborated with city officials to transform the Chicago waterfront from an industrial site into one of beauty, tourism, and leisure. Powerful figures from the city's Commercial Club, like architect and planner Burnham, argued that creating beautiful public spaces on the lakeshore and riverbanks would promote tourism and foster social harmony in a city ravaged by bloody class conflicts at sites like Haymarket Square and Pullman. Drawing inspiration from the nineteenth-century parks movement and the 1893 World's Fair, Burnham and the Commercial Club drafted a blueprint for the beautification of the entire city, the 1909 *Plan of Chicago*. Burnham's plan called on city officials to build a grand boulevard on the riverbank and construct parks, piers, and civic monuments along a long stretch of the Lake Michigan shoreline. In so doing, it raised a key question: Were beautiful, tourist-friendly shoreline parks and waterborne commerce compatible?[18]

The city of Chicago addressed that question by constructing the massive, publically owned Municipal Pier. In 1908, Chicago Mayor Fred Busse worried about the economic effects of beautifying the lakeshore at a time when the city's port traffic was dwindling. He assembled a group of the nation's foremost engineers and experts on harbors, known collectively as the Chicago Harbor Commission, to examine how the city could maintain or perhaps improve its position as one of the world's leading ports. The commission counseled the city to create public dock facilities to promote shipping and spur tourism alike.

The city of Chicago completed Municipal Pier in 1916. With the continued growth of the Calumet River harbor and persistent competition from railroads and trucks, waterborne commerce dwindled. Municipal Pier, in turn, became a crucial site for leisure and tourism for the rest of the century. At the close of the twentieth century, Municipal Pier—since renamed Navy Pier—was among the city's biggest tourist attractions, drawing between 3.5 and 4 million visitors per year.[19]

From the time of the construction of the Illinois and Michigan Canal, to the completion of Navy Pier, and, more recently, the creation of Millennium Park, government leaders collaborated with private business leaders to move earth and water and establish regulations to ensure that the city's waterscape would facilitate profit-making.

Politicians and business leaders have consistently determined, moreover, that the waterfront be comprised of public space. Their vision of a public waterfront was informed, in part, by altruism. At the same time, many of Chicago's political and economic elite have also regarded public space as a means to further their economic agendas—as a means of making resources accessible to business, spurring tourism, and fostering social harmony.

Today, the word "public" often has populist overtones, implying, in the positive sense, a thing that is good, inclusive, and not-for-profit. In the worst sense, public has become synonymous with governmental inefficiency. In any case, these meanings of the word "public" stand in stark opposition to the supposedly efficient, sometimes cutthroat private marketplace. The history of Chicago's waterfront, though, suggests the lines between public spaces and private markets bled, and still bleed, into one another. Public and private agendas hence often remain symbiotic and inseparable.

Business and political leaders usually regarded Chicago's public space with an instrumental, money-making logic, but their actions had other, unintended consequences. The act of creating "public" places or establishing "public" powers unleashed forces businesspeople could not control, a Pandora's Box. Throughout the twentieth century, legislators, environmentalists, and citizens alike imbued the public powers and spaces established on Chicago's waterfront with new meanings, some of which were surprisingly democratic.

The Supreme Court's ruling in *Munn v. Illinois* (1877), for example, led to a dramatic expansion in the power of state legislatures to regulate American business.[20] Chief Justice Morrison Waite's ruling created a new basis for regulation, extending state powers beyond passing nuisance laws and establishing terms of operation in corporations' charters. After *Munn*, a state legislature—a democratically elected body—could enact statutes regulating the practices of a business deemed to be "affected with a public interest."[21] The Supreme Court often applied "affectation doctrine" in cases dealing with transportation. In two cases during the 1890s, for instance, the court upheld laws in North Dakota and New York that set maximum rates for grain handling at elevators, aboard ocean liners, and on canal boats.[22] The Supreme Court sometimes cited the affectation doctrine to validate regulations in other industries, as it did in *German Alliance Insurance Co. v. Lewis* (1914). The court held the state of Kansas could set maximum fire insurance rates because they were a matter of public concern.[23]

The court's broader application of this doctrine begged the question: How would jurists determine which industries were affected with a public interest—and which were not? In a 1934 case concerning the constitutionality of regulations on the price of milk, the court stopped trying to make that distinction, abandoning the "affectation doctrine." In *Nebbia v. New York* (1934), the justices held that state legislatures could use their police powers to intervene in the economy when it was deemed crucial to the public welfare.[24] Elected officials thus gained even greater authority to regulate business than they had from Waite's ruling in *Munn*.

Justice Stephen Field's ruling in *Illinois Central v. Illinois* (1892) had unforeseen implications for the environmental movement. The arch conservative Field invoked the "public trust doctrine" to break the railroad's monopoly
on the Chicago harbor. He reasoned that the city of Chicago would use its
power to build a harbor. As legal scholar Joseph L. Sax has noted, Field's ruling has become "the lodestar in American public trust law." Field's instrumental use of the public trust doctrine has had, ironically, a distinctly
antidevelopmental legacy. Twentieth-century environmentalists have successfully argued that if the state must hold certain lands and waterways in
trust for the public, it must also protect their ecological condition.[25]

The case of California's Mono Lake provides a vivid example of the public
trust doctrine's environmental ramifications. Situated just north of the Owens
River Valley in the Sierra Nevada Mountains, Mono Lake is one of the world's
rare alkaline lakes. It is so distinct from most earthly landscapes that NASA
scientists have even used it as a staging ground for experiments to determine
if life is possible on Mars.[26] Mono Lake teems with wildlife, including rare
shrimp and birds that were put in jeopardy beginning in 1941, when the city
of Los Angeles began diverting water from streams that fed the lake to the
Owens Valley Aqueduct. Los Angeles's diversions slowly reduced the area of
Mono Lake by twenty-seven square miles. In the 1980s, an environmental
group named the Mono Lake Committee and the Audubon Society invoked
the public trust doctrine as a basis to prevent Los Angeles from entirely
draining the lake, as it had nearby Owens Lake. In 1994, after years of litigation, the California Water Resources Control Board issued an order to protect Mono Lake and its tributaries by reducing Los Angeles's diversions.
Water levels have subsequently risen.[27]

Urban environments, too, have been affected by Field's ruling in *Illinois
Central*. When Field confirmed Chicago's rights to the lakeshore, he empowered the city to build key features of Burnham's 1909 *Plan of Chicago*, including shoreline museums, lagoons, and parks. The success of Burnham's
masterpiece has inspired urban planners, notably those seeking to establish
cultural hegemony. Edwin Luyten and Albert Speer drew on Burnham's use
of monuments and grand, symmetrical structures in their designs for British
Imperial New Delhi and Nazi Berlin.[28] Critics like Lewis Mumford have been
quick to deride Burnham's plan for its compatibility with the aims of industrial capitalists, imperialists, and fascists.[29]

Cultural hegemony certainly ranked among the aims of the supporters of
the *Plan of Chicago*, but Burnham's *Plan* was more democratic than Mumford

allowed. While Burnham was trying to create an inclusive, if hegemonic, landscape, political leaders in other places were driving the underclass and racial minorities out of public places altogether. Whites in southern states, for example, forced physical segregation on African Americans. Burnham's vision of people from all classes and ethnicities congregating in the same spaces looks even more democratic in light of trends in the middle of the twentieth century, when many Americans moved to racially and economically exclusive suburbs that lacked any public space.[30] The public places that Burnham created, meanwhile, remain critical sites of democratic protest and celebration. Grant Park was a key rallying place for both opponents of the Vietnam War in 1968 and supporters of President Barack Obama in 2008.

The economic fortunes of Chicago are still tied to its waterscape and to the answers to several looming questions: Should the barrier between the Great Lakes and the Mississippi River watersheds—the one that canal builders traversed in 1848—be restored to protect the Great Lakes from invasive species? Can the city spur real estate development and lure tourists by building additional parks, boathouses, bike trails, and other amenities along the Chicago River? What are the future industrial uses of Chicago's watershed? Does industrial pollution pose a critical threat to leisure, tourism, and the health of the water supply? And, what do climate change and the increasing global scarcity of fresh water mean for Chicago?

These questions are just the latest environmental dilemmas to confront the residents of a city whose history is one long, continuous struggle to mold and exploit an ever-changing waterscape. That waterscape is a product of the past, a canvas layered with the brush strokes of human engineering and their unforeseen consequences. It is also—as it has always been—key to the city's future.

NOTES

—

Introduction

1. Bessie Louise Pierce, *A History of Chicago: The Beginning of a City, 1673–1848*, vol. 1 (Chicago: University of Chicago Press, 1937), 3–5. During some very wet seasons, it would have been possible to cross the portage by boat. Major S. H. Long reported in 1823 that the portage was usually between four and nine miles long. See Long, cited in Alfred Theodore Andreas, *History of Chicago from the Earliest Period to the Present Time*, vol. 1 (Chicago: A. T. Andreas, 1884), 166.

2. During the Wisconsin Glacial Episode, from 110,000 to 10,000 years ago, great sheets of ice created a series of moraines, or glacially formed accumulations of sediment, across what is now the Chicago region. The ridge that formed the divide between the Great Lakes and Mississippi watersheds was part of a moraine at the very edge of a large glacier (William Cronon, *Nature's Metropolis: Chicago and the Great West* [New York: Norton, 1991], 24; Joel Greenberg, *A Natural History of the Chicago Region* [Chicago: University of Chicago Press, 2002], 1–8; Libby Hill, *The Chicago River: A Natural and Unnatural History* [Chicago: Lake Claremont Press, 2000], 12; David M. Solzman, *The Chicago River: An Illustrated History and Guide to the River and Its Waterways*, 2nd ed. [Chicago: University of Chicago Press, 2006], 6).

3. Hill, *The Chicago River*, 13.

4. Ibid., 121.

5. On the Indians living in the Chicago region before 1833 see Ann Durkin Keating, *Rising Up From Indian Country: The Battle of Fort Dearborn and the Birth of Chicago* (Chicago: University of Chicago Press, 2012), introduction, passim.

6. Chicago grew from approximately 350 residents in 1833 to 3,376,438 in 1930 (Hill, *The Chicago River*, 121).

7. Norman Mailer, *Miami and the Siege of Chicago: An Informal History of the Republican and Democratic Conventions of 1968* (New York: World Publishing Company, 1968), 90.

8. This discussion of the debate over planning in Chicago history is based on Carl Smith, *The Plan of Chicago: Daniel Burnham and the Remaking of the American City* (Chicago: University of Chicago Press, 2006), 5.

9. William Bross, *Chicago and the Sources of Her Past and Future Growth* (Chicago: Jansen, McClurg, 1880), 3.

10. J. Paul Goode, "Chicago: A City of Destiny," Lecture to the Geographical Society of Chicago, Chicago, Illinois, 1923.

11. Cronon, *Nature's Metropolis*.

12. Harold Mayer, "Chicago: City of Decisions," Lecture to the Geographical Society of Chicago, Chicago, Illinois, 1955.

13. Harold M. Mayer and Richard C. Wade, *Chicago: Growth of a Metropolis* (Chicago: University of Chicago Press, 1969); Harold L. Platt, *Shock Cities: The Environmental Transformation and Reform of Manchester and Chicago* (Chicago: University of Chicago Press, 2005); Louis P. Cain, *Sanitation Strategy for a Lakefront Metropolis: The Case of Chicago* (DeKalb: Northern Illinois University Press, 1978); and Robert Lewis, *Chicago Made: Factory Networks in the Industrial Metropolis* (Chicago: University of Chicago Press, 2008).

14. Scholars have argued that the power of elites is often predicated on their ability to control water resources, particularly in areas requiring substantial water infrastructure projects. See Karl August Wittfogel, *Oriental Despotism: A Comparative Study of Total Power* (New Haven, Conn.: Yale University Press, 1957); and Donald Worster, *Rivers of Empire: Water, Aridity, and the Growth of the American West* (New York: Oxford University Press, 1985).

15. In the last twenty-five years, environmental historians have increasingly turned their attention from wilderness landscapes to those rigorously managed by humans. Richard White, for instance, has studied the Columbia River, which he calls an "organic machine" in recognition of the fact that it is a creation of both nonhuman nature and human engineering. Geographer Matthew Gandy and writer Robert Gottlieb have argued that cities do not eradicate nature. Rather, humans who build cities rework elements of nature into a new form, a mixture of public space, environmental amenities, and services that they have dubbed "metropolitan nature." Historian Theodore Steinberg has, moreover, studied the role of nature within human economies. Historians such as Colin Fisher, meanwhile, have studied the recreational, social, and cultural uses of urban nature (William Cronon, "The Trouble with Wilderness; or Getting Back to the Wrong Nature," in *Uncommon Ground: Rethinking the Human Place in Nature*, ed. William Cronon [New York: Norton, 1995], 69–90; Colin Fisher, *Urban Green: Nature, Recreation, and the Working Class in Industrial Chicago* [Chapel Hill: University of North Carolina Press, 2015]; Matthew Gandy and Robert Gottlieb, *Concrete and Clay: Reworking Nature in New York City* [Cambridge, Mass.: MIT Press, 2002]; Theodore Steinberg, *Nature Incorporated: Industrialization and the Waters of New England* [New York: Cambridge University Press, 1991]; and Richard White, *The Organic Machine: The Remaking of the Columbia River* [New York: Hill and Wang, 1995]).

16. Munn v. Illinois, 94 U.S. 113 (1877). On *Munn v. Illinois* see Charles Fairman, "The So-Called Granger Cases, Lord Hale, and Justice Bradley," *Stanford Law Review* 5 (1952): 587–679; Walton H. Hamilton, "Affectation with Public Interest," *Yale Law Journal* 39 (1930): 1089–1112; Harry Scheiber, "The Road to Munn: Eminent Domain and the Concept of Public Purpose in the State Courts," in *Perspectives in American History*, vol. 5., ed. Donald Fleming and Bernard Bailyn (Cambridge, Mass.: Charles Warren Center for Studies in American History at Harvard University, 1971), 327–402.

17. Illinois Central Railroad v. Illinois, 146 U.S. 387 (1892). Environmentalists in the 1980s used the public trust doctrine to help stop the city of Los Angeles from draining the waters of Mono Lake, a unique wildlife habitat in the Sierra Nevada Mountains. See John Hart, *Storm Over Mono: The Mono Lake Battle and the California Water Future* (Berkley: University of California Press, 1996); Gary D. Liebcap, *Owens Valley Revisited: A Reassessment of the West's First Great Water Transfer* (Palo Alto, Calif.: Stanford University Press, 2007), 132–154.

18. Daniel H. Burnham and Edward H. Bennett, *Plan of Chicago* (Chicago: Commercial Club of Chicago, 1909). On the significance of the plan, see Peter Hall, *Cities of Tomorrow: An Intellectual History of Urban Planning and Design in the Twentieth Century*, 3rd ed. (Malden, Mass.: Blackwell Publishing, 2003).

19. This characterization of historians' interpretations of American political development is informed by Brian Balogh's 2009 study, *A Government Out of Sight*. Balogh contends that one of the most resilient myths in American history is that the state was weak in the nineteenth century and grew larger and stronger only amid bursts of reform, including those associated with the Progressive Era, the New Deal, and the Great Society. He contends that this powerful interpretation originated in the works of progressive historians like Charles Beard and was amplified by prominent twentieth-century historians, including Arthur M. Schlesinger Jr. Balogh notes, further, that many contemporary liberals and conservatives alike tend to agree with this view of state development. They differ, though, in their assessment of it. Conservatives often seek a return to what they view as an era of unregulated, laissez faire capitalism, whereas modern liberals point to the late nineteenth century as a model of markets run amok. Historian William Novak, meanwhile, has observed that the myth of the weak American state persists in some of the prominent historical writing of the twenty-first century. In many instances, Novak notes, the history of the American state is told as one of "relative powerlessness—a usually benign tale of legal-political self-abnegation, emphasizing constitutional restraints such as federalism, checks and balances, the separation of powers, limited government, the rule of law, and laissez faire." In the positive sense, Novak argues, the story of American history is framed as a quest for freedom from slavery and the rise of political, civil, and economic rights. In those narratives, "property, contract, and freedom of speech, press, and association form the constitutional backbone of a free market, a vigorous civil society, and a democratic polity—hallmarks of a free people." These narratives, thus, emphasize limitations of the state, rather than its powers—even as the nation conquered North America and became, in the twentieth century, a global superpower. See, Brian Balogh, *A Government Out of Sight: The Mystery of National Authority in Nineteenth Century America* (New York: Cambridge University Press, 2009), 1–2; William J. Novak, "The Myth of the 'Weak' American State," *The American Historical Review* 113, 3 (June 2008): 752–772, quotes from 752. Some notable works about American history as a story of the expansion of individual freedoms include Eric Foner, *The Story of American Freedom* (New York: Norton, 1999); Sara M. Evans, *Born for Liberty: A History of Women in America* (New York: Free Press, 1997); Melvin I. Urofsky and Paul Finkelman, *A March of Liberty: A Constitutional History of the United States* (New York: Oxford University Press, 2001); David Hackett Fischer, *Liberty and Freedom: A Visual History of America's Founding Ideas* (New York: Oxford University Press, 2004); and David M. Kennedy, *Freedom from Fear: The American People in Depression and War, 1929–1945* (New York: Oxford University Press, 2001).

20. Richard Schneirov, "Thoughts on Periodizing the Gilded Age: Capital Accumulation, Society, and Politics, 1873–1898," *Journal of the Gilded Age and Progressive Era* 5, 3 (July 2006): 194; Rebecca Edwards, *New Spirits: Americans in the Gilded Age, 1865–1905* (New York: Oxford University Press, 2006); and Mark Twain and Charles Dudley Warner, *The Gilded Age: A Tale of Today* (Chicago: American Publishing Company, 1873).

21. For examples of texts that place individuals at the center of the history of industrialization, see Allan Nevins, *Study in Power: John D. Rockefeller, Industrialist and Philanthropist* (New York: Scribner, 1959) and Matthew Josephson, *The Robber Barons: The Great American Capitalists, 1861–1901* (New York: Harcourt, Brace and Company, 1934). The work of Alfred Chandler helped shift business historians' emphasis from individuals to firms (Alfred D. Chandler, *Strategy and Structure: Chapters in the History of the American Industrial Enterprise* [Frederick, Md.: Beard Books, 1962]; Alfred D. Chandler, *The Visible Hand: The Managerial Revolution in American Business* [Cambridge, Mass.: Harvard University Press, 1977]; and Alfred D. Chandler, *Scale*

and Scope: The Dynamics of Industrial Capitalism [Cambridge, Mass.: Belknap/Harvard University Press, 1990]).

22. Peter B. Evans, Dietrech Rueschemeyer, and Theda Skocpol eds., *Bringing the State Back In* (New York: Cambridge University Press, 1985); Charles Tilly, *Coercion, Capital, and European States AD 990–1990* (Oxford, U.K.: B. Blackwell, 1990); and Stephen Skowronek, *Building a New American State: The Expansion of National Administrative Capacities, 1877–1920* (New York: Cambridge University Press, 1982).

23. There is a fantastic literature on how nineteenth-century policymakers created markets and spurred economic growth. See, for instance, Richard Franklin Bensel, *The Political Economy of American Industrialization, 1877–1900* (New York: Cambridge University Press, 2000); Richard John, *Network Nation: Inventing American Telecommunications* (Cambridge, Mass.: Belknap/Harvard University Press, 2010); Steven Usselman, *Regulating Railroad Innovation: Business, Technology, and Politics in America, 1840–1920* (New York: Cambridge University Press, 2002); Richard White, *"It's Your Misfortune and None of My Own": A History of the American West* (Norman: University of Oklahoma Press, 1991); and Richard White, *Railroaded: The Transcontinentals and the Making of Modern America* (New York: Norton, 2011).

24. William J. Novak suggests that one reason the American state has sometimes been perceived as "weak" is because political leaders have so often used "the private sector to accomplish public objectives" (Novak, "The Myth of the 'Weak' American State," 769). Other examples of fine scholarship on the blurring of lines between public governmental and private economic actors include Balogh, *A Government Out of Sight*; Sven Becket, *Empire of Cotton: A Global History* (New York: Knopf, 2014); and Hendrik Hartog, *Public Property and Private Power: The Corporation of the City of New York in American Law, 1730–1870* (Ithaca, N.Y.: Cornell University Press, 1983).

25. Carl Sandburg, "Chicago," in *Carl Sandburg: Selected Poems* (New York: Random House, 1992), 17. Sandburg originally published "Chicago" in March 1914 in *Poetry*.

Chapter 1

1. The Frenchmen had paddled from St. Ignac in what is now Michigan to the site of Green Bay, Wisconsin, ascended the Fox River, and portaged to the Wisconsin River, a tributary of the Mississippi River that they explored as far south as the mouth of the Arkansas River. On the advice of natives, they returned via a shorter route, ascending the Illinois River, Des Plaines River, and making the portage to the Chicago River, which emptied into Lake Michigan (Bessie Louise Pierce, *A History of Chicago: The Beginning of a City, 1673–1848*, vol. 1 [Chicago: University of Chicago Press, 1937], 3–7).

2. Jolliet lost his maps and journals when his canoe capsized. Consequently, he made only a verbal report to the governor of Quebec. His views on the canal were recorded about a year afterward by Father Claudius Dablon. Dablon quote of Jolliet in Alfred Theodore Andreas, *History of Chicago from the Earliest Period to the Present Time*, vol. 1 (Chicago: A. T. Andreas, 1884), 165.

3. La Salle quoted in Donald Miller, *City of the Century: The Epic of Chicago and the Making of America* (New York: Simon and Schuster, 1996), 46.

4. La Salle letter to Louis de Buade de Frontenac partially reprinted in Andreas, *History of Chicago*, 64.

5. Milo Quaife, *Chicago and the Old Northwest, 1673–1835* (Chicago: University of Illinois Press, 2001, originally published in 1913), 2–7, 31; John Reda, "Joining the Union: Land, Race,

and Sovereignty in the Illinois Country, 1763–1825" (Ph.D., dissertation, University of Illinois at Chicago, 2009), 22–33.

6. On the imperial history of the Illinois Country see Ann Durkin Keating, *Rising Up From Indian Country: The Battle of Fort Dearborn and the Birth of Chicago* (Chicago: University of Chicago Press, 2012) and John Reda, *From Furs to Farms: The Transformation of the Mississippi Valley, 1763–1825* (DeKalb: Northern Illinois University Press, 2016).

7. Pierce, *A History of Chicago*, 12–13.

8. Keating, *Rising Up From Indian Country*, chap. 2, passim, and 54–56.

9. Ibid., 1. For more about the Black Hawk War and the complex relationship between the federal government and the various American Indian groups of the Great Lakes and Upper Mississippi River Valley, see John Hall, *Uncommon Defense: Indian Allies and the Blackhawk War* (Cambridge, Mass.: Harvard University Press, 2009) and Quaife, *Chicago and the Old Northwest*.

10. The region's native population also lost British military and financial support after the war ended in 1814, leaving them alone to resist increasingly hostile white Americans (Keating, *Rising Up From Indian Country*, 197–198).

11. Reda, *From Furs to Farms*.

12. Keating, *Rising Up From Indian Country*, 226–234; Robert G. Spinney, *City of Big Shoulders: A History of Chicago* (DeKalb: Northern Illinois University Press, 2000), 26–29.

13. Jeffrey Adler, *Yankee Merchants and the Making of the Urban West: The Rise and Fall of St. Louis* (New York: Cambridge University Press, 1991), 132; Spinney, *City of Big Shoulders*, 31–32.

14. James E. Davis, *Frontier Illinois: A History of the Trans-Appalachian Frontier* (Bloomington: Indiana University Press, 1998), 160–162.

15. Andreas, *History of Chicago*, 166.

16. Pope quoted in Davis, *Frontier Illinois*, 160–162.

17. Adler, *Yankee Merchants and the Making of the Urban West*, 142.

18. The canal and lake frontage were not the only reasons Pope asked for a border extension. He also wanted to increase population and gain access to the lead deposits in and around Galena. Pope first asked for a ten-mile border extension on the basis that Congress had done the same for Indiana in 1816, but he later decided to make a more ambitious request for forty miles (Davis, *Frontier Illinois*, 160–162).

19. Andreas, *History of Chicago*, 167; William Cronon, *Nature's Metropolis: Chicago and the Great West* (New York: Norton, 1991), 64.

20. Harold M. Mayer and Richard C. Wade, *Chicago: Growth of a Metropolis* (Chicago: University of Chicago Press, 1969), 12.

21. Spinney, *City of Big Shoulders*, 33–34.

22. Some legislators suggested building a railroad in lieu of a canal (Andreas, *History of Chicago*, 168).

23. Andreas, *History of Chicago*, 167; Cost projections in Libby Hill, *The Chicago River: A Natural and Unnatural History* (Chicago: Lake Claremont Press, 2000), 65.

24. A similar channel was completed between the Calumet River and the Sanitary and Ship Canal in 1922. It is called the "Cal-Sag Channel."

25. The quotations are paraphrases of Gurdon S. Hubbard cited in Hill, *The Chicago River*, 65. Hill notes that Hubbard's statements were remembered by the nineteenth-century federal judge Henry W. Blodgett and cited in Caroline M. McIlvaine's introduction to Gurdon Saltonsall

Hubbard, *The Autobiography of Gurdon Saltonsall Hubbard, Pa-pa-ma-ta-be, "The Swift Walker"* (Chicago: R. R. Donnelly & Sons, 1911), xix–xx.

26. Andreas, *History of Chicago*, 168.

27. The railroad would dissect the state, running north from Cairo at the confluence of the Mississippi and Ohio Rivers to Bloomington and the western end of the Illinois and Michigan Canal. From the canal, the Illinois Central would travel northwest to the mining town of Galena on the Mississippi River. The state legislature also planned two east-west railroads, a Northern Cross Railroad from Quincy to Springfield and Indiana and a Southern Cross Railroad from Alton to Shawneetown, as well as several shorter roads to link various towns to the system. Chicago, however, was excluded because its low, wet land would be too hard to drain and the town would have boat connections to the railroad via the Illinois and Michigan Canal (Davis, *Frontier Illinois*, 230–232).

28. John Lauritz Larson, *Internal Improvement: National Public Works and the Promise of Popular Government in the Early United States* (Chapel Hill: University of North Carolina, 2001), 219.

29. Larson, *Internal Improvement*, 201–202, 214–217.

30. When the Illinois and Michigan was completed, two 160-horsepower steam engines pumped seven thousand cubic feet of water per minute out of the south branch of the Chicago River into the canal (Andreas, *History of Chicago*, 170–172).

31. Larson, *Internal Improvement*, 204, 215.

32. William K. Ackerman, *History of the Illinois Central Railroad Company and Representative Employees* (Chicago: Historical Railroad Company, 1900), 27.

33. The city of New York similarly sold access to the waterfront to encourage private parties to develop the harbor. See Hendrik Hartog, *Public Property and Private Power: The Corporation of the City of New York in American Law, 1730–1870* (Ithaca, N.Y.: Cornell University Press, 1983).

34. Andreas, *History of Chicago*, 238–239; Robin L. Einhorn, *Property Rules: Political Economy in Chicago, 1833–1872* (Chicago: University of Chicago Press, 1991), 54–57.

35. Einhorn, *Property Rules*, 40.

36. In 1837, the Illinois Supreme Court ruled that the absence of the city's official seal on leases held by businessman John Kinzie rendered his wharf leases null and void. In 1845, the Common Council Committee on the Judiciary argued that the case set a legal precedent for dealing with abrogated contracts, which presumably lacked the official seal as well (Kinzie v. Chicago, 3 Ill. 188 [1837]); "Report of Committee on Judiciary in Favor of Surrender of Wharfing Leases," January 2, 1845, Chicago City Council Papers, Doc. 2338.

37. The Common Council also requested amendments to the city's charter to enable it to lease wharfing privileges again for a period of ten years at a rate of 4 percent of the assessed value of the riverfront lot ("Order in Relation to Amendments to City Charter and Order in Relation to Wharfing Privileges," December 18, 1846, Chicago City Council Papers, Doc. 3531).

38. Murray Floyd Tuley, *Laws and Ordinances Governing the City of Chicago* (Chicago: Bulletin Printing Company, 1873), 629–630.

39. Andreas, *History of Chicago*, 239.

40. Jesse B. Thomas, *Statistical Report*, in *Chicago River-and-Harbor Convention*, ed. Robert Fergus (Chicago: Fergus Printing Co., 1882), 184.

41. Andreas, *History of Chicago*, 239.

42. Ibid., 198.

43. Ibid., 198.

44. Alderman Henry Rucker, "Report of Committee on Streets and Bridges on the Dearborn Street Bridge," 1838, Chicago City Council Papers, Doc. 501.

45. Andreas, *History of Chicago*, 198; William H. Stow, "Report of Committee on Streets and Bridges in Reference to the Removal of Dearborn Street Bridge," 1839, Chicago City Council Papers, Doc. 735.

46. *Chicago Times* in Andreas, *History of Chicago*, 198.

47. Ira Miltimore, "Report of Committee on Streets and Bridges on Changing Location of Bridge from Clark to Wells Street," April 6, 1840, Chicago City Council Papers, Doc. 944.

48. Einhorn, *Property Rules*, 59.

49. *Chicago Times* in Andreas, *History of Chicago*, 198.

50. "Resolutions for Removal of Clark Street Bridge to Dearborn Street," May 4, 1841, Chicago City Council Papers, Doc. 1159.

51. Andreas, *History of Chicago*, 199; Einhorn, *Property Rules*, 59, 105.

52. Joel Greenberg, *A Natural History of the Chicago Region* (Chicago: University of Chicago Press, 2002), 140.

53. Henry R. Schoolcraft quoted in Andreas, *History of Chicago*, 233.

54. William Howard survey in J. H. Eaton, *Letter from the Secretary of War transmitting a survey and estimate for the improvement of the Harbor of Chicago, on Lake Michigan*, 21st Cong., 1st Sess., 1830, H. Doc. 69, serial 197, 1.

55. William Howard survey in Eaton, *Letter from the Secretary of War*, 2.

56. This description of the river is based on the March 4, 1817 account of Stephen Long in Hill, *The Chicago River*, 6.

57. Hill, *The Chicago River*, 70.

58. William Howard survey in Eaton, *Letter from the Secretary of War*, 3.

59. Andreas, *History of Chicago*, 234, 238; Joshua Salzmann, "The Lakefront's Last Frontier: The Turnerian Mythology of Streeterville," *Journal of Illinois History* 9 (Autumn 2006): 201–214.

60. Miller, *City of the Century*, 60–61.

61. Chicago Common Council Committee on the Judiciary in Betsy Mendelsohn, "The Federal Hand in Urban Harbor Development: Chicago Harbor Before the Civil War," *Prologue* 30 (1998): 259.

62. Robin L. Einhorn, "A Taxing Dilemma: Early Lake Shore Protection," *Chicago History* 18 (1989): 36–38.

63. Lois Wille, *Forever Open, Clear and Free: The Struggle for Chicago's Lakefront*, 2nd ed. (Chicago: University of Chicago Press, 1991), 22–23; Timothy J. Gilfoyle, *Millennium Park: Creating a Chicago Landmark* (Chicago: University of Chicago Press, 2006), 4.

64. City of Chicago, *Petition of the Mayor and Common Council of the City of Chicago, Praying an appropriation to protect that city from the encroachments of Lake Michigan*, 26th Cong., 1st Sess., 1840, S. Doc. 195, serial 357, 1.

65. City of Chicago, *Memorial of the Corporate Authorities of the City of Chicago the State of Illinois Praying the completion of the harbor at that place*, 27th Cong., 2nd Sess., 1842, S. Doc. 65, 2, 4.

66. Ibid.

67. Mendelsohn, "The Federal Hand in Urban Development," 259.

68. Common Council of the City of Chicago, *Proceedings*, cited in United States v. Chicago, 48 U.S. 185 (1849) at 186.

69. *United States v. Chicago*, 48 U.S. at 185.

70. Mendelsohn, "The Federal Hand in Urban Development," 260–261.

71. James K. Polk, "Veto Message," August 3, 1846, Gerhard Peters and John T. Woolley, *The American Presidency Project*, accessed October 31, 2016, http://www.presidency.ucsb.edu/ws/?pid=67936.

72. Ibid.

73. Andrew Jackson, "Veto Message," May 27, 1830, Gerhard Peters and John T. Woolley, *The American Presidency Project*, accessed October 31, 2016, http://www.presidency.ucsb.edu/ws/?pid=67036; Larson, *Internal Improvement*, 183–184; David J. Russo, "The Major Political Issues of the Jacksonian Period and the Development of Party Loyalty in Congress, 1830–1840," *Transactions of the American Philosophical Society* 62 (1972): 9.

74. Whig critics argued that it was nearly impossible to differentiate between improvements that had local versus national significance. See, for instance, Horace Greeley, "The Great River-and-Harbor Convention at Chicago," *New York Semi-Weekly Tribune*, July 17, 1847, in Fergus, ed., *Chicago River-and-Harbor Convention*, 146.

75. Larson, *Internal Improvement*, 239.

76. Polk, "Veto Message," August 3, 1846.

77. Larson, *Internal Improvement*, 191, 239–240.

78. Polk, "Veto Message," August 3, 1846.

79. *Chicago Daily Journal*, August 12, 1846 in Robert Fergus, ed., *Chicago River-and-Harbor Convention*, 14–16.

80. Davis, *Frontier Illinois*, 228.

81. Einhorn, *Property Rules*, 72–73. On Wentworth, see Don Fehrenbacher, *Chicago Giant: A Biography of "Long John" Wentworth* (Champagne: University of Illinois Press, 1983).

82. Joel Stone, "The 1847 Harbor and River Convention at Chicago and the Politics of Internal Improvement," *Journal of Illinois History* 10 (Summer 2007): 114.

83. Einhorn, *Property Rules*, 63.

84. These quotes are drawn from a statement of convention aims drafted by a committee of organizers that included John Wentworth, J. Young Scammon, George Manierre, Isaac T. Arnold, and Grant Goodrich and is reprinted in Andreas, *History of Chicago*, 236.

85. Boone in Einhorn, *Property Rules*, 64. Einhorn contends that 1833–1847 marked a "booster" phase in city governance in which residents shared many of the costs of infrastructure development because they considered economic growth to be beneficial to nearly all Chicagoans. Between 1847 and 1871, Einhorn argues, a "segmented system" prevailed in which the city levied special assessments on those particular residents who stood to benefit from public works.

86. "Communication from N. B. Judd Enclosing Proceedings of Citizens Meeting in Relation to River and Harbor Convention," June 18, 1847, Chicago City Council Papers, Doc. 3925.

87. Thomas, *Statistical Report on Chicago Illinois* in Fergus, ed., *Chicago River-and-Harbor Convention*, 183.

88. Einhorn, *Property Rules*, 63–65.

89. Cronon, *Nature's Metropolis*, 62.

90. Thurlow Weed, "A Trip to Chicago Lake-and Harbor Convention," *Albany Evening Journal*, July 14, 1847, in Fergus, ed., *Chicago River-and-Harbor Convention*, 147.

91. Ibid., 148–149.

92. Cronon, *Nature's Metropolis*, 148–206.

93. Ibid., 147–149; Resolutions of the Convention, "The Great River-and-Harbor Convention at Chicago," in Fergus, ed., *Chicago River-and-Harbor Convention*, 81–86.

94. Horace Greeley, "The Great River-and-Harbor Convention at Chicago," *New York Semi-Weekly Tribune*, July 17, 1847, in Fergus, ed., *Chicago River-and-Harbor Convention*, 139.

95. The precise number of people who attended the convention is unknown. Primary and secondary accounts cite numbers ranging from 2,054, to 10,000, to as many as 20,000. Greeley claims that between 10,000 and 20,000 people attended (Greeley, "The Great River-and-Harbor Convention at Chicago," 139). For a discussion of convention attendance see Stone, "The 1847 Harbor and River Convention at Chicago and the Politics of Internal Improvement," 117.

96. Greeley, "The Great River-and-Harbor Convention at Chicago," 139.

97. Ibid.

98. Field was treated so rudely during his speech that the delegates later issued a resolution stating "the Delegates to this Convention are pained at the expression of ill-feeling evinced this morning during the time that David Dudley Field of New York, occupied by invitation the stand" (Resolutions of the Convention, "The Great River-and-Harbor Convention at Chicago," in Fergus, ed., *Chicago River-and-Harbor Convention*, 81).

99. Greeley, "The Great River-and-Harbor Convention at Chicago," 140.

100. Ibid., 141.

101. Sedgwick in Marvin Meyers, *The Jacksonian Persuasion: Politics and Belief* (New York: Vintage Books, 1957), 166.

102. David Dudley Field, "Speech given at the Chicago Rivers-and-Harbor Convention," July 5, 1847, reprinted in *The United States Democratic Review* 21 (September 1847): 94.

103. Ibid., 101.

104. Ibid., 91.

105. Chief Justice Marshall in ibid., 96; Gibbons v. Ogden, 22 U.S. 1 (1824).

106. Field, "Speech given at the Chicago Rivers-and-Harbor Convention," 97.

107. Ibid., 98.

108. Ibid., 99.

109. Greeley noted that the delegates "sharply interrogated" Field about his views (Greeley, "The Great River-and-Harbor Convention at Chicago," 141).

110. Field's exaggerated scenario of government manipulation of commodity prices would be the goal of Franklin D. Roosevelt's Agricultural Adjustment Act (AAA) nine decades later (Field, "Speech given at the Chicago Rivers-and-Harbor Convention," 99; on the AAA see David M. Kennedy, *Freedom from Fear: The American People in Depression and War, 1929–1945* [New York: Oxford University Press, 2001], 143–144, 203).

111. Field, "Speech given at the Chicago Rivers-and-Harbor Convention," 102.

112. John C. Spencer, "Remarks at the Chicago Rivers and Harbor Convention," July 1847, in Fergus, ed., *Chicago River-and-Harbor Convention*, 132–133.

113. Greeley, "The Great River-and-Harbor Convention at Chicago," 147.

114. Historian Robert Johnston has criticized several prominent "new western" historians, William Cronon, Richard White, Patricia Limerick, and Donald Worster, for "naturalizing capitalism" in their accounts of the development of the American West and of Chicago (Robert Johnston, "Beyond the 'West': Regionalism, Liberalism and the Evasion of Politics in the New Western History," *Rethinking History* 2 [1998]: 239–277).

115. The Illinois and Michigan Canal was, on average, about eight feet above the level of Lake Michigan.

116. *Chicago Daily Journal*, April 11, 1848, 2; Andreas, *History of Chicago*, 172.

117. Chicago Board of Trade, *First Annual Statement, 1858*, 43, University of Illinois at Chicago Special Collections, Chicago, Ill.; Board of Trade, *Fourth Annual Statement, 1861*, 62–63; Andreas, *History of Chicago*, 172.

118. Pierce, *A History of Chicago, From Town to City, 1848–1871*, vol. 2. (New York: Alfred A. Knopf, 1940), 37–39.

119. Einhorn, *Property Rules*.

120. Rufus Blanchard in Andreas, *History of Chicago*, 200.

121. "The Flood at Chicago," *Maine Farmer*, April 5, 1849, 2. There are conflicting statistics about the number of ships destroyed in the flood in both nineteenth-century press and contemporary historians' accounts. David Young, for instance, notes that the flood destroyed four steamboats, four propeller ships, twenty-four brigs, twenty-seven canal boats, and two sloops (David Young, *Chicago Maritime: An Illustrated History* [DeKalb: Northern Illinois University Press, 2001], 63).

122. According to historian Robin Einhorn, the city's newfound efficiency owed to its use of a form of subscription financing in which "those [property owners] who wanted bridges paid for them, while those who opposed such investments did not." Chicagoans, Einhorn argues, thus "transformed bridges from public goods into private investments." Historian Harold Platt, however, disputes this conclusion. Platt contends that Chicago Mayor Woodworth "extorted" contributions of one-third of the cost of bridges from business owners; if they did not pay, Woodworth would threaten to move the span to another location where their rivals would make the "less-than-voluntary" contributions and reap the benefits of the new bridge. With the power to extort, Platt argues, the mayor channeled private investment to help "advance the general welfare of the community." Platt's idea that bridges or other infrastructure served the general welfare—and that there was a general welfare at all—echoes the views of many Whig attendees of the 1847 Chicago River and Harbor Convention (Einhorn, *Property Rules*, 105–107, and Harold L. Platt, *Shock Cities: The Environmental Transformation and Reform of Manchester and Chicago* [Chicago: University of Chicago Press, 2005], 103).

123. On the legal status of the corporation see Herbert Hovenkamp, *Enterprise and American Law, 1836–1937* (Cambridge, Mass.: Harvard University Press, 1991).

124. Ackerman, *History of the Illinois Central Railroad*, 27.

125. *Illinois Laws*, 1851, 61, in Illinois Central Railroad v. Illinois, 146 U.S. 398 (1892); Andreas, *History of Chicago*, 252–253.

126. Munn v. Illinois, 94 U.S. 113 (1877); *Illinois Central Railroad*, 146 U.S. at 387.

Chapter 2

1. Libby Hill, *The Chicago River: A Natural and Unnatural History* (Chicago: Lake Claremont Press, 2000), 121.

2. Robert G. Spinney, *City of Big Shoulders: A History of Chicago* (DeKalb: Northern Illinois University Press, 2000), 74.

3. Theodore J. Karamanski, *Schooner Passage: Sailing Ships and the Lake Michigan Frontier* (Detroit: Wayne State University Press, 2000), 127. In 1871, 12,330 ships carried 3,096,101 tons of freight to Chicago. In that same year, 12,312 ships carried 3,082,235 tons of freight away from the city (Chicago Board of Trade, *Annual Report for 1871*, 109, University of Illinois at Chicago Special Collections, Chicago Ill.).

4. William Cronon, *Nature's Metropolis: Chicago and the Great West* (New York: Norton, 1991), 173.

5. Ibid., 110.

6. Stanton quoted in Theodore J. Karamanski, *Rally 'round the Flag: Chicago and the Civil War* (Chicago: Nelson-Hall, 1993), 173.

7. Spinney, *City of Big Shoulders*, 74.

8. James K. Edsall, "Briefs for the Defendants in Error," October Term, 1874, in *Landmark Briefs and Arguments of the United States: Constitutional Law*, ed. Philip B. Kurland and Gerhard Casper (Arlington, Va.: University Publications of America, 1975), 612. The grain trade was one of the most significant commodity trades for Chicago. In 1875, for example, the Board of Trade documented shipments of corn (21,850,652 bushels), wheat (16,061,054 bushels), and oil cake (4,563,630 pounds), and receipts of lumber (1,077,955,000 feet), shingles (420,298,000 no.), and pig iron (53,507 tons), among other items (Chicago Board of Trade, *Annual Report for 1875*, 154–155); Scott Reynolds Nelson, *A Nation of Deadbeats: An Uncommon History of America's Financial Disasters* (New York: Knopf, 2012), chap. 9, passim.

9. Cronon, *Nature's Metropolis*, chap. 2, passim.

10. The phrase "well regulated" is from William J. Novak, *The People's Welfare: Law and Regulation in Nineteenth Century America* (Chapel Hill: University of North Carolina Press, 1996), 1.

11. Munn v. Illinois, 94 U.S. 113 (1877); Illinois Central Railroad v. Illinois, 146 U.S. 387 (1892).

12. *Munn*, 94 U.S. at 113, 132.

13. C. Peter Magrath, "A Foot in the Door," *American Heritage* 15, 2 (February 1964): 44; Cronon, *Nature's Metropolis*, chap. 3, passim.

14. Richard John, "Robber Barons Redux: Antimonopoly Reconsidered," *Enterprise and Society* 13 (March 2012): 3–5.

15. Cronon, *Nature's Metropolis*, 111.

16. Edmund W. Kitch and Clara Ann Bowler, "The Facts of *Munn v. Illinois*," *The Supreme Court Review* 1978 (1978): 313.

17. "The Northwestern Railroad Elevator," *Chicago Tribune*, March 25, 1862, 4; Magrath, "A Foot in the Door," 44–45.

18. Robin L. Einhorn, *Property Rules: Political Economy in Chicago, 1833–1872* (Chicago: University of Chicago Press, 1991), 66.

19. Cronon, *Nature's Metropolis*, 114–118; William G. Ferris, "The Disgrace of Ira Munn," *Journal of the Illinois State Historical Society* 68, 3 (June 1975): 205.

20. Harold D. Woodman, "Chicago Businessmen and the 'Granger' Laws," *Agricultural History* 36, 1 (January 1962): 19.

21. "Munn and Scott," *Chicago Tribune*, November 26, 1872, 2.

22. Magrath, "A Foot in the Door," 45. *Debates and Proceedings of the Constitutional Convention of the State of Illinois*, vol. 2 (Springfield, Ill.: E. L. Merritt & Brother, 1870), 1622.

23. Cronon, *Nature's Metropolis*, 135.

24. "The Warehouse Business," *Chicago Tribune*, November 26, 1872, 4.

25. Magrath, "A Foot in the Door," 46.

26. Woodman, "Chicago Businessmen and the 'Granger' Laws," 21.

27. *Munn*, 94 U.S. at 113; Chicago, Burlington & Quincy Railroad Company v. Iowa, 94 U.S. 155

(1876); Peik v. Chicago & Northwestern Railway Company, 94 U.S. 164 (1876); Chicago, Milwaukee & St. Paul Railroad Company v. Ackley, 94 U.S. 179 (1876); Winona & St. Peter Railroad Company v. Blake, 94 U.S. 180 (1876); Stone v. Wisconsin, 94 U.S. 181 (1876); Railroad Company v. Husen, 95 U.S. 465 (1877); and Wabash v. Illinois, 118 U.S. 557 (1886). On the *Granger Cases* see, George H. Miller, *Railroads and the Granger Laws* (Madison: University of Wisconsin Press, 1971).

28. *Munn*, 94 U.S. at 113, 132.

29. Magrath, "A Foot in the Door," 46.

30. Cronon, *Nature's Metropolis*, 119.

31. "Inspection and Warehousing of Gran," *Chicago Tribune* December 15, 1873, 3; Magrath, "A Foot in the Door," 46.

32. Chicago Board of Trade president quoted in Magrath, "A Foot in the Door," 46; on the conflict within the Board of Trade see Woodman, "Chicago Businessmen and the 'Granger' Laws," 19.

33. Woodman, "Chicago Businessmen and the 'Granger' Laws," 21.

34. *Debates and Proceedings of the Constitutional Convention of the State of Illinois*, 1623, 1625, Illinois State Library, Springfield, Ill.

35. Ibid., 1625.

36. Illinois Constitution of 1870 in *Debates and Proceedings of the Constitutional Convention of the State of Illinois*, 1879.

37. Magrath, "A Foot in the Door," 48; Woodman, "Chicago Businessmen and the 'Granger' Laws," 22.

38. *Munn*, 94 U.S. at 113; "The Warehouse Law," *Chicago Tribune*, March, 2, 1877, 2.

39. Woodman, "Chicago Businessmen and the 'Granger' Laws," 24.

40. Cronon, *Nature's Metropolis*, 121–127, quote on 125.

41. Ferris, "The Disgrace of Ira Munn," 205.

42. "Inspection and Warehousing of Grain," *Chicago Tribune*, 3; Magrath, "A Foot in the Door," 48.

43. "Inspection and Warehousing of Grain," *Chicago Tribune*, 3; Magrath, "A Foot in the Door," 48.

44. Ferris, "The Disgrace of Ira Munn," 208–209.

45. "Corners of the Past," *Chicago Tribune*, September 30, 1888, 2.

46. "Munn and Scott," *Chicago Tribune*, November 28, 1872, 3; "Expelled," *Chicago Tribune*, December 4, 1872, 3.

47. Ferris, "The Disgrace of Ira Munn," 212.

48. "The Warehouse Law," 2.

49. "The Warehouse Decision," *Chicago Tribune*, February 16, 1874, 4.

50. Richard White, *Railroaded: The Transcontinentals and the Making of Modern America* (New York: Norton, 2011), 110–112.

51. William C. Goudy also served as counsel for the warehousemen.

52. Stephen S. Gregory and Edward T. Lee, "In Memorium: John Nelson Jewett, 1827–1904," University of Illinois at Chicago Special Collections, Chicago, Ill.

53. John N. Jewett, "Ira Y. Munn and George L. Scott, vs. the People of the State of Illinois: Further Brief for Plaintiffs in Error, October Term, 1874," in Kurland and Casper, *Landmark Briefs and Arguments of the Supreme Court of the United States*, vol. 7, 662.

54. Paul Kens, *Justice Stephen Field: Shaping Liberty from the Gold Rush to the Gilded Age* (Lawrence: University of Kansas Press, 1997), 155.

55. James K. Edsall, "Ira Y. Munn and George L. Scott, vs. the People of the State of Illinois: Brief for the Defendants in Error, October Term, 1874," in Kurland and Casper, *Landmark Briefs and Arguments of the Supreme Court of the United States*, vol. 7, 642, 649. Edsall became a member of the state legislature in 1880 where he played an influential role in drafting legislation to regulate the business activities of warehouses and railroads ("James K. Edsall Dead," *Chicago Tribune*, June, 20 1892, 7).

56. Charles Fairman, *The Oliver Wendell Holmes Devise: History of the Supreme Court of the United States Volume VII Reconstruction and Reunion*, part 2 (New York: Macmillan, 1987), 5, 75–79.

57. *Munn*, 94 U.S. at 113, 132.

58. Scheiber, "The Road to *Munn*."

59. Waite cites Lord Hale's treatise *De Portibus Maris* extensively in *Munn v Illinois*, 94 U.S. 113 (1877).

60. Harry Scheiber, "The Road to Munn: Eminent Domain and the Concept of Public Purpose in the State Courts," in *Perspectives in American History*, vol. 5, ed. Donald Fleming and Bernard Bailyn (Cambridge, Mass.: Charles Warren Center for Studies in American History at Harvard University, 1971), 334–335.

61. Hale cited in *Munn*, 94 U.S. at 113, 127. Hale's treatise was not an obscure text. According to Scheiber, Hale's concept of the public interest was in the "consciousness of American lawyers and judges since early in the nineteenth century" (Scheiber, "The Road to *Munn*," 334–335).

62. *Munn*, 94 U.S. at 113, 125.

63. *Munn*, 94 U.S. at 113, 133.

64. Field also believed that the state should protect public safety, health, and morals (Charles W. McCurdy, "Justice Field and the Jurisprudence of Government-Business Relations: Some Parameters of Laissez Faire Constitutionalism, 1863–1897," *Journal of American History* 61 [1975]: 974).

65. Robert G. McCloskey, *American Conservatism in the Age of Enterprise: A Study of William Graham Sumner, Stephen J. Field and Andrew Carnegie* (Cambridge: Harvard University Press, 1951), 89–90.

66. Horace Greeley, "The Great River-and-Harbor Convention at Chicago," *New York Semi-Weekly Tribune*, in *Chicago River-and-Harbor Convention*, ed. Robert Fergus (Chicago: Fergus Printing Co., 1882), 142.

67. Kens, *Justice Stephen Field*, 95–96.

68. Timothy L. Hall, *Supreme Court Justices: A Biographical Dictionary* (New York: Facts on File, 2001), 149–152.

69. Slaughterhouse Cases, 83 U.S. 36, 83 (1872), Field dissenting.

70. Lochner v. New York, 198 U.S. 45 (1905); Kens, *Justice Stephen Field*, 255; Paul Kens, *Judicial Power and Reform Politics: The Anatomy of Lochner v. New York* (Lawrence: University Press of Kansas), 94.

71. McCloskey, *American Conservatism in the Age of Enterprise*, 1. *Slaughterhouse Cases*, 83 U.S. at 36, 83.

72. *Munn*, 94 U.S. at 113, 136.

73. Ibid., at 113, 139.

74. Ibid., at 113, 136.

75. Ibid., at 113, 138.

76. Miller in Herbert Hovenkamp, *Enterprise and American Law, 1836–1937* (Cambridge, Mass.: Harvard University Press, 1991), 128–129.

77. *Illinois Central Railroad*, 146 U.S. at 387.

78. "Proposition of the Illinois Central Railroad Company for its Track to Come into Chicago on the Lake Shore," December 19, 1851, Chicago City Council Papers, Illinois Regional Archives Depository, Northeastern Illinois University, Chicago, Ill., Doc. 1338; William Howard survey in J. H. Eaton, *Letter from the Secretary of War transmitting a survey and estimate for the improvement of the Harbor of Chicago*, 21st Cong., 1st Sess., 1830, H. Doc. 69, serial 197, 3; Alfred Theodore Andreas, *History of Chicago from the Earliest Period to the Present Time*, vol. 1 (Chicago: A. T. Andreas, 1884), 234, 238.

79. Lois Wille, *Forever Open, Clear and Free: The Struggle for Chicago's Lakefront*, 2nd ed. (Chicago: University of Chicago Press, 1991), 26–29.

80. Ibid., 28–29.

81. Robin L. Einhorn, "A Taxing Dilemma: Early Lake Shore Protection," *Chicago History* 18 (1989): 39–41, 44–45; Bessie Louise Pierce, *A History of Chicago: The Beginning of a City, 1673–1848*, vol. 1 (Chicago: University of Chicago Press, 1937), 414, 416.

82. Michigan Avenue property owners also challenged the legality of special assessments with limited success (Einhorn, "A Taxing Dilemma," 39–41, 44–45).

83. Ibid., 46.

84. *Illinois Laws*, 1851, 61, in *Illinois Central Railroad*, 146 U.S. at 397, 398.

85. "Communication from the Illinois Central Railroad in Relation to a Proposition of the Common Council," December 29, 1851, Chicago City Council Papers, Doc. 1376.

86. Ibid.

87. Ibid.

88. Wille, *Forever Open, Clear, and Free*, 29.

89. "Ordinance Concerning Entry by the Illinois Central Railroad Company into the City," December 29, 1851, Chicago City Council Papers, Doc. 1377.

90. William H. Russell in Wille, *Forever Open, Clear, and Free*, 27, 29–31; Timothy J. Gilfoyle, *Millennium Park: Creating a Chicago Landmark* (Chicago: University of Chicago Press, 2006), 9.

91. Joseph D. Kearny and Thomas W. Merrill, "The Origins of the American Public Trust Doctrine: What Really Happened in Illinois Central," *University of Chicago Law Review* 71 (2004): 827.

92. Kearny and Merrill, "The Origins of the American Public Trust Doctrine," 827.

93. Martin v. Waddell, 41 U.S. 367 (1842); Pollard v. Hagan, 44 U.S. 212 (1845); Kearny and Merrill, "The Origins of the American Public Trust Doctrine," 828.

94. Kearny and Merrill, "The Origins of the American Public Trust Doctrine," 828–829.

95. The Propeller Genesee Chief v. Fitzhugh, 53 U.S. 443 (1852); Kearny and Merrill, "The Origins of the American Public Trust Doctrine," 831.

96. Kearny and Merrill, "The Origins of the American Public Trust Doctrine," 832.

97. Middleton v. Pritchard, 4 Ill. 509 (1842); Kearny and Merrill, "The Origins of the American Public Trust Doctrine," 829.

98. Seaman v. Smith, 24 Ill. 521 (1860); Kearny and Merrill, "The Origins of the American Public Trust Doctrine," 832.

99. *Seaman*, 24 Ill. at 521; Kearny and Merrill, "The Origins of the American Public Trust Doctrine," 832.

100. Congress in "Who Owns Lake Park?," *Chicago Tribune*, June 23, 1867, 2.

101. "Who Owns Lake Park?," 2.

102. Wille, *Forever Open Clear and Free*.

103. "Who Owns Lake Park?," 2.

104. Ibid.; House Committee on Judiciary, *The Lake Front At Chicago, Ill.*, 49th Cong., 1st Sess., 1887.

105. "The Chicago Dock Bill," *Chicago Tribune*, February 15, 1867, 2.

106. In addition to Fuller and Shepard, several other Chicago businessmen tried to gain title to the submerged lands and Lake Park (Kearny and Merrill, "The Origins of the American Public Trust Doctrine," 838–842).

107. Merritt Starr, "Address to the Illinois State Bar Association: The Chicago Lake Front Case," *American Lawyer* 2 (1894): 243.

108. "The Lake-Park and Front Bills," *Chicago Tribune*, January 16, 1869, 2; Kearny and Merrill, "The Origins of the American Public Trust Doctrine," 857.

109. Joshua C. Knickerbocker, "Minority Report of the Committee on Municipal Affairs and Insurance in Relation to House Bill No. 373," in "The Chicago Harbor Bill," *Chicago Tribune*, February 10, 1869, 2.

110. "The Chicago Harbor Bill," 2. In his ruling, Field alluded to the possibility that the Illinois Central bribed the state legislature. He noted, "the circumstances attending the passage of the act . . . were . . . the subject of much criticism" (*Illinois Central Railroad*, 146 U.S. at 387, 451).

111. "The Lake Front Bill and Its Effects-Objections to the Bill," *Chicago Tribune*, February 24, 1869, 2.

112. Knickerbocker estimated that 1,500 would come to the meeting, but Kearny and Merrill suggest that only a third of that number were present and that the crowd lacked enthusiasm (Kearny and Merrill, "The Origins of the American Public Trust Doctrine," 867).

113. "The Lake Park Question," *Chicago Tribune*, February 18, 1869, 4.

114. Ibid.

115. Daniel Bluestone, *Constructing Chicago* (New Haven, Conn.: Yale University Press, 1991), 26.

116. "The Lake Park Question," 4.

117. Illinois Legislature, *Journal of the House* 2 (Springfield, 1869): 704–705; Illinois Legislature, *Journal of the Senate* 3 (Springfield, 1869).

118. John M. Palmer, "Message of Governor John M. Palmer Returning H.B. No. 373 to the House of Representatives Without His Signature and Approval," April 14, 1869, Illinois Legislature, *Journal of the House*, 517–528.

119. Illinois Legislature, *Journal of the House*, 704–705; Illinois Legislature, *Journal of the Senate*. In spite of the bill's passage, Alderman Knickerbocker remained defiant. At his urging, the city refused the railroad's first payment for North Lake Park (Chicago City Council, "Communication from Alderman Knickerbocker Concerning Preambles and Resolutions on Lakefront Bill," May 17, 1869, Chicago City Council Papers, Chicago, Ill.).

120. Maj. J. B. Wheeler in Army Corps of Engineers, *Report of the Chief of Engineers*, "Annual Report of Major G. L. Gillespie, Corps of Engineers, for the Fiscal Year Ending June 30, 1876," 44th Cong., 2nd Sess., 1876, 435.

121. Army Corps of Engineers, *1876 Report of the Chief of Engineers*, 435.

122. Committee on Chicago Harbor and Port Survey, *The Harbor Plan of Chicago* (Commercial Club of Chicago, 1927), 13; Army Corps of Engineers, *1876 Report of the Chief of Engineers*, 435–436.

123. Kearny and Merrill, "The Origins of the American Public Trust Doctrine," 896.

124. Ibid., 903–904.

125. House Committee on Judiciary, *The Lake Front At Chicago, Ill.*

126. *Illinois Laws*, 1873, 115; "It's Our Lake Front," *Chicago Evening Journal*, December 5, 1892, 1; Miller, *Railroads and the Granger Laws.*

127. "The State Capital," *Chicago Tribune*, March 27, 1873, 5.

128. Ibid.

129. Ibid.

130. "The State Capital," *Chicago Tribune*, April 10, 1873, 5.

131. Christine Meisner Rosen, *The Limits of Power: Great Fires and the Process of City Growth in America* (New York: Cambridge University Press, 1986), 92.

132. Dennis Cremin, "Building Chicago's Front Yard: Grant Park, 1836–1936" (Ph.D. dissertation, Loyola University, 1999), 82–83.

133. Chicago Board of Trade, *Annual Report for 1885*, 172–173.

134. These developments, combined with a large slip built in 1867 by Chicago businessman William Ogden just north of the mouth of the Chicago River, provided additional dock space for ships.

135. On the relationship between property rights and economic development, see Douglass C. North, *Structure and Change in Economic History* (New York: W. W. Norton, 1981).

136. Kearny and Merrill, "The Origins of the American Public Trust Doctrine," 910.

137. Illinois v. Illinois Central Railroad Co., 33 F. 730 (C.C.N.D. Ill. 1888).

138. "History of the Litigation," *Chicago Tribune*, December 6, 1892, 1.

139. James W. Ely Jr., *The Chief Justiceship of Melville Fuller, 1888–1910* (Columbia: University of South Carolina Press, 1995).

140. In *Allgeyer v. Louisiana* (1897), for instance, the court struck down a statute preventing the purchase of marine insurance from companies that did not have an agent located in Louisiana on the grounds that the law deprived individuals of their contractual liberty. The state law was intended to combat fraud (Allgeyer v. Louisiana, 165 U.S. 578 [1897]).

141. Lochner v New York, 198 U.S. 45 (1905); Kens, *Judicial Power and Reform Politics.*

142. *Illinois Central Railroad*, 146 U.S. at 387.

143. Ibid.

144. "For Use by the Public," *Chicago Record*, December 6, 1892, 1.

145. *Slaughterhouse Cases*, 83 U.S. at 36, 83; *Munn*, 94 U.S. at 113, 136.

146. Jewett was never convinced by Field's arguments. In 1902, two years before his death, Jewett criticized the ruling in a lecture to his students at the John Marshall Law School. He asked the students to imagine themselves in the positions of the litigants: "One of you conveys to the other by deed a piece of ground today . . . Tomorrow you file a declaration revoking the grant." Jewett continued, "According to this opinion of the court . . . the result would be to . . . reinvest it [the title] in the grantor by his mere repudiation of it tomorrow." There is, he concluded, "no law and no reason for such a proposition" (John Jewett, "The Lakefront Litigation: Part II," *The John Marshall Law Quarterly* 3 [June 1938]: 225).

147. *Illinois Central Railroad*, 146 U.S. at 387, 453.

148. McCurdy, "Justice Field and the Jurisprudence of Government-Business Relations," 994–995.

149. *Illinois Central Railroad*, 146 U.S. at 387, 454.

150. Ibid.

151. Ibid., at 387, 453.

152. Brown sided with the majority in *Lochner*, 198 U.S. at 45.

153. *Illinois Central Railroad*, 146 U.S. at 387, 467, Shiras dissenting.

154. Ibid., at 387, 461.

155. Jacksonian Democrats critical of the special privileges granted by states to corporations pushed for general incorporation laws between the 1850s and 1870s. According to legal scholar Morton Horwitz, free incorporation gradually undermined the grant theory of the corporation. Horwitz contends that late nineteenth-century jurists increasingly began to view the corporation as an extended form of business partnership, but not, as many scholars have claimed, a "natural entity," such as a person. While many scholars date the emergence of corporate personhood to the Supreme Court's 1886 *Santa Clara v. Southern Pacific Railroad* ruling, Horwitz argues that corporate personhood did not fully emerge until the early twentieth century (Morton J. Horwitz, "Santa Clara Revisited: The Development of Corporate Theory," *West Virginia Law Review* 88 [1985–1986]: 181–183; Morton J. Horwitz, *The Transformation of American Law 1870–1960: The Crisis of Legal Orthodoxy* [New York: Oxford University Press, 1992], 66–77). On contractual theories of the corporation, also see Hovenkamp, *Enterprise and American Law*, chaps. 20–21, passim. Hovenkamp argues the modern corporation emerged much earlier than does Horwitz.

156. *Illinois Central Railroad,* 146 U.S. at 387, 451.

157. Ibid., at 387, 458.

158. Ibid., at 387, 455.

159. Kearny and Merrill, "The Origins of the American Public Trust Doctrine," 930.

Chapter 3

1. Most of the material in this chapter was first published in an article, Joshua A. T. Salzmann, "The Creative Destruction of the Chicago River Harbor," *Enterprise and Society* 13, 2 (June 2012): 235–275. It is copyrighted by Oxford University Press, 2012, and reprinted with permission of the press. The Port of Chicago consisted of the Chicago River, the Calumet River, and small portions of the Lake Michigan shoreline at the mouths of the two rivers. The Chicago River handled the majority of freight in the Port of Chicago until 1906. The Chicago River carried a particularly large amount of tonnage in 1889. The average yearly tonnage for most years from the late 1880s to the late 1890s was about seven million tons. For annual tonnage statistics see Table 2. The assertion that the Port of Chicago was the fourth largest in the world is based on Elliott Flower, "Chicago's Great River-Harbor," *Century Magazine* 4 (1902): 487. Flower cites tonnage data from the year 1900. Another source of world port statistics shows that the Port of Chicago was also fourth in tonnage among world ports in 1870. See "Report of J. Paul Goode to the Chicago Harbor Commission," in Chicago Harbor Commission, *Report to the Mayor and Aldermen of the City of Chicago* (H. G. Adair, 1909), 68.

2. Gerome Loving, *The Last Titan: A Life of Theodore Dreiser* (Berkeley: University of California Press, 2005), 28.

3. Dreiser, "Smallest and Busiest River," in *Selected Magazine Articles of Theodore Dreiser: Life and Art in the American 1890s*, vol. 2, ed. Yoshinobu Hakutani (Rutherford, N.J.: Farleigh Dickinson University Press, 1987), 84, 87–88; Lieut. Col. George A. Zinn in U.S. House Committee on Rivers and Harbors, *Chicago Harbor and Adjacent Waterways*, 62nd Cong., 2nd sess., April 22, 1912, 20–21.

4. James J. Waite, "The Lumber Interests of Chicago," *Harper's Weekly* October 20, 1883, 666.

5. Dreiser, "Smallest and Busiest River," 86.

6. Libby Hill, *The Chicago River: A Natural and Unnatural History* (Chicago: Lake Clare-mont Press, 2000), 67.

7. Dreiser, "Smallest and Busiest River," 87.

8. Flower, "Chicago's Great River-Harbor," 484.

9. Dreiser, "Smallest and Busiest River," 88.

10. Ibid., 88. Dreiser's discussion raises the often neglected issue of the history of sound. See Peter A. Coates, "The Strange Stillness of the Past: Toward an Environmental History of Sound and Noise," *Environmental History* 10 (2005): 636–665.

11. Association for the Improvement of the Chicago River, *Chicago!: Where Railroad Traffic and Lake Transportation Meet: Snap Shots from Proceedings of River Improvement Meeting, at Great Northern Hotel,* March 13, 1896, 23.

12. Maj. W. L. Marshall, Army Corps of Engineers, *Report of the Chief of Engineers,* "Annual Report of Maj. W. L. Marshall, Corps of Engineers, for the Fiscal Year Ending June 30, 1893," 53rd Cong., 2nd Sess., 1893, 2798.

13. The theory of creative destruction was first advanced by Karl Marx. Joseph Schumpeter adapted and popularized the idea (Joseph Schumpeter, *Capitalism, Socialism, and Democracy* 2nd ed. [New York: Harper and Brothers, 1947], 81–86; Thomas McCraw, *Prophet of Innovation: Joseph Schumpeter and Creative Destruction* [Cambridge: Belknap Press of Harvard University, 2007]).

14. Robert Lewis, *Chicago Made: Factory Networks in the Industrial Metropolis* (Chicago: University of Chicago Press, 2008), 32–33, 37, 39. On the decentralization of industry and cities in the nineteenth and early twentieth century, see Ann Durkin Keating, *Chicagoland: City and Suburbs in the Railroad Age* (Chicago: University of Chicago Press, 2005); Robert Lewis, *Manu-facturing Montreal: The Making of an Industrial Landscape: 1850–1930* (Baltimore: Johns Hopkins University Press, 2000); Glenn McLaughlin, *Growth of American Manufacturing Areas: A Comparative Analysis with Special Emphasis on Trends in the Pittsburgh District* (Pittsburgh: Bureau of Business Research, University of Pittsburgh, 1938); Christine Meisner Rosen, *The Limits of Power: Great Fires and the Process of City Growth in America* (New York: Cambridge University Press, 1986); Graham Taylor, *Satellite Cities: A Study of Industrial Suburbs* (New York: Appleton, 1915).

15. Association for the Improvement of the Chicago River, *Annual Report and Constitution, 1897* (Chicago: Chicago Legal News Co., 1897).

16. This assertion is based on the statistics in Table 2.

17. Lewis, *Chicago Made,* 32–37, 46, 53–59.

18. Chicago Harbor Commission, *Report to the Mayor and Aldermen of the City of Chicago,* 280.

19. Association for the Improvement of the Chicago River, *Chicago!,* 29.

20. Joseph W. Konvitz, "The Crises of Atlantic Port Cities, 1880–1920," *Comparative Studies in Society and History: An International Quarterly* 36, 2 (1994): 299.

21. Theodore J. Karamanski, *Schooner Passage: Sailing Ships and the Lake Michigan Frontier* (Detroit: Wayne State University Press, 2000), 22, 210.

22. Osborne Howes Jr., "Commerce on the Great Lakes," *Harper's Weekly,* April 13, 1889, 293–296.

23. Karamanski, *Schooner Passage,* 210.

24. Table 2.

25. The assertion that the number of steamboats surpassed the number of sailboats on the

Great Lakes in 1888 is based on David Young, *Chicago Maritime: An Illustrated History* (DeKalb: Northern Illinois University Press, 2001), 76.

26. Association for the Improvement of the Chicago River, *Chicago!*, 27–29.

27. These calculations are based on the statistics in Table 3.

28. Chicago Department of Public Works, *1898 Annual Report*, 37, Harold Washington Public Library, Chicago, Ill.

29. William B. Harper in U.S. House Committee on Rivers and Harbors, *Chicago River*, 54th Cong., 1st Sess., February 28, 1896, 16; Association for the Improvement of the Chicago River, *Chicago!*, 17–18.

30. A. J. Earling in Association for the Improvement of the Chicago River, *Chicago!*, 9–10.

31. Army Corps of Engineers, *Report of the Chief of Engineers*, "Annual Report of Maj. W. L. Marshall, Corps of Engineers, for the Fiscal Year Ending June 30, 1896," 54th Cong., 2nd Sess., 1896, 2574, 2586.

32. Marshall noted in his 1892 report that there were "influences at work that will either diminish the uses of the Chicago River and increase the demands upon the Calumet Harbor . . . or . . . require the . . . rectification of the Chicago River to accommodate the enormous commerce . . . upon . . . that stream." Among those "influences" were the increase in ship size and physical barriers to navigation on the Chicago River. By 1896, Marshall had determined that it was prudent to divert in transit freight traffic from the Chicago River to the Calumet. He argued that "there seems no good reason why business merely in transit at Chicago should be allowed to obstruct communications across Chicago River" (Army Corps of Engineers, *Report of the Chief on Engineers*, "Annual Report of Maj. W. L. Marshall, Corps of Engineers, for the Fiscal Year Ending June 30, 1892," 52nd Cong., 2nd Sess., 1892, 2246; Army Corps of Engineers, *1896 Annual Report of the Chief of Engineers*, 2574–2575).

33. Army Corps of Engineers, *1896 Annual Report of the Chief of Engineers*, 2586.

34. Wheeler in Army Corps of Engineers, *1876 Annual Report of the Chief of Engineers*, 441.

35. Wheeler in Army Corps of Engineers, *Report of the Chief of Engineers*, "Annual Report of Maj. D. C. Houston, Corps of Engineers, for the Fiscal Year Ending June 30, 1871," 42nd Cong., 2nd Sess., 1871, 117.

36. Maj. W. L. Marshall, *Survey of Calumet Harbor, Illinois*, 54th Cong., 1st Sess., March 4, 1896, 3.

37. Mayor Dewitt C. Creiger in Chicago Department of Public Works, *1889 Annual Report*, vi.

38. Marshall, "Survey of Calumet Harbor, Illinois," March 4, 1896, 3–4.

39. George A. Tripp, "Relations of Calumet Harbor to Chicago's Commerce Explained by George A. Tripp," *Chicago Commerce* 5, 33 (1909): 8.

40. Lewis, *Chicago Made*, 54–55.

41. U.S. House Committee on Rivers and Harbors, *Chicago River*, 1896.

42. Association for the Improvement of the Chicago River, *Chicago!*, 4.

43. Richard White, *"It's Your Misfortune and None of My Own": A History of the American West* (Norman: University of Oklahoma Press, 1991), 405.

44. Chicago Commercial Association, "Final Report of Real Estate Board on River Improvement," *The Bulletin* 2, 5 (1906): 5; Association for the Improvement of the Chicago River, *1897 Annual Report and Constitution*, 5.

45. Flower, "Chicago's Great River-Harbor," 483.

46. A civic association comprised of well-to-do Chicagoans called the Citizens Association

of Chicago monitored smoke emissions and whistle usage during the 1880s and 1890s and lobbied city leaders to reduce both. See Citizen's Association of Chicago, *1883 Annual Report*, 6; Citizen's Association of Chicago, *1890 Annual Report*, 12. On smoke abatement in Chicago, see Rosen, "Businessmen Against Pollution," 351–397.

47. Dreiser, "Smallest and Busiest River," 84.

48. Marshall in Dreiser, "Smallest and Busiest River," 89–90.

49. Flower, "Chicago's Great River-Harbor," 484.

50. Duddleston in "Petition Urging the City Council to Pass a Resolution Asking Congress to Deepen and Widen the Chicago River," December 13, 1897, Chicago City Council Papers, Box 213, Docs. 281–307.

51. "Petition Presented to the Honorable Committee of Harbors, Viaducts and Bridges," January 22, 1898, Chicago City Council Papers, Box 213, Docs. 281–307.

52. "Citizens of the West Side in Opposition to the Present Scheme of Widening the Chicago River," December 13, 1897, Chicago City Council Papers, Box 213, Docs. 281–307.

53. In nineteenth-century Chicago public works were often paid for only by the people who stood to benefit from them most directly. See Robin L. Einhorn, *Property Rules: Political Economy in Chicago, 1833–1872* (Chicago: University of Chicago Press, 1991).

54. Army Corps of Engineers. *1893 Annual Report of the Chief of Engineers*, 2798.

55. Dreiser, "Smallest and Busiest River," 89.

56. Burnham in Hill, *Chicago River*, 155.

57. Louis P. Cain, *Sanitation Strategy for a Lakefront Metropolis: The Case of Chicago* (DeKalb: Northern Illinois University Press, 1978), 69–71.

58. Army Corps of Engineers, *1893 Annual Report of the Chief of Engineers*, 2798–2800.

59. Hill, *Chicago River*, 182–183; Karamanski, *Schooner Passage*, 168.

60. Chicago Department of Public Works, *1894 Annual Report*, 104.

61. Dreiser, "Smallest and Busiest River," 84.

62. Ibid., 88.

63. Ibid., 84.

64. "Ordinance Prescribing Rules and Regulations Governing Rivers and Harbors," July 7, 1902, Chicago City Council Papers, Box 254, Doc. 1587.

65. Chicago Department of Public Works, *1893 Annual Report*, 37.

66. Karamanski, *Schooner Passage*, 134–135.

67. "Ordinance Prescribing Rules and Regulations Governing Rivers and Harbors," July 7, 1902, Chicago City Council Papers, Box 254, Doc. 1587.

68. Dreiser, "Smallest and Busiest River," 88.

69. Chicago Department of Public Works, *1896 Annual Report*, 138; Citizens' Association of Chicago, *1881 Annual Report*, 11.

70. Hill, *Chicago River*, 121; Frank J. Piehl, "Shall We Gather at the River," *Chicago History* 2 (1973): 203.

71. Piehl, "Shall We Gather at the River," 203; Chicago Department of Public Works, *1881 Annual Report*, 78.

72. "Veto of Bridge Ordinance as Passed," October 12, 1885, Chicago City Council Papers, Box 102, Doc. 990.

73. Escanaba Company v. Chicago, 107 U.S. 678 (1883).

74. Munn v. Illinois, 94 U.S. 113 (1877), Field dissenting.

75. On teamsters and other workers in the "craft economy," see Andrew Wender Cohen, *The*

Racketeer's Progress: Chicago and the Struggle for the Modern American Economy, 1900–1940 (Cambridge: Cambridge University Press, 2004), 16.

76. *Escanaba Company*, 107 U.S. at 678, 682.

77. In the three decades following the *Escanaba* ruling, the number of bridges increased. By the early twentieth century, ships had to pass through twenty-six bridges to reach the Sanitary and Ship Canal from Lake Michigan and twenty-two to reach Belmont Avenue on the city's north side (Maj. Thomas H. Rees, "Preliminary Examination of Chicago Harbor, ILL., and Adjacent Waterways," August 28, 1909, in *Chicago Harbor and Adjacent Waterways*, 62nd Cong., 2nd Sess., 1912, 8).

78. Chicago Department of Public Works, *1883 Annual Report*, 39.

79. "Crisis in Lake Traffic," *Chicago Tribune*, July 26, 1897, 12.

80. Keith in Chicago Harbor Commission, *Report to the Mayor and Aldermen of the City of Chicago*, 329–330. Many vessel owners sank under the weight of tug fees. In 1912, the City Council applied that rule to steamships loaded with more than twelve hundred tons of freight. Under the new law, one steamboat line incurred a ten-fold increase in annual tug fees from twenty-five hundred to twenty-five thousand dollars, adding significantly to the cost of doing business on the Chicago (Lieut. Col. George A. Zinn, Army Corps of Engineers, "Survey of Chicago Harbor, ILL., and Adjacent Waterways," October 7, 1911, in *Chicago Harbor and Adjacent Waterways*, 57).

81. Lewis, *Chicago Made*, 282. "Petition of Chicago Commercial Association for Building Bascule Bridges and Widening Chicago River," February 25, 1901, Chicago City Council Papers, Box 236.

82. Piehl, "Shall We Gather at the River," 196.

83. Maj. W. L. Marshall, Army Corps of Engineers, *Preliminary Examination of Chicago River, Illinois*, 56th Cong., 1st Sess., 1899, 8.

84. By 1904, the Sanitary District had built two-hundred-thousand-dollar bascule bridges at State, Randolph, Indiana, Taylor, Canal, Main, and Ashland (Statement of Hon. Joseph C. Braden, Chairman of the Engineering Committee of the Board of Trustees of the Sanitary District of Chicago in *Chicago River Tunnels: Hearings Before the Committee on Interstate and Foreign Commerce*, 58th Cong., 2nd sess., December 18, 1903–March 11, 1904, 47).

85. W. H. Bixby, Chief of Engineers, U.S. Army, *Chicago Harbor and Adjacent Waterways: Report of the Board of Engineers for Rivers and Harbors on Survey*, 63rd Cong., 1st Sess., 1913, 234.

86. Frank J. Piehl, "Our Forgotten Streetcar Tunnels," *Chicago History* 4 (1975): 134–135.

87. Donald Miller, *City of the Century: The Epic of Chicago and the Making of America* (New York: Simon and Schuster, 1996), 268–269.

88. Ibid., 269.

89. Theodore Dreiser, *The Titan* (New York: John Lane Company, 1914), 170.

90. Piehl, "Our Forgotten Streetcar Tunnels," 135–136; "Ordinance Authorizing Use of La-Salle Street Tunnel," *Chicago City Council Proceedings*, July 19, 1886; "Ordinance Authorizing Use of Washington Street Tunnel," *Chicago City Council Proceedings*, February 1, 1886; "Van Buren Street Tunnel," *Chicago City Council Proceedings*, April 2, 1888, in U.S. House Committee on Interstate and Foreign Commerce, *Chicago River Tunnels Obstructions to Navigation, Etc.*, March 23, 58th Cong., 2nd Sess., 1904, 74, 76, 78.

91. Flower, "Chicago's Great River-Harbor," 485.

92. Delos F. Wilcox, *Municipal Franchises: A Description of the Terms and Conditions Upon Which Private Corporations Enjoy Special Privileges in the Streets of American Cities*, vol. 2 (New York: Engineering News Publishing, 1911), 148–150.

93. Miller, *City of the Century*, 270–273.

94. William Mavor, Chairman of the Finance Committee of the City Council of Chicago, in U.S. House Committee on Interstate and Foreign Commerce, *Chicago River Tunnels Obstructions to Navigation*, 8.

95. Dering in U.S. House Committee on Interstate and Foreign Commerce, *Chicago River Tunnels Obstructions to Navigation*, 23.

96. Livingstone in U.S. House Committee on Interstate and Foreign Commerce, *Chicago River Tunnels Obstructions to Navigation*, 45.

97. Bennett in U.S. House Committee on Interstate and Foreign Commerce, *Chicago River Tunnels Obstructions to Navigation*, 20.

98. Foreman in U.S. House Committee on Interstate and Foreign Commerce, *Chicago River Tunnels Obstructions to Navigation*, 29.

99. "Chicago Victor in Tunnel Case," *Chicago Tribune*, April 10, 1906, 4. The city of Chicago and the traction companies tried to avoid paying to comply with the congressional mandate. The city ordered the financially strapped Union Traction Company to finance the work. The company, in turn, challenged that order in a 1906 hearing before the United States Supreme Court. Justice John Harlan rejected the company's challenge. After the ruling, the traction company agreed to lower the tunnels in exchange for the right to turn their cable lines into electric trolleys. Subsequently, Chicago's mayor George Dunne brokered a settlement to the city's traction question. Private companies continued to run the railways, but the city assumed greater regulatory powers and the right to purchase the system at any time.

100. Carr in U.S. House Committee on Interstate and Foreign Commerce, *Chicago River Tunnels Obstructions to Navigation*, 52–53.

101. J. B. McClure, *Stories and Sketches of Chicago* (Chicago: Rhodes and McClure, 1880), 171.

102. Hill, *Chicago River*, 100.

103. Alfred Theodore Andreas, *History of Chicago from the Earliest Period to the Present Time*, vol. 1 (Chicago: A. T. Andreas, 1884), 595.

104. "Reports of Physicians on Cholera Cases," July 18, 1849, Chicago City Council Papers, Doc. 5438A.

105. Harold L. Platt, *Shock Cities: The Environmental Transformation and Reform of Manchester and Chicago* (Chicago: University of Chicago Press, 2005), 80.

106. Historians cite death tolls ranging from 1,500 to 1,700 (Einhorn, *Property Rules*, 137); Lois Wille, *Forever Open, Clear and Free: The Struggle for Chicago's Lakefront*, 2nd ed. (Chicago: University of Chicago Press, 1991), 25.

107. "Gem of the Prairie," in Andreas, *History of Chicago*, 190.

108. Hill, *Chicago River*, 100; Cain, *Sanitation Strategy*, 24–29.

109. Cain, *Sanitation Strategy*, 37, 46.

110. Ibid., 64. Cain noted that as much as 12 percent of the city's population died as a result of waterborne illness in 1885. That figure is much higher than the actual number of deaths, which has been exaggerated by various public officials, writers, and journalists over time—some of whom Cain cite. On the causes of misinformation about the epidemic see Libby Hill, "The Chicago Epidemic of 1885: An Urban Legend?," *Journal of Illinois History* 9 (2006): 154–174.

111. Cain, *Sanitation Strategy*, 69–70.

112. Dunham in U.S. House Committee on Rivers and Harbors, *Chicago River*, February 28, 1896, 4, 6.

113. In 1893, Marshall recommended that "no improvement in the Chicago River should be made by the General Government . . . so long as the city of Chicago uses it as a dumping ground for its filth" (Army Corps of Engineers, *1893 Annual Report of the Chief of Engineers*, 2799).

114. Elkins in Dreiser, "Smallest and Busiest River," 85.

115. Chicago Department of Public Works, *1877–1900 Annual Reports*.

116. Madden in U.S. House Committee on Rivers and Harbors, *Chicago River*, February 28, 1896, 13.

117. Hill, *Chicago River*, 186–187; State of Wisconsin, et al. v. State of Illinois et al., 281 U.S. 179 (1930).

118. Hill, *Chicago River*, 183.

119. Keith in Chicago Harbor Commission, *Report to the Mayor and Aldermen of the City of Chicago*, 329.

120. The current led many boatmen to use tugs to guide their ships through the channel, which, in turn, added to the cost of shipping goods via the Chicago River (Chicago Harbor Commission, *Report to the Mayor and Aldermen of the City of Chicago*, 33).

121. Busse message to the Chicago City Council in Chicago Harbor Commission, *Report to the Mayor and Aldermen of the City of Chicago*, 6.

122. "Death Closes Varied Career of Fred Busse," *Chicago Tribune*, July 10, 1914, 5; John W. Leonard, ed., *The Book of Chicagoans: A Biographical Dictionary of Leading Living Men of the City of Chicago* (Chicago: A. N. Marquis and Company, 1905), 98.

123. Chicago Harbor Commission, *Report to the Mayor and Aldermen of the City of Chicago*, 11.

124. Table 4.

125. Johnson in Chicago Harbor Commission, *Report to the Mayor and Aldermen of the City of Chicago*, 353.

126. Tables 5 and 6.

127. Table 5.

128. Tables 5 and 6.

129. Homer Hoyt, *One Hundred Years of Land Values in Chicago: The Relationship of the Growth of Chicago to the Rise in Its Land Values, 1830–1933* (Chicago: University of Chicago Press, 1933), 214.

130. "Elevators at South Chicago," *American Elevator and Grain Trade*, March 10, 1892, 301.

131. Wheeler in Army Corps of Engineers, *1876 Annual Report of the Chief of Engineers*, 441.

132. Hoyt, *One Hundred Years of Land Values in Chicago*, 214.

133. After 1915, there was a precipitous drop in grain tonnage carried on both the Chicago and Calumet Rivers. It is not clear why this occurred. It is possible that it had something to do with crop failure, the war preparedness movement, or the success of the railroad and trucking industries.

134. Table 6. The Calumet River did not show increases in building materials. Since lumber comprised the majority of building materials, it is likely that the denuding of Midwestern forests prevented the Calumet River from becoming a significant port for building materials. On the destruction of Midwestern forests see William Cronon, *Nature's Metropolis: Chicago and the Great West* (New York: Norton, 1991), 200–206.

135. Lewis, *Chicago Made*, 55, 37.

136. Lieut. Col. W.H. Bixby, Corps of Engineers, "Preliminary Examination of Calumet River, Illinois, from One Hundred and Twenty-Second Street, Chicago, to Its Forks," in House

Committee on Rivers and Harbor, *Calumet River, Illinois*, 60th Cong., 1st Sess., December 16, 1907, 3–4.

137. Kremer in Chicago Harbor Commission, *Report to the Mayor and Aldermen of the City of Chicago*, 325.

138. Daniel H. Burnham and Edward H. Bennett, *Plan of Chicago* (Chicago: Commercial Club of Chicago, 1909).

Chapter 4

1. Frederick Jackson Turner, "The Significance of the Frontier in American History," 1893, reprinted in *History, Frontier, and Section: Three Essays by Fredrick Jackson Turner*, ed. Martin Ridge (Albuquerque: University of New Mexico Press, 1993), 1–11, 59, 61, 82. Turner was born in 1861 to a school teacher turned homemaker and a newspaper editor turned politician in Portage, Wisconsin. He witnessed firsthand how small, landed proprietary capitalists civilized a frontier town full of Indians, loggers, and ruffians. Turner took advantage of the education that his white, middle-class status afforded him; he attended the University of Wisconsin and then went on to graduate school at Johns Hopkins University. At Johns Hopkins, Turner studied with Herbert Baxter Adams. A leading historian, Adams advanced a "germ theory" of history that located key characteristics of American institutions in medieval tribal structures. Ironically, Adams himself set the stage for an event that would present the greatest challenge to his germ theory when he invited his former student, Turner, by then a professor at the University of Wisconsin, to present a paper to the American Historical Association meeting at the Chicago World's Fair. Turner's address, "The Significance of the Frontier in American History," transformed how many Americans thought about their nation's past. Rooted in his own life experiences in the small town of Portage, Wisconsin, Turner's thesis attacked the prevailing views of the East Coast-based, German-trained historians. Turner argued that American institutions had been shaped by the unique conditions of life on the frontier more than by their European origins.

2. Harlow N. Higginbotham, *Report of the President to the Board of Directors of the World's Columbian Exposition, 1892–1893* (Chicago: Rand, McNally, and Company, 1898), 9.

3. Turner, "The Significance of the Frontier in American History," 59.

4. Ibid., 88.

5. Historian Nell Irvin Painter has aptly described the nation as "standing at Armageddon" (Nell Irvin Painter, *Standing at Armageddon: The United States, 1877–1919* [New York: Norton, 1989]).

6. James Green, *Death in the Haymarket: A Story of Chicago, the First Labor Movement, and the Bombing that Divided Gilded Age America* (New York: Pantheon, 2006); Carl Smith, *Urban Disorder and the Shape of Belief: The Great Chicago Fire, the Haymarket Bomb, and the Model Town of Pullman* (Chicago: University of Chicago Press, 2007).

7. On smoke, see Christine M. Rosen, "Businessmen Against Pollution in Late Nineteenth Century Chicago," *Business History Review* 69, 3 (Fall 1995): 351–397. On sanitation, see Louis P. Cain, *Sanitation Strategy for a Lakefront Metropolis: The Case of Chicago* (DeKalb: Northern Illinois University Press, 1978). On inequality, see Richard Schneirov, *Labor and Urban Politics: Class Conflict and the Origins of Modern Liberalism in Chicago, 1864–97* (Urbana: University of Illinois Press, 1998) and Green, *Death in the Haymarket*.

8. "Lake Park in Vision," *Chicago Tribune*, March 28, 1897, 1.

9. Frederick Jackson Turner, *The Frontier in American History* (New York: Henry Holt and

Company, 1921), 32. Historians have shown that even though landscape architects attempted to use parks as a means of social control, working-class people often appropriated parks and put them to very different uses than their designers had intended. See, for example, Roy Rosenzweig and Elisabeth Blackmar, *The Park and the People: A History of Central Park* (Ithaca, N.Y.: Cornell University Press, 1998).

10. William Cronon, *Nature's Metropolis: Chicago and the Great West* (New York: Norton, 1991).

11. Biographical material from S. B. Sutton, ed., *Fredrick Law Olmsted Civilizing American Cities: A Selection of Frederick Law Olmsted's Writings on City Landscapes* (Cambridge, Mass.: MIT Press, 1971), 2–10. On Central Park, see Rosenzwieg and Blackmar, *The Park and The People*.

12. Frederick Law Olmsted, "The Structure of Cities: A Historical View," 1868, reprinted in *Civilizing American Cities: A Selection of Frederick Law Olmsted's Writings on City Landscapes*, ed. S. B. Sutton (Cambridge, Mass.: MIT Press, 1971), 36.

13. Ibid., 40.

14. Ibid., 40.

15. Cleveland in Daniel Bluestone, *Constructing Chicago* (New Haven, Conn.: Yale University Press, 1991), 22.

16. Bross in Bluestone, *Constructing Chicago*, 26. Also see, *The Papers of Frederick Law Olmsted: The California Frontier 1863–1865*, vol. 5, ed. Victoria Post Ranney, Gerard J. Rauluk, and Carolyn F. Hoffman (Baltimore: Johns Hopkins University Press, 1990), 438. In the spring of 1866, Olmsted sent Bross his San Francisco parks report. Bross, who "wanted a like improvement for Chicago," estimated that Chicagoans could be "brought up to the determination of doing something handsome at the next meeting of the legislature." In 1869, the Illinois State Legislature established three park commissions in the city, one each for the North, West, and South Sides of Chicago.

17. Bluestone, *Constructing Chicago*, 22.

18. Bross in ibid., 24.

19. Daniel H. Burnham and Edward H. Bennett, *Plan of Chicago* (Chicago: Commercial Club of Chicago, 1909).

20. Bluestone, *Constructing Chicago*, 24.

21. I. J. Bryan, "A History of Lincoln Park," in Commissioners of Lincoln Park, *Report of the Commissioners* (Chicago, 1898–1899).

22. Glen E. Holt, "Private Plans for Public Spaces: The Origins of Chicago's Park System, 1850–1875," *Chicago History* 8, 3 (Fall 1979): 177.

23. John H. Rauch, M.D., *Public Parks: Their Effects upon the Moral, Physical and Sanitary Condition of the Inhabitants of Large Cities: With special reference to Chicago* (Chicago: S. C. Griggs and Company, 1869), 31.

24. Ibid., 8.

25. Ibid., 31.

26. Ibid., 32.

27. Ibid., 83.

28. Ibid., 83.

29. The Chicago South Park Commission established by the February 24, 1869, law provided for the creation of the South Park; its members were appointed by the governor of Illinois (*Private Laws of the State of Illinois*, Passed by the Twenty-Sixth General Assembly, Convened January 4, 1869, vol. 1 [Springfield, Ill.: Journal Printing Office, 1869], 358–366).

30. Holt, "Private Plans for Public Spaces," 178.

31. Ibid., 178–179.

32. Olmsted, Vaux & Co. to Chicago South Park Commission, March 1871, "Landscape Themes for a Park in Chicago," *The Papers of Frederick Law Olmsted: The Years of Olmsted, Vaux & Co., 1865–1874*, vol. 6, ed. Charles E. Beveridge and Carolyn R. Hoffman (Baltimore: Johns Hopkins University Press, 1992), 235.

33. Olmsted, Vaux & Co. to William Edward Dorsheimer, October 1, 1868, "First Park System of Olmsted, Vaux and Co.," *The Papers of Frederick Law Olmsted,*" 162.

34. Ibid., 162, 163, 167; Fredrick Law Olmsted, "Chicago: Taming the Waterfront," 1871, in *Frederick Law Olmsted Civilizing American Cities: A selection of Frederick Law Olmsted's Writings on City Landscapes*, ed. S. B. Sutton (Cambridge, Mass.: MIT Press, 1971), 183.

35. Holt, "Private Plans for Public Spaces," 181.

36. Colin Fisher, *Urban Green: Nature, Recreation, and the Working Class in Industrial Chicago* (Chapel Hill: University of North Carolina Press, 2015), 14.

37. For a discussion of beauty as a response to the class conflicts of the Gilded Age, see Alan Trachtenberg, *The Incorporation of America: Culture and Society in the Gilded Age* (New York: Hill and Wang, 1982), 217.

38. Olmsted, "Chicago: Taming the Waterfront," 183.

39. "Lake-Front Set Aside," *Chicago Tribune*, August 20, 1890, 1.

40. Ibid.

41. Olmsted, "Chicago: Taming the Waterfront," 183.

42. Higginbotham, President of the Columbian Exposition, *Report of the President to the Board of Directors of the World's Columbian Exposition*, 20. Also see, "Lake Front Advocates," *Chicago Tribune*, March 2, 1890, 3.

43. "Lake-Front Set Aside," *Chicago Tribune,* 1; "The Lake-Front and the Exposition," *Chicago Tribune*, January 18, 1891, 12.

44. "Lake Front Advocates," *Chicago Tribune,* 3.

45. "Lake-Front Set Aside," *Chicago Tribune,* 1.

46. Illinois Central Railroad v. Illinois, 146 U.S. 387 (1892).

47. Higginbotham, *Report of the President to the Board of Directors of the World's Columbian Exposition*, 23.

48. Ibid., 33.

49. Thomas S. Hines, *Burnham of Chicago: Architect and Planner* (New York: Oxford University Press, 1974), 5.

50. Hines, *Burnham of Chicago*, 16.

51. Robert W. Rydell, "World's Columbian Exposition," *The Encyclopedia of Chicago*, ed. James R. Grossman, Ann Durkin Keating, and Janice L. Reiff (Chicago: University of Chicago Press, 2004), 898–902.

52. Rydell, "World's Columbian Exposition," 898–902.

53. Schneirov, *Labor and Urban Politics*, 335–342; Smith, *Urban Disorder and the Shape of Belief*.

54. Smith, *Urban Disorder and the Shape of Belief*.

55. H. G. Wells in Fisher, *Urban Green*, 41.

56. Lois Wille, *Forever Open, Clear and Free: The Struggle for Chicago's Lakefront*, 2nd ed. (Chicago: University of Chicago Press, 1991), 71–73; Joseph D. Kearney and Thomas Merrill,

"Private Rights in Public Lands: The Chicago Lakefront, Montgomery Ward, and the Public Dedication Doctrine," *Northwestern Law Review* 105, 4 (Fall, 2011): 1417–1529.

57. Wille, *Forever Open, Clear and Free*, 73–74.

58. *Illinois Central Railroad*, 146 U.S. at 387.

59. William H. Wilson, *The City Beautiful Movement* (Baltimore: Johns Hopkins University Press, 1994).

60. "Career of Success," *Chicago Tribune*, November 23, 1893, 3. Quote in "Museum Has a Boom," *Chicago Tribune*, November 21, 1893, 12.

61. "Museum Has a Boom," 12.

62. "Career of Success," 3.

63. "His Plan for a Park," *Chicago Tribune*, January 18, 1895, 1.

64. "Is Against Porter," *Chicago Tribune*, December 12, 1893, 4.

65. "Dream of an Artist," *Chicago Tribune*, November 28, 1894, 8.

66. According to Louis Menand and Michael Schudson individual rights were far less important to late nineteenth- and early twentieth-century Americans than they have been to Americans since the late twentieth century (Louis Menand, *The Metaphysical Club: A Story of Ideas in America* [New York: Farrar, Strauss and Giroux, 2001] and Michael Schudson, *The Good Citizen: A History of American Civic Life* [New York: The Free Press, 1998]). According to Lizabeth Cohen, consumerism, not common landscapes, fostered unity among culturally diverse groups. See Lizabeth Cohen, *Making a New Deal: Industrial Workers in Chicago, 1919–1939* (Cambridge: Cambridge University Press, 1990).

67. Carl Smith, *The Plan of Chicago: Daniel Burnham and the Remaking of the American City* (Chicago: University of Chicago Press, 2006), 43.

68. Addams led efforts to expose urban youth to healthy landscapes, nature, and games (Fisher, *Urban Green*, 22–23, 66–67).

69. Andrew Wender Cohen, *The Racketeer's Progress: Chicago and the Struggle for the Modern American Economy, 1900–1940* (Cambridge: Cambridge University Press, 2004), 13–17.

70. "League Under Way," *Chicago Tribune*, October 27, 1894, 14.

71. Ibid.

72. "Plan for New Park," *Chicago Inter Ocean*, August 10, 1895, 9.

73. Bluestone, *Constructing Chicago*, 189.

74. "His Lake Front Plan," *Chicago Tribune*, November 30, 1894, 4.

75. Smith, *The Plan of Chicago*, chap. 4, passim.

76. "Lake-Front Is Won," *Chicago Tribune*, October 22, 1895, 1.

77. "Position of the I.C.," *Chicago Inter Ocean*, August 10, 1895, 6.

78. "Ready for a Vote," *Chicago Tribune*, September 16, 1895, 1.

79. "Lake Front Passes," *Chicago Inter Ocean*, October 22, 1895, 1.

80. "Why Fight the Lake-Front Park?," *Chicago Tribune*, June 30, 1895, 12; "Lake Front Passes," 1.

81. "Lake-Front on Top," *Chicago Tribune*, September 17, 1895, 1.

82. "Has a Good Appetite for Refuse," *Chicago Tribune*, April 13, 1896, 1.

83. "Accepts the Lake-Front," *Chicago Tribune*, October 15, 1896, 7.

84. Dennis H. Cremin, "Building Chicago's Front Yard: Grant Park 1836 to 1936" (Ph.D. diss., Loyola University Chicago, 1999), 223–224.

85. "No Finer on Earth," *Chicago Tribune*, June 4, 1895, 1.

86. "Plans for Lake Front Park and South Shore Drive," *Chicago Inter Ocean*, October 11, 1896, 25.

87. Ibid.

88. Ibid.

89. "City's New Year Needs," *Chicago Tribune*, January 3, 1897, 37.

90. Ibid.

91. Smith, *The Plan of Chicago*, 54.

92. Ibid., 65.

93. Ibid., 65.

94. Ibid., 64.

95. "Make a Fine Park," *Chicago Tribune*, December 30, 1894, 1.

96. "Lake Park in Vision," 1.

97. Smith, *The Plan of Chicago*, 67.

98. Chicago Commercial Club, "History of the Chicago Plan." Not dated. Chicago Commercial Club Collection, Chicago History Museum, Chicago, Ill. Box 26. Folder 2.

99. Ibid.

100. Ibid. For more on this discussion, see Smith, *The Plan of Chicago*, 67–70.

101. Chicago Commercial Club, "History of the Chicago Plan."

102. Smith, *The Plan of Chicago*, 71.

103. Chicago Commercial Club, Committee on Plan of Chicago, "Message to Subscribers," June 11, 1907. Chicago Commercial Club Collection, Chicago History Museum, Chicago, Ill. Box 26. Folder 2, 1.

104. Chicago Commercial Club, Committee on Plan of Chicago, "Message to Subscribers," 2.

105. Ibid., 3; Illinois State Legislature, Law of 1903 cited in Chicago Harbor Commission, *Report to the Mayor and Aldermen of the City of Chicago* (Chicago: H. G. Adair, 1909), 255.

106. Smith, *The Plan of Chicago*, 2.

107. "Explain Details of Great Chicago," *Chicago Tribune*, July 4, 1909, 1.

108. Burnham and Bennett, *Plan of Chicago*, 1.

109. James C. Scott, *Seeing Like A State: How Certain Schemes to Improve the Human Condition Have Failed* (New Haven, Conn.: Yale University Press, 1999); David Jordan, *Transforming Paris: The Life and Labors of Baron Haussman* (New York: Free Press, 1995).

110. Burnham, *Plan of Chicago*, 18.

111. Special Park Commission, *Report of the Special Park Commission to the City Council of Chicago on the Subject of a Metropolitan Park System*, 1904, compiled by Dwight Heald Perkins (Chicago: printed by W.J. Hartman, Co, 1905).

112. Burnham, *Plan of Chicago*, 44.

113. Ibid., 47–48.

114. Ibid., 50.

115. Ibid., 53.

116. Ibid., 50–52.

117. Ibid., 110.

118. Ibid., 112.

119. Ibid., 68, 111.

120. Wille, *Forever Open, Clear and Free*, 77–79; Kearney and Merrill, "Private Rights in Public Lands."

121. Wille, *Forever Open, Clear and Free*, 80–81; Kearney and Merrill, "Private Rights in Public Lands."

122. Chicago Commercial Club, Committee on Plan of Chicago, "Message to Subscribers," 2.

Chapter 5

1. Fred Busse, "Copy of Mayor Busse's Letter to the Secretary of War Transmitted to the Council in Connection with the Mayor's Special Message of January 6, 1908," and "Copy of Resolution Creating the Chicago Harbor Commission, Passed by the City Council January 6, 1908," in Chicago Harbor Commission, *Report to the Mayor and Aldermen of the City of Chicago*, 7–9, University of Illinois at Chicago Special Collections, Chicago, Ill.

2. Ibid., 6.

3. John W. Leonard, ed., *The Book of Chicagoans: A Biographical Dictionary of Leading Living Men of the City of Chicago* (Chicago: A. N. Marquis and Company, 1905); Albert Nelson Marquis, ed., *The Book of Chicagoans: A Biographical Dictionary of Leading Living Men and Women of the City of Chicago* (Chicago: A. N. Marquis and Company, 1917), 470, 698.

4. Douglas Bukowski, *Navy Pier: A Chicago Landmark* (Chicago: Metropolitan Pier and Exposition Authority, 1996).

5. Chicago Commercial Association, "From Great Lakes to the Gulf: Fundamental Elements of the Great Deep Waterway Proposition Exhaustively and Impartially Formulated by the Chicago Commercial Association," *The Bulletin* 2, 9 (July 13, 1906): 4–5; Chicago Harbor Commission, *Report to the Mayor and Aldermen of the City of Chicago*, 18.

6. Ibid., 18.

7. Libby Hill, *The Chicago River: A Natural and Unnatural History* (Chicago: Lake Claremont Press, 2000), 197. On the prospects of the Lakes to the Gulf, see Chicago Harbor Commission, *Report to the Mayor and Aldermen of the City of Chicago*, 22.

8. J. Paul Goode, "The Development of Commercial Ports: Report to the Chicago Harbor Commission," November 10, 1908, in Chicago Harbor Commission, *Report to the Mayor and Aldermen of the City of Chicago*, 151.

9. John Lauritz Larson, *Bonds of Enterprise: John Murray Forbes and Western Development in America's Railway Age* (Iowa City: University of Iowa Press, 2001); Chicago Harbor Commission, *Report to the Mayor and Aldermen of the City of Chicago*, 18.

10. Maj. J. B. Wheeler, in Army Corps of Engineers, *1876 Annual Report of the Chief of Engineers*, 435, U. S. Congressional Serial Set.

11. Army Corps of Engineers, *1893 Annual Report of the Chief of Engineers*, 2791.

12. Chicago Harbor Commission, *Report to the Mayor and Aldermen of the City of Chicago*, 11.

13. John C. Scales, "Chicago's Harbor Problem," August 23, 1911, in *Chicago Harbor and Adjacent Waterways*, 63rd Cong., 1st Sess., September 15, 1913, 188; Lyman E. Cooley, in Chicago Harbor Commission, *Report to the Mayor and Aldermen of the City of Chicago*, 380; Chicago Harbor Commission, *Report to the Mayor and Aldermen of the City of Chicago*, 42.

14. Louis P. Cain, *Sanitation Strategy for a Lakefront Metropolis: The Case of Chicago* (DeKalb: Northern Illinois University Press, 1978).

15. Lyman E. Cooley in Chicago Harbor Commission, *Report to the Mayor and Aldermen of the City of Chicago*, 380; Chicago Harbor Commission, *Report to the Mayor and Aldermen of the City of Chicago*, 42.

16. Chicago Commercial Association, "Mr. C.L. Dering on River Improvement," *Chicago Commerce* 4, 14 (August 14, 1908): 16.

17. George G. Tunell, "The Volume and Trend of Traffic to and from the Central West," in Chicago Harbor Commission, *Report to the Mayor and Aldermen of the City of Chicago*, 241.

18. Tunell, "The Volume and Trend of Traffic to and from the Central West," 238–239.

19. Edward Hines Lumber Company, "Letter of the Edward Hines Lumber Company to Lieut. Col. George A. Zinn," January 31, 1911, in U.S. House Committee on Rivers and Harbors, *Chicago Harbor and Adjacent Waterways*, 170.

20. Chicago Commercial Association, "Lake Harbor or Lake Park?," *Chicago Commerce* 3, 35 (January 10, 1908): 19.

21. Engineer Ellis Chesbrough reversed the Chicago River in 1871, but it sometimes flowed backward into Lake Michigan when water levels were high.

22. Daniel H. Burnham and Edward H. Bennett, *Plan of Chicago* (Chicago: Commercial Club of Chicago, 1909), 8; *Chicago Tribune*, cited in Chicago Commercial Association, "Lake Harbor or Lake Park?," *Chicago Commerce*, 17–18.

23. *Chicago Daily News* and *Chicago Tribune*, cited in Chicago Commercial Association, "Lake Harbor or Lake Park?," *Chicago Commerce*, 17.

24. Chicago Harbor Commission, *Report to the Mayor and Aldermen of the City of Chicago*, 40–42.

25. Ibid., 251.

26. Ibid., 41–42.

27. Ibid., 11.

28. Georg Leidenberger, *Chicago's Progressive Alliance: Labor and the Bid for Public Streetcars* (DeKalb: Northern Illinois University Press, 2006); Delos F. Wilcox, *Municipal Franchises: A Description of the Terms and Conditions Upon Which Private Corporations Enjoy Special Privileges in the Streets of American Cities*, vol. 2 (New York: Engineering News Publishing, 1911), 464–483.

29. This assessment of trends is based on a keyword search for the phrase "public utility" in the *Chicago Tribune*, 1857–1898.

30. Alderman Charles Foell, "Report of Committee on Harbors, Wharves, and Bridges on the Report of the Chicago Harbor Commission," *Journal of the Proceedings of the City Council of the City of Chicago, Illinois*, March 21, 1910, 3542.

31. Goode, "The Development of Commercial Ports," in Chicago Harbor Commission, *Report to the Mayor and Aldermen of the City of Chicago*, 62.

32. Foell, "Report of Committee on Harbors, Wharves, and Bridges on the Report of the Chicago Harbor Commission," 3550.

33. Goode, "The Development of Commercial Ports," 116, 121.

34. Foell, "Report of Committee on Harbors, Wharves, and Bridges on the Report of the Chicago Harbor Commission," 3548.

35. Ibid., 2556.

36. Ibid., 3551, 3556.

37. *Yesler v. Washington Harbor Line Commissioners*, 146 U.S. 646 (1892).

38. Washington Harbor Line Commission, in "Report of Committee on Harbors, Wharves, and Bridges on the Report of the Chicago Harbor Commission," *Journal of the Proceedings of the City Council of the City of Chicago, Illinois*, 3560.

39. Foell, "Report of Committee on Harbors, Wharves, and Bridges on the Report of the Chicago Harbor Commission," 3561.

40. Chicago Harbor Commission, *Report to the Mayor and Aldermen of the City of Chicago*, 103.

41. Goode, "The Development of Commercial Ports," 103–105.

42. Ibid., 74.

43. Ibid., 105.

44. Foell, "Report of Committee on Harbors, Wharves, and Bridges on the Report of the Chicago Harbor Commission," 3543.

45. Ibid., 3564–3565.

46. Ibid., 3558–3561.

47. Ibid., 3562; George C. Sikes, "Obstacles to Chicago's Water Shipping Development," October 1908, in Chicago Harbor Commission, *Report to the Mayor and Aldermen of the City of Chicago* (Chicago: H. G. Adair, 1909), 170.

48. Foell, "Report of Committee on Harbors, Wharves, and Bridges on the Report of the Chicago Harbor Commission," 3563; Sikes, "Obstacles to Chicago's Water Shipping Development," 170; William Cronon, *Nature's Metropolis: Chicago and the Great West* (New York: Norton, 1991), 55–96.

49. Chicago Harbor Commission, *Report to the Mayor and Aldermen of the City of Chicago*, 3; Marquis, *The Book of Chicagoans*, 622.

50. Sikes, "Obstacles to Chicago's Water Shipping Development,"189.

51. Ibid., 192.

52. Sikes, "Obstacles to Chicago's Water Shipping Development,"190–91.

53. *Chicago Daily News*, January 20, 1910, in Chicago Commercial Association, "Forces Inducing Decline of Water Shipments Between Chicago and Atlantic Seaboard," *Chicago Commerce* 5, 37 (January 21, 1910): 15.

54. Sikes, "Obstacles to Chicago's Water Shipping Development," 190–191.

55. *Chicago Daily News*, "Forces Inducing Decline of Water Shipments Between Chicago and Atlantic Seaboard,"15.

56. Chicago Board of Trade, *1913 Annual Report*, xxx, University of Illinois at Chicago Special Collections, Chicago, Ill.

57. Sikes, "Obstacles to Chicago's Water Shipping Development," 195; Chicago Board of Trade, *1915 Annual Report*, xxx.

58. Chicago Board of Trade, *1913 Annual Report*, xxxi; Chicago Board of Trade, *1915 Annual Report*, xxvii; Chicago Board of Trade, *1916 Annual Report*, xxx-xxxi. For railroad defense, see "Chicago is Loser in Rates Fight," *Chicago Tribune*, April 13, 1911, 10; for the ongoing controversy over rates, see, "Say Roads Drive Grain Off Lakes," *Chicago Tribune*, December 15, 1910, 16; "Tells Grain Rate Secret," *Chicago Tribune*, December 17, 1910, 16.

59. Sikes, "Obstacles to Chicago's Water Shipping Development," 198.

60. Frederic Rex, Assistant City Statistician, Chicago, Illinois, in J. A. Bensel et al., "Notes on Municipal Government: Port Administration and Harbor Facilities: A Symposium," *Annals of the American Academy of Political and Social Sciences* 29 (March 1907): 120.

61. Col. E. S. Conway in Chicago Commercial Association, "Ways and Means Hears Argument for Outer Harbor for Passenger and Package Traffic," *Chicago Commerce* 7, 24 (October 20, 1911): 19.

62. "Letter written by H.C. Barlow, Traffic Director, and approved by Charles L. Dering, Chairman, Rivers and Harbors Committee and E.S. Conway, Chairman, Special Outer Harbor

Committee, of the Chicago Association of Commerce to the Army Corps of Engineers Lieut. Col. George A. Zinn," May 15, 1911, in U.S. House Committee on Rivers and Harbors, *Chicago Harbor and Adjacent Waterways*, 199.

63. "Chicago's Harbor Bills Face Crisis at Capital Today," *Chicago Tribune*, April 19, 1911, 1, 4.

64. "B. F. Kleeman Dead; Attorney, Ex-Legislator," *Chicago Tribune*, September 5, 1934, 14.

65. "Calumet Harbor Called a 'Grab,'" *Chicago Tribune*, May 13, 1913, 4.

66. Chicago Commercial Association, "How Obstruction to Outer Harbor Legislation Threatens Welfare of City and State," *Chicago Commerce* 6, 50 (April 21, 1911): 8

67. "See Realty Grab in Kleeman Bill for Calumet Port," *Chicago Tribune*, May 24, 1911, 1.

68. Ibid.

69. "Kleeman Defends his Measure to Create Calumet Harbor," *Chicago Tribune*, June 12, 1913, 6.

70. "B. F. Kleeman, In a Second Article, Defends the Calumet Harbor Measure," *Chicago Tribune*, June 13, 1913, 6.

71. Chicago Harbor Commission, *Report to the Mayor and Aldermen of the City of Chicago*, 57.

72. On the legislative wrangling over the Kleeman, Juul, and O'Connor Bills, see "Kleeman Bill in Vote Trade Deal?," *Chicago Tribune*, April 25, 1911, 9 ; "Crisis for Outer Harbor," *Chicago Tribune*, May, 17, 1911, 4; and "Juul Harbor Bill Beaten," *Chicago Tribune*, May 18, 1911, 7.

73. "Governor Signs Many Big Bills; Vetoes Several," *Chicago Tribune*, June 12, 1911, 1.

74. Cain, *Sanitation Strategy for a Lakefront Metropolis*, 84–106.

75. "Mayor Asks Subway Men to Plan a Harbor," *Chicago Tribune*, November 14, 1911, 3.

76. W. H. Bixby, "Report to Henry L. Stimson, Secretary of War," April 20, 1912, in *Chicago Harbor and Adjacent Waterways*, 2, 5.

77. Bukowski, *Navy Pier*, 15; "Senate Approves of Outer Harbor," *Chicago Tribune* April 25, 1913, 4.

78. "City Port Halted by 'Joker' in Law," *Chicago Tribune* June 26, 1912, 1.

79. Ibid.

80. "Senate Approves of Outer Harbor," 4.

81. "Reports Outer Harbor Bill," *Chicago Tribune* May 8, 1913, 4.

82. "B. F. Kleeman, In a Second Article, Defends the Calumet Harbor Measure," 6.

83. "Will Dunne Sign? Suffrage Waits," *Chicago Tribune* June 24, 1913, 2; Chicago Department of Public Works, *1914 Annual Report*, lxxxv.

84. "Gov. Dunne Vetoes Kleeman Bill for Calumet Harbor," *Chicago Tribune* June 17, 1913, 1.

85. Chicago Department of Public Works, *1921 Annual Report*, 137; Arend Van Vlissingen, *Plan and Report: Lake Calumet Harbor* (Chicago: Chicago City Council, Committee on Harbors, Wharves, and Bridges, 1920).

86. David M. Solzman, *The Chicago River: An Illustrated History and Guide to the River and Its Waterways*, 2nd ed. (Chicago: University of Chicago Press, 2006), 182.

87. Illinois Central Railroad v. Illinois, 146 U.S. 387 (1892).

88. Burnham, *Plan of Chicago*.

89. During the latter half of the late nineteenth century and the first two decades of the twentieth century, architects including Burnham decorated urban landscapes with beaux-arts style buildings, parks, and boulevards. Granger and his new partner Charles Sumner Frost followed suit, designing railroad stations in the beaux-art fashion in Chicago and across the Midwest. In 1910, the architects' partnership dissolved when Granger moved to Philadelphia. After

his French-trained collaborator left for the East Coast, Frost continued working in the beaux-art style. Like many architects of his age, Frost considered the beaux-art style well-suited for large, monumental, civic structures like Municipal Pier (Bukowski, *Navy Pier*, 16).

90. House Committee on Rivers and Harbors, *Hearings on the Subject of Improvement of Chicago Harbor, Ill.*, 64th Cong., 1st Sess., December 13, 1915, 6.

91. Bukowski, *Navy Pier*, 17–20; Ira W. Hoover, "The Chicago Municipal Pier: Charles S. Frost, Architect," *Brickbuilder* 25 (October 1916): 261–264.

92. U.S. House Committee on Rivers and Harbors, *Hearings on the Subject of Improvement of Chicago Harbor and River, Ill.*, 63rd Cong., 6th Sess., December 12, 1914, 6, 10.

93. U.S. House Committee on Rivers and Harbors, *Hearings on the Subject of Improvement of Chicago Harbor, Ill.*, 6.

94. The Harbor and Subway Commission of the City of Chicago, *Report on Dock and Pier Development, Harbor District No. 1* (Chicago: Chicago City Council, February 7, 1912), 5.

95. Bukowski, *Navy Pier*, 20.

96. Chicago Department of Public Works, *1917 Annual Report of the Department of Public Works*, 17.

97. Bukowski, *Navy Pier*, 33.

98. Committee on Chicago Harbor and Port Survey of the Commercial Club of Chicago, *The Harbor Plan of Chicago* (Chicago: Commercial Club of Chicago, 1927), 47.

99. Chicago Department of Public Works, *1917 Annual Report*, 17.

100. Perry Duis, *The Saloon: Public Drinking in Chicago and Boston, 1880–1920* (Chicago: University of Illinois Press, 1998).

101. Carl Smith, *The Plan of Chicago: Daniel Burnham and the Remaking of the American City* (Chicago: University of Chicago Press, 2006), 43.

102. "Spend Your Vacation on the $5,000,000 Municipal Pier," September 10 (Chicago: Bentley Murray and Co., 1918), 1.

Epilogue

1. Blair Kamin, "The Millennium Park Effect," *Chicago Tribune*, June 26, 2005.

2. Daniel Burnham, in "Lake Park in Vision," *Chicago Tribune*, March 28, 1897, 1.

3. Timothy J. Gilfoyle, *Millennium Park: Creating a Chicago Landmark* (Chicago: University of Chicago Press, 2006), 81–82.

4. Marc Doussard, Jamie Peck, and Nik Theodore, "After Deindustrialization: Uneven Growth and Economic Inequality in "Postindustrial" Chicago," *Economic Geography* 85, 2 (April, 2009): 183–207.

5. David M. Solzman, *The Chicago River: An Illustrated History and Guide to the River and Its Waterways*, 2nd ed. (Chicago: University of Chicago Press, 2006), 160.

6. Doussard, Peck, and Theodore, "After Deindustrialization," 184, 187.

7. R. C. Longworth, "City on the Brink," *Chicago Tribune*, May 10, 1981, 1.

8. Francis Cairncross, *The Death of Distance: How the Communications Revolution Is Changing Our Lives* (Cambridge, Mass.: Harvard Business Review Press, 2001); Thomas L. Friedman, *The World Is Flat: A Brief History of the Twenty-First Century* (New York: Farrar, Straus and Giroux, 2005), 216.

9. Gilfoyle, *Millennium Park*, 83.

10. "A Success Story: A Survey of Chicago," *Economist*, March 18, 2006, 4.

11. Blair Kamin, "Millennium Park: 10 Years Old and a Boon for Art, Commerce, and the

Cityscape," *Chicago Tribune*, July 12, 2014, accessed March 24, 2015, http://www.chicagotribune
.com/news/columnists/ct-millennium-park-at-10-kamin-0713-met-20140712-column
.html#page=1.

12. Gilfoyle, *Millennium Park,* chaps. 9, 12 *passim.*

13. "A Success Story: A Survey of Chicago," 1.

14. Richard Florida, *Who's Your City?: How the Creative Economy Is Making Where to Live
the Most Important Decision of Your Life* (New York: Basic Books, 2008), 52. The term "global
city" was used by Saskia Sassen to describe a city that is a center of world economic and political power (Saskia Sassen, *The Global City: New York, London, Tokyo* [Princeton: Princeton University Press, 1992]). In consultation with Sassen, the Chicago Council on Global
Affairs, the journal *Foreign Policy*, and the Chicago-based consulting firm A. T. Kearny published a ranking of global cities in 2008. A. T. Kearny has continued to publish the rankings,
and Chicago consistently ranks high. It was seventh in the world in 2014. See A. T. Kearny,
2014 Global Cities Index and Emerging Cities Outlook, accessed March 24, 2015, http://www
.atkearney.com/documents/10192/4461492/Global+Cities+Present+and+Future-GCI+2014
.pdf/3628fd7d-70be-41bf-99d6-4c8eaf984cd5.

15. Florida, *Who's Your City?*

16. The Metropolitan Tenants Organization, for instance, criticized Daley for using Tax In-
crement Financing funds intended for poor areas to finance construction of Millennium Park
(Gilfoyle, *Millennium Park*, 159).

17. Munn v. Illinois, 94 U.S. 113 (1877); Illinois Central Railroad v. Illinois, 146 U.S. 387
(1892).

18. Daniel H. Burnham and Edward H. Bennett, *Plan of Chicago* (Chicago: Commercial
Club of Chicago, 1909).

19. Douglas Bukowski, *Navy Pier: A Chicago Landmark* (Chicago: Metropolitan Pier and
Exposition Authority, 1996), 87.

20. Paul Kens, *Judicial Power and Reform Politics: The Anatomy of Lochner v. New York*
(Lawrence: University Press of Kansas); Robert G. McCloskey, *American Conservatism in the
Age of Enterprise: A Study of William Graham Sumner, Stephen J. Field and Andrew Carnegie*
(Cambridge: Harvard University Press, 1951).

21. The affectation doctrine was subsequently weakened by the court's ruling in Wabash, St.
Louis & Pacific Railroad Company v. Illinois, 118 U.S. 557 (1886). The ruling stripped states of
many of their powers to regulate interstate commerce. It also inspired Congress to create the
Interstate Commerce Commission.

22. Budd v. New York, 143 U.S. 517 (1892); Brass v. North Dakota, 153 U.S. 391 (1894).

23. German Alliance Insurance Company v. Kansas, 233 U.S. 389 (1914).

24. Nebbia v. New York, 291 U.S. 502 (1934).

25. Joseph L. Sax, "The Public Trust Doctrine in Natural Resource Law: Effective Judicial
Intervention," *Michigan Law Review*, 68 (January 1970): 489. For more on the public trust doc-
trine see, Molly Selvin, *This Tender and Delicate Business: The Public Trust Doctrine in American
Law, 1789–1920* (New York: Garland, 1987).

26. Tony Phillips, "A New Form of Life," Science @ NASA, accessed December 15, 2007,
http://science.nasa.gov/headlines/y2003/30jul_monolake.htm.

27. John Hart, *Storm Over Mono: The Mono Lake Battle and the California Water Future*
(Berkley: University of California Press, 1996).

28. Peter Hall, *Cities of Tomorrow: An Intellectual History of Urban Planning and Design in the Twentieth Century*, 3rd ed. (Malden, Mass.: Blackwell Publishing, 2003), 198, 212.

29. Ibid., 195.

30. Kevin Kruse, *White Flight: Atlanta and the Making of Modern Conservatism* (Princeton: Princeton University Press, 2007) chap. 4, passim.

Adams, Charles Francis, 46
Adams Street, 135
Addams, Jane, 132, 213n68
Adler, Dankmar, 128
Adler, Max, 144
Adler Planetarium, 144, 175
affectation doctrine, 4, 55, 59, 183, 220n21. See also *Munn v. Illinois* (1877)
Allen, James, 26
Allen Law, 101
American Railway Union, 129
American Revolution, 13
American System, 31
Angell, Joseph, 67–68
Antwerp, 153, 156
Army Corps of Engineers: construction of breakwaters on lakeshore, 72, 74; developing the Calumet River Harbor, 91–93, 181; dredging of the sandbar at the mouth of the Chicago River, 26, 61, 81; dredging of waterways in the Great Lakes region, 88; improvement of the Chicago River, 84, 86. See also Calumet River; Chicago River
Art Institute of Chicago, 117
AT&T Plaza, 178
Athens, 136, 141
Atlantic Ocean, 1, 11–12, 34, 86, 180
Atwood, Charles B., 135

Baltimore, 154
Barlow, H. C., 163
Battle of Fallen Timbers, 13
Bender, George, 26
Bennett, Edward, 140–41
Bennett, Frank, 102
Berlin, 184
Bilbao, 175

Black Hawk, 13–14, 27, 191n9
Bluestone, Daniel, 121
Board of Railroad and Warehouse Commissioners, 50
Boeing, 178
Boone, Levi, 33–34
Boston, 77–78, 83, 125, 161
Bowen, James, 93
BP Pedestrian Bridge, 178
Brayman, Mason, 63–64
breakwaters, 60–64, 69, 72, 74, 134, 167, 171–72, 180. See also Army Corps of Engineers; Illinois Central Railroad
Brewer, David, 76
bridges: "the bridge war," 23–24; delays, 94–98, 181, 207n77; financing and construction 23–24, 40–41, 196n122; replacement of center pier bridges, 99, 207n84. See also Calumet River; Chicago River
British Empire, 13, 24, 184, 191n10
Bronson, Arthur, 19–20
Bross, William, 2, 70–71, 120–21, 123, 130, 211n16
Brown, Henry Billings, 76, 78
Bryan, Thomas B., 117
Bubbly Creek, 84. See also Chicago River
Buffalo, 34, 39, 91, 102, 157–59, 161–62
Burnham, Daniel: advocate of civic beautification, 116, 118, 121, 123, 132–33, 135, 150–51, 174–76, 178, 181–82; background, 127–28; Columbian Exposition plans, 124–25, 127–28; creation and elements of the 1909 *Plan of Chicago*, 95, 116, 135–45; critics, 146–47, 184–85; legacy 3–4, 184–85; Municipal Pier, 146–47, 150–51, 167, 169–71. See also *Plan of Chicago*; World's Columbian Exposition

Busse, Fred, 106, 146–47, 149, 182
Butler, Edward B., 140

Cahill, Edward T., 171–72
Cairncross, Frances, 177–78
Cairo, 42, 63, 192n27
Cal-Sag Canal, 18, 166, 168
Calumet and Chicago Canal and Dock Com-
    pany, 93, 165
Calumet River: annual tonnage, 106–9, 112–
    15, 181, 203n1, 209n133, 209n134; harbor
    construction, 82, 84–87, 90, 92, 164;
    maps, 12, 87; as possible route for the
    Illinois and Michigan Canal, 18; ship-
    ping rates, 102; steel industry, 114–15, 177.
    See also Cal-Sag Canal; Calumet and
    Chicago Canal and Dock Company
Campbell, James L., 131
canals. See Cal-Sag Canal; Illinois and Michi-
    gan Canal
Carr, Harvey, 102
Carson, Pirie, Scott and Company, 163
Carter, Leslie, 140
Cary, William, 49
Centralia, 42
Central Park, 120–21, 123
Charleston, 43
Chesbrough, Ellis Sylvester, 104, 149
Chicago: antebellum land boom, 16–17;
    changes in industrial geography, 85,
    114–16; colonial era, 10–13; competition
    with St. Louis, 14, 43; current economic
    and environmental issues, 185; deindus-
    trialization 176–77; economic growth, 2,
    7, 43–44, 83; global economic signifi-
    cance in the early twenty first century,
    178–79; historical interpretations of
    city's growth, 2–3, 6–7; legacies of the
    city's economic and environmental his-
    tory, 183–85; maps, 11–12, 17, 75, 87; plat-
    ting of the city, 15–16; population, 2, 43,
    97–98; public library, 130; tensions in
    urban life, 117–19. See also Chicago
    Common Council
Chicago Architectural Club, 133
Chicago Association of Commerce, 99, 101,
    162–63. See also Chicago River Improve-
    ment Association
Chicago Board of Trade: founding, 47; rail-
    road and grain elevator rate regulation

49–50; shipping, 91, 161–62. See also
    Munn v. Illinois (1877)
Chicago Commercial Club: advocates of civic
    beauty, 118, 130; members, 132, 137; work
    on the Plan of Chicago, 133, 137–40, 151.
    See also Burnham, Daniel; Plan of
    Chicago
Chicago Common Council (also known as
    the "City Council"): bridge funding, 24,
    41, 99; bridge regulation, 97–98; Com-
    mittee on Harbors, Wharves, and
    Bridges, 152–53, 157, 169; conflict with
    federal officials over lakeshore erosion
    and harbor funding, 28–30; Chicago
    River improvement, 94; Chicago River
    tunnels, 101–2; financing of the River and
    Harbor Convention, 33; managing the
    decline of Chicago River traffic, 106, 146;
    negotiations for right of way with Illinois
    Central Railroad, 63–65; park construc-
    tion, 134–35, 142; tug boat regulation,
    207n80; wharves, 21–23, 192n36, 192n37
Chicago Department of Public Works, 34, 89,
    98, 172
Chicago Fire of 1871, 74, 126
Chicago Harbor Commission: findings 148–
    51, 158–62; formation, 106, 146; port
    statistics, 108–13; recommendations, 155,
    165, 173, 182. See also Busse, Fred; Mu-
    nicipal Pier; Plan of Chicago
Chicago Iron and Steel Company, 93
Chicago Portage, 1, 9–10, 12–15, 179. See also
    Chicago River; Illinois and Michigan
    Canal
Chicago River: bridges, 23–24, 96–100; con-
    nection to Illinois and Michigan Canal,
    16, 18, 20, 39, 190n1, 192n30; current, 105;
    federal funding for improvements, 29–
    30, 93–95; flood of 1849, 40; industry
    and commercial traffic on the river,
    72–73, 83, 86, 144–45, 176, 181, 203n1;
    literary description of, 83–84; main
    branch, 1, 23, 30, 44, 52, 84, 97, 145; maps,
    11–12, 17, 87, 75; migration of industry
    from Chicago River to Calumet River,
    84, 86, 106–11, 114–16, 205n32; north
    branch, 22, 26, 91, 95, 115, 176; reversal,
    16, 104, 149–51; sandbar at the mouth,
    1–2, 9–10, 13–14, 25–27, 179–80; sewage,
    103, 105, 143, 150–51; size of ships on the

river, 90–91; source, 1; south branch, 1, 20, 25, 39, 40, 44, 83, 95–96, 98, 101–2, 104, 145, 192n30; tunnels, 100–102; wharves and docks, 20–22, 162; bridges, 23–24, 96–100; federal funding for improvements, 29–30, 93–95; flood of 1849, 40; industry and commercial traffic on the river, 72–73, 83, 86, 144–45, 176, 181, 203n1; migration of industry from Chicago River to Calumet River, 84, 86, 106–111, 114–16, 205n32; size of ships on the river, 90–91; tunnels, 100–102; sewage, 103, 105, 143, 150–51; current, 105; main branch, 1, 23, 30, 44, 52, 84, 97, 145; north branch, 22, 26, 91, 95, 115, 176; south branch, 1, 20, 25, 39, 40, 44, 83, 95–96, 98, 101–102, 104, 145, 192n30.

Chicago River and Harbor Convention, 33–38, 58, 179. *See also* internal improvements

Chicago River Improvement Association, 85, 91, 93, 99, 104, 115. *See also* Chicago Association of Commerce; Chicago River

Chicago Times, 23–24

Chicago Tribune, 54, 70, 74, 99, 138, 152, 165, 167–68, 175, 177

Chicago Union Stockyards, 84

Chisholm, Thomas H., 52–53

Cincinnati, 43

City Beautiful Movement, 116, 129–30, 141, 169–70, 176. *See also* Burnham, Daniel; *Plan of Chicago*

Civil War, 43–44

Clark Street, 23–24, 40–41

class conflict, 5–6, 116, 118, 128, 132, 174, 182

Clay, Henry, 31, 36

Cleveland, 44, 102, 125, 138, 157

Cleveland, H. W. S., 120

Clinton, Bill, 176

Cloud Gate, 178

coal, 88, 98–99, 102, 106–7, 110–14

Cobb, Henry Ives, 128, 169

Congress: confirmation of judges, 56, 58; establishing Illinois as a territory, 15, 191n18; harbor improvement funding, 25–26, 28–32, 72, 85, 91–95, 104–5, 115, 167, 170–72, 181; land grants, 42, 69; regulation of commerce, 37, 55, 57, 101–2, 220n21

Constitution of the United States, 36–38, 42, 54, 58, 73, 76, 98, 183, 189n19. See also

Illinois Central v. Illinois (1892); *Munn v. Illinois* (1877)

Conway, E. S., 162

Coolbaugh, William, 50

Cooley, Lyman, 150–51

Cornell, Paul, 65, 121, 123

the corporation, 41–42, 56, 59–60, 63–64, 78–79, 139, 177, 183, 203n155. See also *Illinois Central v. Illinois* (1892); *Munn v. Illinois* (1877)

Coughlin, John, 163

Counselman, Charles, 114

Crear Library, 133, 142

creative destruction, 85–86, 91, 115, 204n13

Cregier, DeWitt, 94, 98

Cronon, William, 3, 51, 119, 195n114

Crown Fountain, 178

Daley, Richard M., 176–79

Dart, Joseph, 46

Dawes, Charles G., 140

Dean, Phillip, 29

Dearborn Park, 27, 36, 61, 130. *See also* Fort Dearborn

Debs, Eugene V., 129

deindustrialization, 176–77

De Jure Maris, 67

Delano, Columbus, 56

Delano, Fredrick, 138–39

Democratic Party, 31–32, 36–38, 40–41, 58, 77, 180, 203n155

Deneen, Charles S., 166

De Portibus Maris, 56

Dering, Charles L., 101–2, 150

Des Plaines River, 1, 9, 12, 40, 95, 104, 190n1

Detroit, 13, 178

Detroit River, 34, 88–89

Diamond, F. J., 52–53

disease, 103–4, 120, 122–23, 142. *See also* pollution

Dodge, John, 62–63

Douglas, Stephen, 20, 32, 40–41, 65

Drainage and Water Supply Commission, 104

Dreiser, Theodore, 83–84, 96, 100

Drummond, Thomas, 72

Duddleston, George, 94

Duluth, 114, 157

Dunham, J. S., 104

Dunne, Edward, 157, 167–68, 208n99

Du Sable, Jean Baptiste Pointe, 13

Earling, A. J., 91
École des Beaux-Arts, 141, 169
Economist, 177–78
Edsall, James, 55, 199n55
Edward Hines Lumber Company, 150
Edwards, Jonathan, 57
Elkins, Stephen B., 105
Ellsworth, James W., 135–36
environment: environmentalism, 184; histo-
     riography, 188n15. *See also* City Beautiful
     Movement; disease; pollution
Erie Canal: canal construction, 19, 34; improve-
     ment, 148; map, 11; shipping rates, 158–59,
     161. *See also* internal improvements
Escanaba Company v. Chicago (1883), 98,
     207n77
Ewen, John, 146

Farwell, John V., 84
Farwell, John V. Jr., 140
Field, David Dudley: influence on Supreme
     Court nomination of Stephen J. Field,
     58; views on internal improvements,
     36–38, 40–41, 195n98, 195n110. *See also*
     Chicago River and Harbor Convention
Field, Marshall, 133, 135, 137, 144
Field Museum, 144, 175
Field, Stanley, 144
Field, Stephen: background, 57–59; dissent in
     Munn, 58–59; legacies, 164, 184; opinion
     in *Escanaba*, 98; opinion in *Illinois Cen-
     tral*, 76–82, 202n146; views on the Four-
     teenth Amendment, 58. See also
     Escanaba Company v. Chicago (1883);
     Illinois Central v. Illinois (1892); *Munn v.
     Illinois* (1877)
Fish, Stuyvesant, 134
Florida, Richard, 179
Flower, Elliott, 94
Foell, Charles, 153, 155, 163, 173
Forbes, John Murray, 149
Foreman, Milton, 102
Fort Dearborn: addition to Chicago, 27–29,
     61–62, 66; map, 17; "massacre" 13–14;
     waterfrontage, 18, 26–27
Fox, 27
French Empire, 9–10, 13, 15, 190n1
Friedman, Thomas, 177–78
Frost, Charles Sumner, 169–70, 218n89
Fuller, Melville, 3, 69–70, 76, 155

Galena, 42, 63, 191n18, 192n27
Garrett, Augustus, 24
Gary, 114, 173
Gehry, Frank, 175, 178
German Alliance Insurance Co. v. Lewis
     (1914), 183
Gibbons v. Ogden (1824), 37
Glasgow, 156
global city, 220n14
Glover, G. O., 72
Gold Coast, 137
Goode, J. Paul, 2–3, 148, 153, 156
Goose Island, 95
grain: city as a hub for grain shipment, 2–4,
     43–45, 51–53; grain elevators, 46–48, 66;
     regulation of the grain trade, 48–51,
     53–60; shipping rates, 91, 102, 158, 162,
     168; tonnage carried to and from the
     city, 107, 110–14, 197n8, 209n133. See also
     Munn v. Illinois (1877)
Granger, Alfred, 169
Granger Cases (1877), 48, 59. See also *Munn v.
     Illinois* (1877)
Grant Park, 135, 140, 142–44, 151, 176, 185. *See
     also* Lake Park
Grant, Ulysses S., 56
Gray, Horace, 76, 78
Great Lakes: economic geography of Great
     Lakes shipping, 158–64; merchant ships,
     86–90; water diversions by Chicago, 105.
     See also Chicago Portage; Illinois and
     Michigan Canal; Lake Michigan
Greeley, Horace, 35, 38, 180, 195n95
Guerin, Jules, 140–43
Guiled Age and Progressive Era, 5–6
Gulf of Mexico, 1, 10–12, 180
Gurnee, Walter, 60–61, 64–65

Hale, Matthew, 56, 59, 67, 199n61
Halsted Street, 44
Hamburg, 83, 156
Harbor and Subway Commission, 166–67,
     169–70, 172. *See also* Municipal Pier
harbors: construction of Chicago River
     wharves, 20–22; debate over building a
     lakeshore harbor in Chicago, 150–51;
     federal funding for harbor dredging, 24,
     30; impediments to the use of the Chi-
     cago River as a harbor, 95–106; local

politics of port development in Chicago, 163–68; map of Chicago region's harbors, 87; private and public ownership and management of global ports, 152–57; rise of the Calumet River as a key regional harbor, 92–93, 106–14; waning demand for industrial harbor facilities, 172–74. *See also* Calumet River; Chicago Harbor Commission; Chicago River; Chicago River and Harbor Convention; Municipal Pier

Harlan, John, 74, 76, 78, 208n99
Harper, William H., 91
Harper's Weekly, 83
Harrison, Carter, 94, 133–34, 166–67
Haussmann, Georges-Eugène, 141
Haymarket Affair, 6, 118, 182
Hibbard, Spencer, Bartlett and Company, 83
Howard, William, 25–26
Hubbard, Gurdon S., 1–2, 6, 14, 16, 18, 191n25
Hull House, 132
Humphrey, W. R., 163

Illinois and Michigan Canal: canal commissioners' dedication of land as "forever free and clear" of buildings, 27, 61, 69, 72, 130, 144; maps, 11–12; opening, 39–40; politics of financing and construction, 14–20, 192n30, 195n115; vision for the canal, 9–10; widening and deepening the Chicago River, 22. *See also* Chicago Portage
Illinois Central Railroad: acquisition of lakeshore lands in Chicago, 60, 70–72; charter, 63; conflicts over access to Lake Michigan with the city of Chicago, 133–34; description of Chicago lakeshore tracks and station, 65–66; litigation over Chicago lakeshore, 74–81; Millennium Park land, 176; repeal of lakeshore grant, 73; right of way in Chicago, 60–66, 53–65. See also *Illinois Central v. Illinois* (1892)
Illinois Central v. Illinois (1892): arguments, 74–76; dissent, 78–79; Illinois Central right of way on the lakefront, 60–66; lakefront grant and repeal, 69–73; legacy, 4, 130, 134, 155, 164, 181, 184; ruling, 76–80. *See also* Field, Stephen; Illinois Central Railroad

Illinois International Port District, 168
Illinois River, 9–11, 25, 69, 190n1
Illinois State Constitutional Convention, 49–50
Illinois State Legislature: grain elevator regulation, 49–50, 60; internal improvements, 16, 18–19, 21, 192n27; lakefront legislation, 69, 71–72, 76–79; parks, 121–24, 140; streetcar franchises, 101
Illinois Steam Forge, 93
Illinois Steel, 115
Illinois Supreme Court, 53–54, 68, 130, 144, 192n36
Illinois Warehouse Act, 50, 53–54
Indiana, 13, 18–20, 82–83, 114–16, 149–50, 191n18
Indiana Harbor, 87, 173
internal improvements, 19, 30–33, 36, 40–41, 179. *See also* Chicago River and Harbor Convention; Illinois and Michigan Canal
Iroquois Iron Company, 115

Jackson, Andrew, 16, 30
Jackson Boulevard, 144
Jackson Park, 124–25, 128, 130, 133, 136, 140, 146, 149
Janin, Fernand, 140–41
Jay Pritzker Pavilion, 178
Jefferson, Thomas, 30, 54, 74
Jenney, William LeBaron, 124, 128
Jewett, John, 54–55, 59, 73–74, 76–77, 81, 202n146
John Marshall Law School, 55
Johnson, Tom, 157
Johnson, William, 106–7
Joliet, Louis, 9–10, 38
Judd, Norman, 33–34

Kamin, Blair, 175
Keith, J. G., 99, 105
Kens, Paul, 58
Kentucky, 15, 30, 36, 71
Kleeman, Benton F., 164–68
Konvitz, Joseph, 86
Kremer, C. E., 115

Lake Calumet, 18, 164–68
Lake Carriers Association, 102
Lake Front Act, 71–73, 76, 78–79

Lake Michigan: beauty 124–25, 142; dimensions of and current in the lake, 25, 38,
62, 180, 187n2; lake levels, 105; lakeshore
and state lines, 15; littoral drift and erosion, 26–30; pollution and drinking
water, 104, 149–51
Lake Park: beautification 134–36; creation, 27,
61–63; filling in the lake, 74, 134–35; Illinois Central tracks, 65–66; litigation
over vice and garbage removal, 129–31;
ownership of and riparian rights, 68–74,
80; as possible site for World's Columbian Exposition, 126–27. *See also* Grant
Park; Illinois and Michigan Canal; *Illi-
nois Central v. Illinois* (1892)
lakeshore. *See* harbors; Illinois Central Rail-
road; Municipal Pier; parks; *Plan of
Chicago*; riparian law
Lakeshore Boulevard, 136
Lakeshore Drive, 135
Lake Steamboat Association, 32
Lakes-to-the Gulf Waterway, 148
Lamar, Joseph, 76
La Salle, René-Robert Cavelier Sieur de, 9–10,
14, 25
LaSalle Street, 42, 100–101
Lawson, Victor F., 140
Lee, Henry W., 166
Lewis, Robert, 3
Lincoln, Abraham, 58
Lincoln Park, 121–24, 136–37
Livingstone, William, 102
Lochner v. New York (1905), 76
Lockport, 39, 95
London, 77, 156
Los Angeles, 184, 188n17
lumber, 39, 43–44, 83, 93, 111–15, 121, 150,
197n8, 209n134
Lurie Gardens, 178
Luyten, Edwin, 184
Lyon, John B., 52–53

Mack, Alonzo, 70
MacVeagh, Franklin, 137–39
Madden, Martin B., 105, 131–32, 134
Madison Street, 27, 61, 127, 135
Maher, Hugh, 52
Mailer, Norman, 2
Mammoth System, 19
Manchester, 156

Manila, 138
Marquette, Jacques, 9
Marshall, John, 37
Marshall, W. L., 84–85, 91–95, 105, 115
Marshall Field and Company, 163
Martin v. Waddell (1842), 67
Mayer, Harold, 3
Maysville Road Bill, 30
McCagg, Ezra, 121, 123
McCloskey, Robert, 58
McCormick, Cyrus, 44
McCormick, Harold, 140
McCormick, Joseph Medill, 138
McCormick Harvesting Machine Company, 83
McCormick Tribune Ice-Rink and Park Grill,
178
McKim, Charles, 128
Medill, Joseph, 74
Mehrberg, Randy, 176
Meigs Field, 178
Merchant Marine League, 115
Merchants Club, 137–39
Merriam, Charles, 146
Metropolitan Sewage District, 166
Miami people, 13
Michigan, 2, 25, 98, 190n1
Michigan Avenue: lake and park views, 61–
65, 69–71, 126; litigation over adjacent
park, 129–30, 150; parks, 27, 29, 74, 176.
See also *Illinois Central v. Illinois* (1892);
Lake Park; Millennium Park
Middleton v. Pritchard (1842), 68
Midway Airport, 1
Millennium Park, 175–76, 178–79, 182, 220n16
Miller, Samuel, 59
Miltimore, Ira, 20, 39
Milwaukee, 85, 157
Minneapolis, 44
Mississippi River, 1, 9–13, 68, 72, 185, 190n1
Missouri River, 14
Mobile, 43
Mono Lake, 184, 188n17
Monroe Street, 134–35
Montgomery Ward and Company, 163
Montreal, 10
Morris, Nelson, 165
Mud Lake, 1, 3, 12, 18, 40
Mumford, Lewis, 184
Municipal Pier: design and construction, 169–
71; politics of pier construction, 163–68,

171–73; rationale for building public piers 146–47, 152, 162–63; shipping and tourism, 173–74, 182. *See also* Navy Pier
Munn, Ira, 45–48. See also *Munn v. Illinois* (1877)
Munn v. Illinois (1877): dissent, 58–60; legacy, 4, 60, 181–83; ruling, 53–57, 60. *See also* grain

Navy Pier, 145–46, 173, 175, 178, 182. *See also* Municipal Pier
Nebbia v. New York (1934), 183
Nelson, Swain, 124
Newberry, Walter, 24
New Delhi, 184
New Orleans, 10–11, 14, 39, 103, 153
New York City: freight rates to and from Chicago, 91, 158–61; geographic and economic connections to Chicago, 11, 15–16, 19–20, 33–34, 47, harbor size and tonnage, 77–78, 83; parks; 120–21; port ownership and management, 154
New York State, 34–39, 68, 76, 127
North Chicago Rolling Mill Company, 177
Northerly Island, 178
Northwest Indian War, 13
Northwest Ordinance, 15
Norton, Charles, 138–39

Obama, Barack, 185
Ogden, William B., 19–20, 24, 45, 202n134
O'Hare International Airport, 177
Ohio, 13, 15, 19–20, 55–56
Ohio Loan Law, 19
Ohio River, 19, 192n27
Olmsted, Frederick Law: background, 119–20; Central Park, 120–21, 123; park advocate, 3, 71, 116, 119–23; Riverside, 124; World's Columbian Exposition, 124–27
Ottawa, 15
Owens River Valley, 184

Palmer, John, 70–72
Panama Canal, 148
Panic of 1837, 18–19, 21, 62
Paris, 116, 141, 169
parks. *See* Central Park; Dearborn Park; Grant Park; Jackson Park; Lake Park; Lincoln Park; Millennium Park; Olmsted, Frederick Law; Washington Park

Patton, Normand S., 132
Pendleton, John, 103
Philadelphia, 33, 43, 100, 125, 154, 161
Pirie, J. T., 163
Plan of Chicago: description of Chicago River, 95; influence of the parks movement and World's Columbian Exposition, 119–21, 127; key ideas and design features, 140–45; legacy, 4, 175, 182, 184; pier construction, 151, 169–70, 174; role of the Chicago Commercial Club, 133, 137–40; social engineering, 132. *See also* Burnham, Daniel; Municipal Pier
Platt, Harold, 3, 196n22
Polk, James K., 30–32, 35, 40–41
Pollard v. Hagen (1845), 67
pollution, 5, 82, 86, 92, 118, 123, 149–52, 185. *See also* disease
Pope, Nathaniel, 14–15
Porter, Washington, 130–31, 133
ports. *See* harbors
Pottawatomie, 29
Propeller Genesee Chief v. Fitzhugh (1851), 67
public and private dualism, 4–7, 182–83, 190n24
public trust doctrine, 77, 81, 184, 188n17. See also *Illinois Central v. Illinois* (1892)
public utilities, 152–53
Pugh, James, 167
Pugh Terminal Warehouse Company, 167
Pullman Palace Car Company, 128, 137, 165
Pullman Strike, 6, 128–29

Quincy, Josiah, 46

railroads. alleged railroad influence on construction of Municipal Pier, 171–73; competition with lake shipping lines, 88, 147, 154–63, 169; connections to Calumet River, 93, 114; Galena and Chicago Union Railroad, 45–46; goods carried to and from Chicago, 39; Pullman Palace Car Company, 128–29; railroad access to proposed lakefront harbor, 150; railroad construction financing, 16, 18–20, 40–42; rate regulation, 50, 59; role in Chicago's economic development, 2–4, 6, 43–44. *See also* Illinois Central Railroad

Randolph, Isham, 146, 150–51
Randolph Street, 60–61, 65–66, 74–75, 130,
    134, 176, 207n84
Rauch, John, 116, 122–24, 130
Regional Port District, 168
Republican Party, 56, 58, 121, 137
Rex, Frederic, 162
Riis, Jacob, 137
riparian law, 66–69, 154–55. See also *Illinois
    Central v. Illinois* (1892)
rivers. *See* Calumet River; Chicago River; Des
    Plaines River; Detroit River; Illinois
    River; Mississippi River; Missouri River;
    Ohio River; Owens River Valley; St.
    Clair River; Thames River
Riverside, 123–24
robber baron, 46
Rome, 141
Roosevelt, Franklin Delano, 138, 195n110
Root, John W., 127–28
Rotterdam, 153
Rucker, Henry, 23
Russell, William H., 65

sailboats, 66, 84–85, 88, 91, 204n25
Saint Lawrence Seaway, 168
Saint Louis, 14, 43–44
Sandburg, Carl, 7
San Francisco, 43, 57, 121, 138
Sanitary and Ship Canal. *See* Sanitary District
    of Chicago
Sanitary District of Chicago: construction of
    Sanitary and Ship Canal, 12, 95, 104, 131;
    construction of the Cal-Sag Canal, 166;
    creation, 95; proposed development of
    Chicago lakefront piers, 166–67; pro-
    posed dredging of Lake Calumet, 164;
    replacement of bridges on the Chicago
    River, 99, 207n84; water diversions from
    Lake Michigan, 105, 149–50
Sassen, Saskia, 179, 220n14
Sauk, 13, 27
Sax, Joseph L., 184
Scammon, J. Young, 29, 33
Schlatter, Charles, 30
Schoolcraft, Henry, 25
Schumpeter, Joseph, 85, 204n13
Scott, George, 45–47, 51–53, 59–60
Seaman v. Smith (1860), 68
Sears, Roebuck, and Company, 144

Sears Tower, 177
Seattle, 155, 178
Sedgwick, Henry, 36
Sedgwick, Robert, 36
Sedgwick, Theodore, 37
Seven Years War, 10
Shankland, Edward, 166
Shedd, C. B., 165
Shedd, E. A., 165
Shedd, John G., 144
Shedd Aquarium, 175
Shepard, Henry, 69
Sherman, Francis, 28
shipping rates, 47, 88, 91, 158–63, 209n109
Shiras, George, 76, 78
Sierra Nevada Mountains, 71, 184, 188n17
Sikes, George, 158, 162
Simpson, James, 163
Skinner, James G., 172
Skocpol, Theda, 6
Slaughterhouse Cases (1873), 58, 77
slavery, 14, 32, 189n19
Smith, Adam, 54
Smith, Carl, 140
Soldier Field, 144, 175
South Park Commission, 123–24, 135, 140,
    144, 146, 211n29
Speer, Albert, 184
Spencer, John, 37
Stanford, Leland, 58
Stanton, Edwin, 44
state power in American historiography, 5–7,
    189n19, 190n23, 190n24
St. Clair River, 34, 88
steamships, 84–86, 88–91, 93, 97, 115, 181,
    207n80
steel: loss of steel industry jobs, 177; rise of
    steel industry 92–93, 107; ships, 84–86,
    88–91; skyscrapers, 124, 170, 176–77;
    tonnage of steel shipped to and from
    Chicago ports, 111, 113–15
streetcars, 101, 118, 152, 157, 181
Streeterville, 26
suburbs, 121, 185
Sullivan, Louis, 128
Supreme Court of the United States. See
    Escanaba Company v. Chicago (1883);
    Illinois Central v. Illinois (1892); *Munn v.
    Illinois* (1877)
Swift, George, 133–35

Tacoma, 155
Taft, William H., 146
taxation. *See* Chicago Common Council; Chicago River and Harbor Convention
Thames River, 77, 156
Thayer, Walter, 159
Thomas, H. W., 131
Thompson, James, 15–17
Thorne, C. H., 163
The Titan, 100
tourism, 7, 118, 144–45, 174–78, 181–82, 185
A Treatise on the Common Law in Relation to Water-Courses, 67
Treaty of Chicago (1833), 14
Treaty of Greenville (1795), 13, 17
Turner, Frederick Jackson, 117–19, 210n1
Twain, Mark, 5
Twelfth Street, 27, 65, 69, 74, 84, 134, 144
Twenty-Second Street, 150
Tyler, John, 37

United States v. Chicago (1849), 30. *See also* Fort Dearborn
U.S. Steel, 114, 165, 176–77

Van Buren, Martin, 27, 36, 61
Van Buren Street, 101, 134
Van Vlissengen, Arend, 168
Vaux, Calvert, 120, 123–24
Vietnam War protest, 185

Wacker, Charles H., 139, 146
Wacker Drive, 145, 175
Waite, Morrison, 45, 55–59, 76, 147, 183
Ward, Aaron Montgomery, 129–30, 144
Warner, Charles Dudley, 5
Washington, Booker T., 137
Washington, D.C., 57, 138–39
Washington Park, 124–25
Washington State, 154–55
Washington Street, 100–101, 127, 135
Weed, Thurlow, 34–35
Wells, H. G., 129
Wells Street, 24, 40
Wentworth, John, 32–33, 41, 61, 70
Western Confederacy, 13
West Park Commission, 123–24
Wheeler, J. B., 72, 92
Whig Party, 31–37, 41, 194n74, 196n122
Wisconsin, 14–15, 44, 99, 117, 190n1, 210n1
Wisner, G. M., 163–65
Woodworth, James, 39–41, 196n122
World's Columbian Exposition: cultural meaning, 117–18, 210n1; fairgrounds, 125–29; influence on lakeshore development plans, 131–33, 136, 142, 169, 182. *See also* Burnham, Daniel; City Beautiful Movement
Wright, Peter, 127, 132
Wrigley Square, 178

Yerkes, Charles Tyson, 100–101, 152
Yesler v. The Harbor Line Commission (1892), 155

ACKNOWLEDGMENTS

I met so many generous and interesting people during the process of writing this book. It pleases me to be able to thank them here.

I began this study while at the University of Illinois at Chicago—amid a lively and supportive group of historians. Richard John led stimulating classes and extracurricular book discussions at the Port Café, in which he showed off his dazzling command of American historiography. His teaching and scholarship piqued my interest in political economy. Richard worked tirelessly, pushing me to refine my arguments and writing. Leon Fink inspired me with his excellent scholarship, personal kindness, and uncanny ability to formulate smart questions. Leon's challenging questions helped me frame this study. His encouragement helped me finish it. Sue Levine, Robert Johnston, Christopher Boyer, and Daniel Hamilton enriched my work with their extraordinary teaching and perceptive commentary, which was often doled out over drinks at Jaks Tap.

I met Sarah Rose and John Reda in Richard John's U.S. History Seminar in 2001. Since then, we have shared numerous meals together and commented on draft after draft of each other's work. I could not be more grateful for what they have taught me about historical scholarship and for their friendship.

Many librarians and archivists helped me navigate the rich collections of Chicago's great repositories, including: the University of Illinois at Chicago Special Collections; the Municipal Reference Collection at the Harold Washington Public Library; the Chicago History Museum; the Newberry Library; and the Illinois Regional Archives Depository at Northeastern Illinois University's Ronald Williams Library.

I am grateful for the institutional support of the Illinois State Historical Society and the Illinois Historic Preservation Agency, which awarded me the King V. Hostick grant to pay for research costs. I would like to thank the Oxford University Press for granting permission to reprint material I originally published in a 2012 article in the journal *Enterprise and Society* in the third chapter of this book. I am also pleased to thank Northeastern Illinois University for supporting my work with a Faculty Summer Research Stipend, which gave me time to work on revisions. Northeastern's Office of the Dean of Liberal Arts and Sciences, led by Dean Wamucii Njogu, also generously paid for the maps made by Jason LaBrosse and for the reproduction of the historical images that appear in this book.

My colleagues at Northeastern Illinois University have offered encouragement, advice, and good humor over the past five years. For these things, I am grateful to: Francesca Morgan; Charles Steinwedel; Christina Bueno; Leo Bacino; Cris Joe; Mateo Farzaneh; Zach Schiffman; Nikolas Hoel; Steven Riess; and Ed Remus. Patrick Miller and Marc Arenberg read several draft chapters of this book and offered smart suggestions for revision. Our department chair, Michael Tuck has been tremendously supportive, helping me to balance my workload and secure funds for my research.

I have also benefitted from the suggestions and encouragement of several scholars I met at conferences and seminars including: Louise Nelson Dyble; Harold Platt; Joel Tarr; and Ann Durkin Keating. Over the past four years, I have had the pleasure of co-coordinating the History of Capitalism Seminar at the Newberry Library with Jeffrey Sklansky. Jeff has enriched my work with his thoughtful comments on the field as well as on my book. My good friend Theo Anderson read several drafts of this book and lent invaluable editing assistance.

I am very grateful for the incredible generosity of Mark Rose. Mark read and commented on drafts of this work from its earliest stages to the end of the process. He helped me refine my narrative and lent sage advice on publishing and navigating the historical profession along the way.

Elizabeth Tandy Shermer was instrumental in helping me revise my manuscript for publication. She read it twice and offered extensive, smart commentary. Robert Lockhart, in turn, helped guide me through the editorial process.

I owe my biggest debt of gratitude to my friends and family, whose love and humor sustain me. Julie, Bob, Ashley, Cheri, Ed, and London, I'm thinking of you. And, Josie, Phoebe, and Dad—my big three—this book is for you.